AGAINST
INTERPRETATION

Susan Sontag is the author of four novels, *In America*,
The Benefactor, *Death Kit*, and *The Volcano Lover*;
I, etcetera, a collection of stories; several plays, including
Alice in Bed; and five works of non-fiction, among them
On Photography and *Illness As Metaphor* and *AIDS
and Its Metaphors*. She lives in New York City.

ALSO BY SUSAN SONTAG

Fiction

The Benefactor
Death Kit
I, etcetera
The Way We Live Now
The Volcano Lover
In America

Essays

Styles of Radical Will
On Photography
Illness as Metaphor
Under the Sign of Saturn
AIDS and Its Metaphors
Where the Stress Falls

Filmscripts

Duet for Cannibals
Brother Carl

Play

Alice in Bed

A Susan Sontag Reader

Susan Sontag

AGAINST INTERPRETATION

V

VINTAGE

Published by Vintage 2001

2 4 6 8 10 9 7 5 3 1

First published in the United States by
Farrar, Straus & Giroux, 1966.

Vintage edition includes the author's note that appeared
originally in the Dell paperback edition published in 1967

Vintage edition 1994

Vintage
Random House, 20 Vauxhall Bridge Road,
London SW1V 2SA

Random House Australia (Pty) Limited
20 Alfred Street, Milsons Point, Sydney,
New South Wales 2061, Australia

Random House New Zealand Limited
18 Poland Road, Glenfield, Auckland 10,
New Zealand

Random House (Pty) Limited
Endulini, 5A Jubilee Road, Parktown 2193,
South Africa

The Random House Group Limited Reg. No. 954009
www.randomhouse.co.uk

A CIP catalogue record for this book
is available from the British Library

ISBN 0 09 938731 X

Papers used by Random House are natural, recyclable
products made from wood grown in sustainable forests. The
manufacturing processes conform to the environmental
regulations of the country of origin

Printed and bound in Great Britain by
Cox & Wyman Limited, Reading, Berkshire

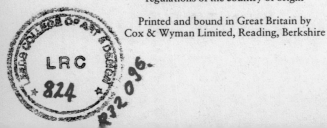

for Paul Thek

A note and some
acknowledgments

THE articles and reviews collected here make up a good part of the criticism I wrote between 1962 and 1965, a sharply defined period in my life. In early 1962 I finished my first novel, *The Benefactor*. In late 1965 I began a second novel. The energy, and the anxiety, that spilled over into criticism had a beginning and an end. That period of search, reflection, and discovery already seemed somewhat remote at the time of the American publication of *Against Interpretation* and seems even more so now, a year later, as the collection is about to be reissued in a paperback edition.

Although in these essays I do talk a great deal about particular works of art and, implicitly, about the tasks of the critic, I am aware that little of what is assembled in the book counts as criticism proper.

Leaving aside a few pieces of journalism, most of it could perhaps be called meta-criticism—if that is not too grand a name. I was writing, with passionate partiality, about *problems* raised for me by works of art, mainly contemporary, in different genres: I wanted to expose and clarify the theoretical assumptions underlying specific judgments and tastes. Although I did not set out to devise a "position" about either the arts or modernity, some kind of general position seemed to take shape and to voice itself with increasing urgency no matter what particular work I wrote about.

I disagree now with a portion of what I wrote, but it is not the sort of disagreement that makes feasible partial changes or revisions. Although I think that I overestimated or underestimated the merit of several works I discussed, little of my present disagreement owes to a shift in particular judgments. Anyway, what value these essays may possess, the extent to which they are more than just case studies of my evolving sensibility, rests not on the specific appraisals made but on the interestingness of the problems raised. I don't, ultimately, care for handing out grades to works of art (which is why I mostly avoided the opportunity of writing about things I didn't admire). I wrote as an enthusiast and a partisan—and with, it now seems to me, a certain naïveté. I didn't understand the gross impact which writing about new or little-known activities in the arts can have in the era of instant "communication." I didn't know—I had yet to learn, painfully—the speed at which a bulky essay in *Partisan Review* becomes a hot tip in *Time*. For all my exhortatory tone, I was not trying to lead anyone into the Promised Land except myself.

For me, the essays have done their work. I see the world differently, with fresher eyes; my conception of my tasks as a novelist is radically changed. I could describe the process this way. Before I wrote the essays I did not believe many of the ideas espoused in them; when I wrote them, I believed what I wrote; subsequently, I have come to disbelieve some of these same ideas again—but from a new perspective, one that incorporates and is nourished by what is true in the argument of the essays. Writing criticism has proved to be an act of intellectual disburdenment as much as of intellectual self-expression.

I have the impression not so much of having, for myself, resolved a certain number of alluring and troubling problems as of having used them up. But no doubt this is illusory. The problems remain, more remains to be said about them by other curious and reflective people, and perhaps this collection of some recent thinking about the arts will have a certain relevance to that.

"Sartre's *Saint Genet*," "The Death of Tragedy," "Nathalie Sarraute and the Novel," "Going to Theater, etc.," "Notes on 'Camp,'" "Marat/Sade/Artaud," and "On Style" originally appeared in *Partisan Review*; "Simone Weil," "Camus' *Notebooks*," Michel Leiris' *Manhood*," "The Anthropologist as Hero," and "Ionesco" appeared in *The New York Review of Books*; "The Literary Criticism of Georg Lukács" and "Reflections on *The Deputy*" in *Book Week*; "Against Interpretation" in *Evergreen Review*; "Piety Without Content," "The Artist as Exemplary Sufferer," and "Happenings: An Art of Radical Juxtaposition" in *The Second Coming*; "Godard's *Vivre Sa Vie*" in *Moviegoer*; "One Culture and the New Sensibility" (in abridged form) in *Mademoiselle*; "Jack Smith's *Flaming Creatures*" in *The Nation*; "Spiritual Style in the Films of Robert Bresson" in *The Seventh Art*; "A Note on Novels and Films" and "Psychoanalysis and Norman O. Brown's *Life Against Death*" in *The Supplement* (*Columbia Spectator*); "The Imagination of Disaster" in *Commentary*. (Some articles appeared under different titles.) I am grateful to the editors of these magazines for permission to reprint.

It is a pleasure to have the opportunity to thank William Phillips for generous encouragement though he often disagreed with what I was saying; Annette Michelson, who has shared her erudition and taste with me in many conversations over the last seven years; and Richard Howard, who very helpfully read over most of the essays and pointed out several errors of fact and rhetoric.

Last, I wish to record my gratitude to the Rockefeller Foundation for a fellowship last year which freed me, for the first time in my life, to write full-time—during which period I wrote, among other things, some of the essays collected in this book.

S. S.
1966

Contents

I

Content is a glimpse of something, an encounter like a flash. It's very tiny—very tiny, content.

                    WILLEM DE KOONING, *in an interview*

It is only shallow people who do not judge by appearances. The mystery of the world is the visible, not the invisible.

                    OSCAR WILDE, *in a letter*

Against
interpretation

THE earliest experience of art must have been that it was incantatory, magical; art was an instrument of ritual. (Cf. the paintings in the caves at Lascaux, Altamira, Niaux, La Pasiega, etc.) The earliest theory of art, that of the Greek philosophers, proposed that art was mimesis, imitation of reality.

It is at this point that the peculiar question of the *value* of art arose. For the mimetic theory, by its very terms, challenges art to justify itself.

Plato, who proposed the theory, seems to have done so in order to rule that the value of art is dubious. Since he considered ordinary material things as themselves mimetic objects, imitations of transcendent forms or structures, even the best painting of a bed would be only an "imitation of an imitation." For Plato, art is neither particularly useful (the painting of a bed is no good to sleep on), nor, in the strict sense, true. And Aristotle's arguments in defense of art do not really challenge Plato's view that all art is an elaborate *trompe l'oeil*, and therefore a lie. But he does dispute Plato's idea that art is useless. Lie or no, art has a certain value according to Aristotle because it is a form of therapy. Art is useful, after all, Aristotle counters, medicinally useful in that it arouses and purges dangerous emotions.

In Plato and Aristotle, the mimetic theory of art goes hand in hand with the assumption that art is always figurative. But advocates of the mimetic theory need not close their eyes to decorative and abstract art. The fallacy that art is necessarily a "realism" can be modified or scrapped without ever moving outside the problems delimited by the mimetic theory.

The fact is, all Western consciousness of and reflection upon art have remained within the confines staked out by the Greek theory of art as mimesis or representation. It is through this theory that art as such—above and beyond given works of art—becomes problematic, in need of defense. And it is the defense of art which gives birth to the odd vision by which something we have learned to call "form" is separated off from something we have learned to call "content," and to the well-intentioned move which makes content essential and form accessory.

Even in modern times, when most artists and critics have discarded the theory of art as representation of an outer reality in favor of the theory of art as subjective expression, the main feature of the mimetic theory persists. Whether we conceive of the work of art on the model of a picture (art as a picture of reality) or on the model of a statement (art as the statement of the artist), content still comes first. The content may have changed. It may now be less figurative, less lucidly realistic. But it is still assumed that a work of art *is* its content. Or, as it's usually put today, that a work of art by definition *says* something. ("What X is saying is . . . ," "What X is trying to say is . . . ," "What X said is . . ." etc., etc.)

2

None of us can ever retrieve that innocence before all theory when art knew no need to justify itself, when one did not ask of a work of art what it *said* because one knew (or thought one knew) what it *did*. From now to the end of consciousness, we are stuck with the task of defending art. We can only quarrel with one or another means of defense. Indeed, we have an obligation to overthrow any means of defending and justifying art which becomes particularly obtuse or onerous or insensitive to contemporary needs and practice.

This is the case, today, with the very idea of content itself. Whatever it may have been in the past, the idea of content is today mainly a hindrance, a nuisance, a subtle or not so subtle philistinism.

Though the actual developments in many arts may seem to be leading us away from the idea that a work of art is primarily its content, the idea still exerts an extraordinary hegemony. I want to suggest that this is because the idea is now perpetuated in the guise of a certain way of encountering works of art thoroughly ingrained among most people who take any of the arts seriously. What the overemphasis on the idea of content entails is the perennial, never consummated project of *interpretation*. And, conversely, it is the habit of approaching works of art in order to *interpret* them that sustains the fancy that there really is such a thing as the content of a work of art.

3

Of course, I don't mean interpretation in the broadest sense, the sense in which Nietzsche (rightly) says, "There are no facts, only interpretations." By interpretation, I mean here a conscious act of the mind which illustrates a certain code, certain "rules" of interpretation.

Directed to art, interpretation means plucking a set of elements (the X, the Y, the Z, and so forth) from the whole work. The task of interpretation is virtually one of translation. The interpreter says, Look, don't you see that X is really—or, really means—A? That Y is really B? That Z is really C?

What situation could prompt this curious project for transforming a text? History gives us the materials for an answer. Interpretation first appears in the culture of late classical antiquity, when the power and credibility of myth had been broken by the "realistic" view of the world introduced by scientific enlightenment. Once the question that haunts post-mythic consciousness—that of the seemliness of religious symbols—had been asked, the ancient texts were, in their pristine form, no longer acceptable. Then interpretation was summoned, to reconcile the ancient texts to "modern" demands. Thus, the Stoics, to accord with their view that the gods had to be moral, allegorized away the rude features of Zeus and his boisterous clan in Homer's epics. What Homer really designated by the adultery of Zeus with Leto, they explained, was the union between power and wisdom. In the same vein, Philo of Alexandria interpreted the literal historical narratives of the Hebrew Bible as spiritual paradigms. The story of the exodus from Egypt, the wandering in the desert for forty years, and the entry into the promised land, said Philo, was really an allegory of the individual soul's emancipation, tribulations, and final deliverance. Interpretation thus presupposes a discrepancy between the clear meaning of the text and the demands of (later) readers. It seeks to resolve that discrepancy. The situation is that for some reason a text has become unacceptable; yet it cannot be discarded. Interpretation is a radical strategy for conserving an old text, which is thought too precious to repudiate, by revamping it. The interpreter, without actually erasing or rewriting the text, is altering it. But he can't admit to doing this. He claims to be only making it intelligible, by disclosing its true meaning. However far the interpreters alter the text (another notorious example is the Rabbinic and Christian "spiritual" interpretations of the clearly erotic Song of Songs), they must claim to be reading off a sense that is already there.

Interpretation in our own time, however, is even more complex. For the contemporary zeal for the project of interpretation is often prompted not by piety toward the troublesome text (which may conceal an aggression), but by an open aggressiveness, an overt contempt for appearances. The old style of interpretation was insistent, but respectful; it erected another meaning on top of the literal one. The modern style of interpretation excavates, and as it excavates, destroys; it digs "behind" the text, to find a sub-text which is the true one. The most celebrated and influential modern doctrines, those of Marx and Freud, actually amount to elaborate systems of hermeneutics, aggressive and impious theories of interpretation. All observable phenomena are bracketed, in Freud's phrase, as *manifest content*. This manifest content must be probed and pushed aside to find the true meaning—the *latent content*—beneath. For Marx, social events like revolutions and wars; for Freud, the events of individual lives (like neurotic symptoms and slips of the tongue) as well as texts (like a dream or a work of art)—all are treated as occasions for interpretation. According to Marx and Freud, these events only *seem* to be intelligible. Actually, they have no meaning without interpretation. To understand *is* to interpret. And to interpret is to restate the phenomenon, in effect to find an equivalent for it.

Thus, interpretation is not (as most people assume) an absolute value, a gesture of mind situated in some timeless realm of capabilities. Interpretation must itself be evaluated, within a historical view of human consciousness. In some cultural contexts, interpretation is a liberating act. It is a means of revising, of transvaluing, of escaping the dead past. In other cultural contexts, it is reactionary, impertinent, cowardly, stifling.

4

Today is such a time, when the project of interpretation is largely reactionary, stifling. Like the fumes of the automobile and of heavy industry which befoul the urban atmosphere, the effusion of interpretations of art today poisons our sensibilities. In a culture whose already classical dilemma is the hypertrophy of the intellect at the expense of energy and sensual capability, interpretation is the revenge of the intellect upon art.

Even more. It is the revenge of the intellect upon the world. To interpret is to impoverish, to deplete the world—in order to set up a shadow world of "meanings." It is to turn *the* world into *this* world. ("This world"! As if there were any other.)

The world, our world, is depleted, impoverished enough. Away with all duplicates of it, until we again experience more immediately what we have.

5

In most modern instances, interpretation amounts to the philistine refusal to leave the work of art alone. Real art has the capacity to make us nervous. By reducing the work of art to its content and then interpreting *that*, one tames the work of art. Interpretation makes art manageable, comfortable.

This philistinism of interpretation is more rife in literature than in any other art. For decades now, literary critics have understood it to be their task to translate the elements of the poem or play or novel or story into something else. Sometimes a writer will be so uneasy before the naked power of his art that he will install within the work itself—albeit with a little shyness, a touch of the good taste of irony—the clear and explicit interpretation of it. Thomas Mann is an example of such an overcooperative author. In the case of more stubborn authors, the critic is only too happy to perform the job.

The work of Kafka, for example, has been subjected to a mass ravishment by no less than three armies of interpreters. Those who read Kafka as a social allegory see case studies of the frustrations and insanity of modern bureaucracy and its ultimate issuance in the totalitarian state. Those who read Kafka as a psychoanalytic allegory see desperate revelations of Kafka's fear of his father, his castration anxieties, his sense of his own impotence, his thralldom to his dreams. Those who read Kafka as a religious allegory explain that K. in *The Castle* is trying to gain access to heaven, that Joseph K. in *The Trial* is being judged by the inexorable and mysterious justice of God. . . . Another oeuvre that has attracted interpreters like leeches is that of Samuel Beckett. Beckett's delicate dramas of the withdrawn consciousness—pared down to essentials, cut off, often represented as physically immobilized—are read as a statement about modern man's alienation from meaning or from God, or as an allegory of psychopathology.

Proust, Joyce, Faulkner, Rilke, Lawrence, Gide . . . one could go on citing author after author; the list is endless of those around whom thick encrustations of interpretation have taken hold. But it should be noted that interpretation is not simply the compliment

that mediocrity pays to genius. It is, indeed, the modern way of
understanding something, and is applied to works of every quality.
Thus, in the notes that Elia Kazan published on his production of
A Streetcar Named Desire, it becomes clear that, in order to direct the play, Kazan had to discover that Stanley Kowalski represented the sensual and vengeful barbarism that was engulfing our
culture, while Blanche Du Bois was Western civilization, poetry,
delicate apparel, dim lighting, refined feelings and all, though a
little the worse for wear to be sure. Tennessee Williams' forceful
psychological melodrama now became intelligible: it was about
something, about the decline of Western civilization. Apparently,
were it to go on being a play about a handsome brute named Stanley Kowalski and a faded mangy belle named Blanche Du Bois, it
would not be manageable.

6

It doesn't matter whether artists intend, or don't intend, for their
works to be interpreted. Perhaps Tennessee Williams thinks
Streetcar is about what Kazan thinks it to be about. It may be that
Cocteau in The Blood of a Poet and in Orpheus wanted the elaborate readings which have been given these films, in terms of Freudian symbolism and social critique. But the merit of these works
certainly lies elsewhere than in their "meanings." Indeed, it is precisely to the extent that Williams' plays and Cocteau's films do
suggest these portentous meanings that they are defective, false,
contrived, lacking in conviction.

From interviews, it appears that Resnais and Robbe-Grillet consciously designed Last Year at Marienbad to accommodate a multiplicity of equally plausible interpretations. But the temptation to
interpret Marienbad should be resisted. What matters in Marienbad is the pure, untranslatable, sensuous immediacy of some of its
images, and its rigorous if narrow solutions to certain problems of
cinematic form.

Again, Ingmar Bergman may have meant the tank rumbling
down the empty night street in The Silence as a phallic symbol.
But if he did, it was a foolish thought. ("Never trust the teller,
trust the tale," said Lawrence.) Taken as a brute object, as an im-

mediate sensory equivalent for the mysterious abrupt armored happenings going on inside the hotel, that sequence with the tank is the most striking moment in the film. Those who reach for a Freudian interpretation of the tank are only expressing their lack of response to what is there on the screen.

It is always the case that interpretation of this type indicates a dissatisfaction (conscious or unconscious) with the work, a wish to replace it by something else.

Interpretation, based on the highly dubious theory that a work of art is composed of items of content, violates art. It makes art into an article for use, for arrangement into a mental scheme of categories.

7

Interpretation does not, of course, always prevail. In fact, a great deal of today's art may be understood as motivated by a flight from interpretation. To avoid interpretation, art may become parody. Or it may become abstract. Or it may become ("merely") decorative. Or it may become non-art.

The flight from interpretation seems particularly a feature of modern painting. Abstract painting is the attempt to have, in the ordinary sense, no content; since there is no content, there can be no interpretation. Pop Art works by the opposite means to the same result; using a content so blatant, so "what it is," it, too, ends by being uninterpretable.

A great deal of modern poetry as well, starting from the great experiments of French poetry (including the movement that is misleadingly called Symbolism) to put silence into poems and to reinstate the magic of the word, has escaped from the rough grip of interpretation. The most recent revolution in contemporary taste in poetry—the revolution that has deposed Eliot and elevated Pound—represents a turning away from content in poetry in the old sense, an impatience with what made modern poetry prey to the zeal of interpreters.

I am speaking mainly of the situation in America, of course. Interpretation runs rampant here in those arts with a feeble and negligible avant-garde: fiction and the drama. Most American novelists and playwrights are really either journalists or gentlemen sociologists and psychologists. They are writing the literary equivalent of program music. And so rudimentary, uninspired, and stagnant has been the sense of what might be done with form in fiction and drama that even when the content isn't simply information, news, it is still peculiarly visible, handier, more exposed. To the extent that novels and plays (in America), unlike poetry and painting and music, don't reflect any interesting concern with changes in their form, these arts remain prone to assault by interpretation.

But programmatic avant-gardism—which has meant, mostly, experiments with form at the expense of content—is not the only defense against the infestation of art by interpretations. At least, I hope not. For this would be to commit art to being perpetually on the run. (It also perpetuates the very distinction between form and content which is, ultimately, an illusion.) Ideally, it is possible to elude the interpreters in another way, by making works of art whose surface is so unified and clean, whose momentum is so rapid, whose address is so direct that the work can be . . . just what it is. Is this possible now? It does happen in films, I believe. This is why cinema is the most alive, the most exciting, the most important of all art forms right now. Perhaps the way one tells how alive a particular art form is, is by the latitude it gives for making mistakes in it, and still being good. For example, a few of the films of Bergman —though crammed with lame messages about the modern spirit, thereby inviting interpretations—still triumph over the pretentious intentions of their director. In *Winter Light* and *The Silence*, the beauty and visual sophistication of the images subvert before our eyes the callow pseudo-intellectuality of the story and some of the dialogue. (The most remarkable instance of this sort of discrepancy is the work of D. W. Griffith.) In good films, there is always a directness that entirely frees us from the itch to interpret. Many old Hollywood films, like those of Cukor, Walsh, Hawks, and countless other directors, have this liberating anti-symbolic quality, no less than the best work of the new European directors, like Truffaut's *Shoot the Piano Player* and *Jules and Jim*, Godard's *Breathless* and *Vivre Sa Vie*, Antonioni's *L'Avventura*, and Olmi's *The Fiancés*. The fact that films have not been overrun by interpreters is in part due simply to the newness of cinema as an art. It also owes to the happy accident that films for such a long time were just movies; in other words, that they were understood to be part of mass, as opposed to high, culture, and were left alone by most people with minds. Then, too, there is always something other than content in the cinema to grab hold of, for those who want to analyze. For the cinema, unlike the novel, possesses a vocabulary of forms—the explicit, complex, and discussable technology of camera movements, cutting, and composition of the frame that goes into the making of a film.

8

What kind of criticism, of commentary on the arts, is desirable today? For I am not saying that works of art are ineffable, that they cannot be described or paraphrased. They can be. The question is how. What would criticism look like that would serve the work of art, not usurp its place?

What is needed, first, is more attention to form in art. If excessive stress on *content* provokes the arrogance of interpretation, more extended and more thorough descriptions of *form* would silence. What is needed is a vocabulary—a descriptive, rather than prescriptive, vocabulary—for forms.* The best criticism, and it is uncommon, is of this sort that dissolves considerations of content into those of form. On film, drama, and painting respectively, I can think of Erwin Panofsky's essay, "Style and Medium in the Motion Pictures," Northrop Frye's essay "A Conspectus of Dramatic Genres," Pierre Francastel's essay "The Destruction of a Plastic Space." Roland Barthes' book *On Racine* and his two essays on Robbe-Grillet are examples of formal analysis applied to the work of a single author. (The best essays in Erich Auerbach's *Mimesis*,

* One of the difficulties is that our idea of form is spatial (the Greek metaphors for form are all derived from notions of space). This is why we have a more ready vocabulary of forms for the spatial than for the temporal arts. The exception among the temporal arts, of course, is the drama; perhaps this is because the drama is a narrative (i.e., temporal) form that extends itself visually and pictorially, upon a stage. . . . What we don't have yet is a poetics of the novel, any clear notion of the forms of narration. Perhaps film criticism will be the occasion of a breakthrough here, since films are primarily a visual form, yet they are also a subdivision of literature.

like "The Scar of Odysseus," are also of this type.) An example of
formal analysis applied simultaneously to genre and author is Walter Benjamin's essay, "The Story Teller: Reflections on the Works
of Nicolai Leskov."

Equally valuable would be acts of criticism which would supply a
really accurate, sharp, loving description of the appearance of a
work of art. This seems even harder to do than formal analysis.
Some of Manny Farber's film criticism, Dorothy Van Ghent's essay "The Dickens World: A View from Todgers'," Randall Jar-
rell's essay on Walt Whitman are among the rare examples of what
I mean. These are essays which reveal the sensuous surface of art
without mucking about in it.

9

Transparence is the highest, most liberating value in art—and in
criticism—today. Transparence means experiencing the luminous-
ness of the thing in itself, of things being what they are. This is the
greatness of, for example, the films of Bresson and Ozu and Renoir's *The Rules of the Game*.

Once upon a time (say, for Dante), it must have been a revolutionary and creative move to design works of art so that they might
be experienced on several levels. Now it is not. It reinforces the
principle of redundancy that is the principal affliction of modern
life.

Once upon a time (a time when high art was scarce), it must
have been a revolutionary and creative move to interpret works of
art. Now it is not. What we decidedly do not need now is further
to assimilate Art into Thought, or (worse yet) Art into Culture.

Interpretation takes the sensory experience of the work of art for
granted, and proceeds from there. This cannot be taken for
granted, now. Think of the sheer multiplication of works of art
available to every one of us, superadded to the conflicting tastes
and odors and sights of the urban environment that bombard our
senses. Ours is a culture based on excess, on overproduction; the
result is a steady loss of sharpness in our sensory experience. All the
conditions of modern life—its material plenitude, its sheer crowdedness—conjoin to dull our sensory faculties. And it is in the light

of the condition of our senses, our capacities (rather than those of another age), that the task of the critic must be assessed.

What is important now is to recover our senses. We must learn to see more, to hear more, to feel more.

Our task is not to find the maximum amount of content in a work of art, much less to squeeze more content out of the work than is already there. Our task is to cut back content so that we can see the thing at all.

The aim of all commentary on art now should be to make works of art—and, by analogy, our own experience—more, rather than less, real to us. The function of criticism should be to show how it is what it is, even that it is what it is, rather than to show what it means.

10
In place of a hermeneutics we need an erotics of art.

[1964]

On
style

L T W O U L D be hard to find any reputable literary critic today who would care to be caught defending as an idea the old antithesis of style versus content. On this issue a pious consensus prevails. Everyone is quick to avow that style and content are indissoluble, that the strongly individual style of each important writer is an organic aspect of his work and never something merely "decorative."

In the practice of criticism, though, the old antithesis lives on, virtually unassailed. Most of the same critics who disclaim, in passing, the notion that style is an accessory to content maintain the duality whenever they apply themselves to particular works of literature. It is not so easy, after all, to get unstuck from a distinction that practically holds together the fabric of critical discourse, and serves to perpetuate certain intellectual aims and vested interests which themselves remain unchallenged and would be difficult to surrender without a fully articulated working replacement at hand.

In fact, to talk about the style of a particular novel or poem at all as a "style," without implying, whether one wishes to or not, that style is merely decorative, accessory, is extremely hard. Merely by employing the notion, one is almost bound to invoke, albeit implicitly, an antithesis between style and something else. Many critics appear not to realize this. They think themselves sufficiently protected by a theoretical disclaimer on the vulgar filtering-off of style from content, all the while their judgments continue to reinforce precisely what they are, in theory, eager to deny.

• •

One way in which the old duality lives on in the practice of criticism, in concrete judgments, is the frequency with which quite admirable works of art are defended as good although what is miscalled their style is acknowledged to be crude or careless. Another is the frequency with which a very complex style is regarded with a barely concealed ambivalence. Contemporary writers and other artists with a style that is intricate, hermetic, demanding—not to speak of "beautiful"—get their ration of unstinting praise. Still, it is clear that such a style is often felt to be a form of insincerity: evidence of the artist's intrusion upon his materials, which should be allowed to deliver themselves in a pure state.

Whitman, in the preface to the 1855 edition of *Leaves of Grass*, expresses the disavowal of "style" which is, in most arts since the last century, a standard ploy for ushering in a new stylistic vocabulary. "The greatest poet has less a marked style and is more the free channel of himself," that great and very mannered poet contends. "He says to his art, I will not be meddlesome, I will not have in my writing any elegance or effect or originality to hang in the way between me and the rest like curtains. I will have nothing hang in the way, not the richest curtains. What I tell I tell for precisely what it is."

Of course, as everyone knows or claims to know, there is no neutral, absolutely transparent style. Sartre has shown, in his excellent review of *The Stranger*, how the celebrated "white style" of Camus' novel—impersonal, expository, lucid, flat—is itself the vehicle of Meursault's image of the world (as made up of absurd, fortuitous moments). What Roland Barthes calls "the zero degree of writing" is, precisely by being anti-metaphorical and dehumanized, as selective and artificial as any traditional style of writing. Nevertheless, the notion of a style-less, transparent art is one of the most tenacious fantasies of modern culture. Artists and critics pretend to believe that it is no more possible to get the artifice out of art than it is for a person to lose his personality. Yet the aspiration lingers—a permanent dissent from modern art, with its dizzying velocity of style changes.

• •

To speak of style is one way of speaking about the totality of a work of art. Like all discourse about totalities, talk of style must rely on metaphors. And metaphors mislead.

Take, for instance, Whitman's very material metaphor. By likening style to a curtain, he has of course confused style with decoration and for this would be speedily faulted by most critics. To conceive of style as a decorative encumbrance on the matter of the work suggests that the curtain could be parted and the matter revealed; or, to vary the metaphor slightly, that the curtain could be rendered transparent. But this is not the only erroneous implication of the metaphor. What the metaphor also suggests is that style is a matter of more or less (quantity), thick or thin (density). And, though less obviously so, this is just as wrong as the fancy that an artist possesses the genuine option to have or not to have a style. Style is not quantitative, any more than it is superadded. A more complex stylistic convention—say, one taking prose further away from the diction and cadences of ordinary speech—does not mean that the work has "more" style.

Indeed, practically all metaphors for style amount to placing matter on the inside, style on the outside. It would be more to the point to reverse the metaphor. The matter, the subject, is on the outside; the style is on the inside. As Cocteau writes: "Decorative style has never existed. Style is the soul, and unfortunately with us the soul assumes the form of the body." Even if one were to define style as the manner of our appearing, this by no means necessarily entails an opposition between a style that one assumes and one's "true" being. In fact, such a disjunction is extremely rare. In almost every case, our manner of appearing is our manner of being. The mask is the face.

I should make clear, however, that what I have been saying about dangerous metaphors doesn't rule out the use of limited and concrete metaphors to describe the impact of a particular style. It seems harmless to speak of a style, drawing from the crude terminology used to render physical sensations, as being "loud" or "heavy" or "dull" or "tasteless" or, employing the image of an argument, as "inconsistent."

• •

The antipathy to "style" is always an antipathy to a given style. There are no style-less works of art, only works of art belonging to different, more or less complex stylistic traditions and conventions.

This means that the notion of style, generically considered, has a specific, historical meaning. It is not only that styles belong to a time and a place; and that our perception of the style of a given work of art is always charged with an awareness of the work's historicity, its place in a chronology. Further: the visibility of styles is itself a product of historical consciousness. Were it not for departures from, or experimentation with, previous artistic norms which are known to us, we could never recognize the profile of a new style. Still further: the very notion of "style" needs to be approached historically. Awareness of style as a problematic and isolable element in a work of art has emerged in the audience for art only at certain historical moments—as a front behind which other issues, ultimately ethical and political, are being debated. The notion of "having a style" is one of the solutions that has arisen, intermittently since the Renaissance, to the crises that have threatened old ideas of truth, of moral rectitude, and also of naturalness.

• •

But suppose all this is admitted. That all representation is incarnated in a given style (easy to say). That there is, therefore, strictly speaking, no such thing as realism, except as, itself, a special stylistic convention (a little harder). Still, there are styles and styles.

Everyone is acquainted with movements in art—two examples: Mannerist painting of the late 16th and early 17th centuries, Art Nouveau in painting, architecture, furniture, and domestic objects —which do more than simply have "a style." Artists such as Parmigianino, Pontormo, Rosso, Bronzino, such as Gaudí, Guimard, Beardsley, and Tiffany, in some obvious way cultivate style. They seem to be preoccupied with stylistic questions and indeed to place the accent less on what they are saying than on the manner of saying it.

To deal with art of this type, which seems to demand the distinction I have been urging be abandoned, a term such as "stylization" or its equivalent is needed. "Stylization" is what is present in a work of art precisely when an artist does make the by no means inevitable distinction between matter and manner, theme and form. When that happens, when style and subject are so distinguished, that is, played off against each other, one can legitimately speak of subjects being treated (or mistreated) in a certain style. Creative mistreatment is more the rule. For when the material of art is conceived of as "subject-matter," it is also experienced as capable of being exhausted. And as subjects are understood to be fairly far along in this process of exhaustion, they become available to further and further stylization.

Compare, for example, certain silent movies of Sternberg (*Salvation Hunters, Underworld, The Docks of New York*) with the six American movies he made in the 1930s with Marlene Dietrich. The best of the early Sternberg films have pronounced stylistic features, a very sophisticated aesthetic surface. But we do not feel about the narrative of the sailor and the prostitute in *The Docks of New York* as we do about the adventures of the Dietrich character in *Blonde Venus* or *The Scarlet Empress*, that it is an exercise in style. What informs these later films of Sternberg's is an ironic attitude toward the subject-matter (romantic love, the *femme fatale*), a judgment on the subject-matter as interesting only so far as it is transformed by exaggeration, in a word, stylized. . . . Cubist painting, or the sculpture of Giacometti, would not be an example of "stylization" as distinguished from "style" in art; however extensive the distortions of the human face and figure, these are not present to make the face and figure *interesting*. But the paintings of Crivelli and Georges de La Tour are examples of what I mean.

"Stylization" in a work of art, as distinct from style, reflects an ambivalence (affection contradicted by contempt, obsession contradicted by irony) toward the subject-matter. This ambivalence is handled by maintaining, through the rhetorical overlay that is stylization, a special distance from the subject. But the common result is that either the work of art is excessively narrow and repetitive, or else the different parts seem unhinged, dissociated. (A good example of the latter is the relation between the visually brilliant denouement of Orson Welles' *The Lady from Shanghai* and the rest of the film.) No doubt, in a culture pledged to the utility (particularly the moral utility) of art, burdened with a useless need to fence off solemn art from arts which provide amusement, the eccentricities of stylized art supply a valid and valuable satisfaction. I have described these satisfactions in another essay, under the name of "camp" taste. Yet, it is evident that stylized art, palpably an art of excess, lacking harmoniousness, can never be of the very greatest kind.

• •

What haunts all contemporary use of the notion of style is the putative opposition between form and content. How is one to exorcise the feeling that "style," which functions like the notion of form, subverts content? One thing seems certain. No affirmation of the organic relation between style and content will really carry conviction—or guide critics who make this affirmation to the recasting of their specific discourse—until the notion of content is put in its place.

Most critics would agree that a work of art does not "contain" a certain amount of content (or function—as in the case of architecture) embellished by "style." But few address themselves to the positive consequences of what they seem to have agreed to. What is "content"? Or, more precisely, what is left of the notion of content when we have transcended the antithesis of style (or form) and content? Part of the answer lies in the fact that for a work of art to have "content" is, in itself, a rather special stylistic convention. The great task which remains to critical theory is to examine in detail the formal function of subject-matter.

• •

Until this function is acknowledged and properly explored, it is inevitable that critics will go on treating works of art as "statements." (Less so, of course, in those arts which are abstract or have largely gone abstract, like music and painting and the dance. In these arts, the critics have not solved the problem; it has been taken from them.) Of course, a work of art can be considered as a statement, that is, as the answer to a question. On the most elementary level, Goya's portrait of the Duke of Wellington may be examined as the answer to the question: what did Wellington look like? *Anna Karenina* may be treated as an investigation of the problems of love, marriage, and adultery. Though the issue of the adequacy of artistic representation to life has pretty much been abandoned in, for example, painting, such adequacy continues to constitute a powerful standard of judgment in most appraisals of serious novels, plays, and films. In critical theory, the notion is quite old. At least since Diderot, the main tradition of criticism in all the arts, appealing to such apparently dissimilar criteria as verisimilitude and moral correctness, in effect treats the work of art as a *statement being made in the form of a work of art.*

To treat works of art in this fashion is not wholly irrelevant. But it is, obviously, putting art to use—for such purposes as inquiring into the history of ideas, diagnosing contemporary culture, or creating social solidarity. Such a treatment has little to do with what actually happens when a person possessing some training and aesthetic sensibility looks at a work of art appropriately. A work of art encountered as a work of art is an experience, not a statement or an answer to a question. Art is not only about something; it is something. A work of art is a thing in the world, not just a text or commentary on the world.

I am not saying that a work of art creates a world which is entirely self-referring. Of course, works of art (with the important exception of music) refer to the real world—to our knowledge, to our experience, to our values. They present information and evaluations. But their distinctive feature is that they give rise not to conceptual knowledge (which is the distinctive feature of discursive or scientific knowledge—e.g., philosophy, sociology, psychology, history) but to something like an excitation, a phenomenon of commitment, judgment in a state of thralldom or captivation. Which is to say that the knowledge we gain through art is an experience of the form or style of knowing something, rather than a knowledge of something (like a fact or a moral judgment) in itself.

This explains the preeminence of the value of expressiveness in works of art; and how the value of expressiveness—that is, of style —rightly takes precedence over content (when content is, falsely, isolated from style). The satisfactions of *Paradise Lost* for us do not lie in its views on God and man, but in the superior kinds of energy, vitality, expressiveness which are incarnated in the poem.

Hence, too, the peculiar dependence of a work of art, however expressive, upon the cooperation of the person having the experience, for one may see what is "said" but remain unmoved, either through dullness or distraction. Art is seduction, not rape. A work of art proposes a type of experience designed to manifest the quality of imperiousness. But art cannot seduce without the complicity of the experiencing subject.

• •

Inevitably, critics who regard works of art as statements will be wary of "style," even as they pay lip service to "imagination." All that imagination really means for them, anyway, is the supersensitive rendering of "reality." It is this "reality" snared by the work of art that they continue to focus on, rather than on the extent to which a work of art engages the mind in certain transformations.

But when the metaphor of the work of art as a statement loses its authority, the ambivalence toward "style" should dissolve; for this ambivalence mirrors the presumed tension between the statement and the manner in which it is stated.

• •

In the end, however, attitudes toward style cannot be reformed merely by appealing to the "appropriate" (as opposed to utilitarian) way of looking at works of art. The ambivalence toward style is not rooted in simple error—it would then be quite easy to uproot—but in a passion, the passion of an entire culture. This passion is to protect and defend values traditionally conceived of as lying "outside" art, namely truth and morality, but which remain in perpetual danger of being compromised by art. Behind the ambivalence toward

style is, ultimately, the historic Western confusion about the relation between art and morality, the aesthetic and the ethical.

For the problem of art versus morality is a pseudo-problem. The
distinction itself is a trap; its continued plausibility rests on not
putting the ethical into question, but only the aesthetic. To argue
on these grounds at all, seeking to defend the autonomy of the aesthetic (and I have, rather uneasily, done so myself), is already to
grant something that should not be granted—namely, that there
exist two independent sorts of response, the aesthetic and the ethical, which vie for our loyalty when we experience a work of art. As
if during the experience one really had to choose between responsible and humane conduct, on the one hand, and the pleasurable
stimulation of consciousness, on the other!

Of course, we never have a purely aesthetic response to works of
art—neither to a play or a novel, with its depicting of human beings choosing and acting, nor, though it is less obvious, to a painting
by Jackson Pollock or a Greek vase. (Ruskin has written acutely
about the moral aspects of the formal properties of painting.) But
neither would it be appropriate for us to make a moral response to
something in a work of art in the same sense that we do to an act in
real life. I would undoubtedly be indignant if someone I knew murdered his wife and got away with it (psychologically, legally), but I
can hardly become indignant, as many critics seem to be, when the
hero of Norman Mailer's *An American Dream* murders his wife and
goes unpunished. Divine, Darling, and the others in Genet's *Our
Lady of the Flowers* are not real people whom we are being asked
to decide whether to invite into our living rooms; they are figures in
an imaginary landscape. The point may seem obvious, but the prev-
alence of genteel-moralistic judgments in contemporary literary
(and film) criticism makes it worth repeating a number of times.

For most people, as Ortega y Gasset has pointed out in *The Dehumanization of Art*, aesthetic pleasure is a state of mind essentially
indistinguishable from their ordinary responses. By art, they understand a means through which they are brought in contact with interesting human affairs. When they grieve and rejoice at human
destinies in a play or film or novel, it is not really different from
grieving and rejoicing over such events in real life—except that the

experience of human destinies in art contains less ambivalence, it is relatively disinterested, and it is free from painful consequences. The experience is also, in a certain measure, more intense; for when suffering and pleasure are experienced vicariously, people can afford to be avid. But, as Ortega argues, "a preoccupation with the human content of the work [of art] is in principle incompatible with aesthetic judgment." *

Ortega is entirely correct, in my opinion. But I would not care to leave the matter where he does, which tacitly isolates aesthetic from moral response. Art is connected with morality, I should argue. One way that it is so connected is that art may yield moral pleasure; but the moral pleasure peculiar to art is not the pleasure of approving of acts or disapproving of them. The moral pleasure in art, as well as the moral service that art performs, consists in the intelligent gratification of consciousness.

• •

What "morality" means is a habitual or chronic type of behavior (including feelings and acts). Morality is a code of acts, and of judgments and sentiments by which we reinforce our habits of acting in a certain way, which prescribe a standard for behaving or trying to behave toward other human beings generally (that is, to all who are acknowledged to be human) as if we were inspired by love. Needless to say, love is something we feel in truth for just a few individual human beings, among those who are known to us in reality and in our imagination. . . . Morality is a form of acting and not a particular repertoire of choices.

If morality is so understood—as one of the achievements of hu-

* Ortega continues: "A work of art vanishes from sight for a beholder who seeks in it nothing but the moving fate of John and Mary or Tristan and Isolde and adjusts his vision to this. Tristan's sorrows are sorrows and can evoke compassion only insofar as they are taken as real. But an object of art is artistic only insofar as it is not real. . . . But not many people are capable of adjusting their perceptive apparatus to the pane and the transparency that is the work of art. Instead, they look right through it and revel in the human reality with which the work deals. . . . During the 19th century artists proceeded in all too impure a fashion. They reduced the strictly aesthetic elements to a minimum and let the work consist almost entirely in a fiction of human realities. . . . Works of this kind [both Romanticism and Naturalism] are only partially works of art, or artistic objects . . . No wonder that 19th century art has been so popular . . . it is not art but an extract from life."

man will, dictating to itself a mode of acting and being in the world —it becomes clear that no generic antagonism exists between the form of consciousness, aimed at action, which is morality, and the nourishment of consciousness, which is aesthetic experience. Only when works of art are reduced to statements which propose a specific content, and when morality is identified with a particular morality (and any particular morality has its dross, those elements which are no more than a defense of limited social interests and class values)—only then can a work of art be thought to undermine morality. Indeed, only then can the full distinction between the aesthetic and the ethical be made.

But if we understand morality in the singular, as a generic decision on the part of consciousness, then it appears that our response to art is "moral" insofar as it is, precisely, the enlivening of our sensibility and consciousness. For it is sensibility that nourishes our capacity for moral choice, and prompts our readiness to act, assuming that we do choose, which is a prerequisite for calling an act moral, and are not just blindly and unreflectively obeying. Art performs this "moral" task because the qualities which are intrinsic to the aesthetic experience (disinterestedness, contemplativeness, attentiveness, the awakening of the feelings) and to the aesthetic object (grace, intelligence, expressiveness, energy, sensuousness) are also fundamental constituents of a moral response to life.

• •

In art, "content" is, as it were, the pretext, the goal, the lure which engages consciousness in essentially formal processes of transformation.

This is how we can, in good conscience, cherish works of art which, considered in terms of "content," are morally objectionable to us. (The difficulty is of the same order as that involved in appreciating works of art, such as The Divine Comedy, whose premises are intellectually alien.) To call Leni Riefenstahl's The Triumph of the Will and The Olympiad masterpieces is not to gloss over Nazi propaganda with aesthetic lenience. The Nazi propaganda is there. But something else is there, too, which we reject at our loss. Because they project the complex movements of intelligence and grace and sensuousness, these two films of Riefenstahl (unique among works of Nazi artists) transcend the categories of propaganda or even reportage. And we find ourselves—to be sure, rather uncomfortably—seeing "Hitler" and not Hitler, the "1936 Olympics" and not the 1936 Olympics. Through Riefenstahl's genius as a film-maker, the "content" has—let us even assume, against her intentions—come to play a purely formal role.

A work of art, so far as it is a work of art, cannot—whatever the artist's personal intentions—advocate anything at all. The greatest artists attain a sublime neutrality. Think of Homer and Shakespeare, from whom generations of scholars and critics have vainly labored to extract particular "views" about human nature, morality, and society.

Again, take the case of Genet—though here, there is additional evidence for the point I am trying to make, because the artist's intentions are known. Genet, in his writings, may seem to be asking us to approve of cruelty, treacherousness, licentiousness, and murder. But so far as he is making a work of art, Genet is not advocating anything at all. He is recording, devouring, transfiguring his experience. In Genet's books, as it happens, this very process itself is his explicit subject; his books are not only works of art but works about art. However, even when (as is usually the case) this process is not in the foreground of the artist's demonstration, it is still this, the processing of experience, to which we owe our attention. It is immaterial that Genet's characters might repel us in real life. So would most of the characters in King Lear. The interest of Genet lies in the manner whereby his "subject" is annihilated by the serenity and intelligence of his imagination.

Approving or disapproving morally of what a work of art "says" is just as extraneous as becoming sexually excited by a work of art. (Both are, of course, very common.) And the reasons urged against the propriety and relevance of one apply as well to the other. Indeed, in this notion of the annihilation of the subject we have perhaps the only serious criterion for distinguishing between erotic literature or films or paintings which are art and those which (for want of a better word) one has to call pornography. Pornography has a "content" and is designed to make us connect (with disgust, desire) with that content. It is a substitute for life. But art does not excite; or, if it does, the excitation is appeased, within the terms of the aesthetic experience. All great art induces contemplation, a dynamic contemplation. However much the reader or listener or spectator is aroused by a provisional identification of what is in the work of art with real life, his ultimate reaction—so far as he is reacting to the work as a work of art—must be detached, restful, contemplative, emotionally free, beyond indignation and approval. It is interesting that Genet has recently said that he now thinks that if his books arouse readers sexually, "they're badly written, because the poetic emotion should be so strong that no reader is moved sexually. Insofar as my books are pornographic, I don't reject them. I simply say that I lacked grace."

A work of art may contain all sorts of information and offer instruction in new (and sometimes commendable) attitudes. We may learn about medieval theology and Florentine history from Dante; we may have our first experience of passionate melancholy from Chopin; we may become convinced of the barbarity of war by Goya and of the inhumanity of capital punishment by An American Tragedy. But so far as we deal with these works as works of art, the gratification they impart is of another order. It is an experience of the qualities or forms of human consciousness.

The objection that this approach reduces art to mere "formalism" must not be allowed to stand. (That word should be reserved for those works of art which mechanically perpetuate outmoded or depleted aesthetic formulas.) An approach which considers works of art as living, autonomous models of consciousness will seem objectionable only so long as we refuse to surrender the shallow distinction of form and content. For the sense in which a work of art has no content is no different from the sense in which the world has no content. Both are. Both need no justification; nor could they possibly have any.

• •

The hyperdevelopment of style in, for example, Mannerist painting and Art Nouveau, is an emphatic form of experiencing the world as an aesthetic phenomenon. But only a particularly emphatic form, which arises in reaction to an oppressively dogmatic style of realism. All style—that is, all art—proclaims this. And the world *is*, ultimately, an aesthetic phenomenon.

That is to say, the world (all there is) cannot, ultimately, be justified. Justification is an operation of the mind which can be performed only when we consider one part of the world in relation to another—not when we consider all there is.

• •

The work of art, so far as we give ourselves to it, exercises a total or absolute claim on us. The purpose of art is not as an auxiliary to truth, either particular and historical or eternal. "If art is anything," as Robbe-Grillet has written, "it is everything; in which case it must be self-sufficient, and there can be nothing beyond it."

But this position is easily caricatured, for we live in the world, and it is in the world that objects of art are made and enjoyed. The claim that I have been making for the autonomy of the work of art —its freedom to "mean" nothing—does not rule out consideration of the effect or impact or function of art, once it be granted that in this functioning of the art object as art object the divorce between the aesthetic and the ethical is meaningless.

I have several times applied to the work of art the metaphor of a mode of nourishment. To become involved with a work of art entails, to be sure, the experience of detaching oneself from the world. But the work of art itself is also a vibrant, magical, and exemplary object which returns us to the world in some way more open and enriched.

• •

Raymond Bayer has written: "What each and every aesthetic object imposes upon us, in appropriate rhythms, is a unique and singular formula for the flow of our energy. . . . Every work of art embodies a principle of proceeding, of stopping, of scanning; an image of energy or relaxation, the imprint of a caressing or destroying hand which is [the artist's] alone." We can call this the physiognomy of the work, or its rhythm, or, as I would rather do, its style. Of course, when we employ the notion of style historically, to group works of art into schools and periods, we tend to efface the individuality of styles. But this is not our experience when we encounter a work of art from an aesthetic (as opposed to a conceptual) point of view. Then, so far as the work is successful and still has the power to communicate with us, we experience only the individuality and contingency of the style.

It is the same with our own lives. If we see them from the outside, as the influence and popular dissemination of the social sciences and psychiatry has persuaded more and more people to do, we view ourselves as instances of generalities, and in so doing become profoundly and painfully alienated from our own experience and our humanity.

As William Earle has recently noted, if *Hamlet* is "about" anything, it is about Hamlet, his particular situation, not about the human condition. A work of art is a kind of showing or recording or witnessing which gives palpable form to consciousness; its object is to make something singular explicit. So far as it is true that we cannot judge (morally, conceptually) unless we generalize, then it is also true that the experience of works of art, and what is represented in works of art, transcends judgment—though the work itself may be judged as art. Isn't this just what we recognize as a feature of the greatest art, like the *Iliad* and the novels of Tolstoy and the plays of Shakespeare? That such art overrides our petty judgments, our facile labelling of persons and acts as good or bad? And that this can happen is all to the good. (There is even a gain for the cause of morality in it.)

For morality, unlike art, *is* ultimately justified by its utility: that it makes, or is supposed to make, life more humane and livable for us all. But consciousness—what used to be called, rather tendentiously, the faculty of contemplation—can be, and is, wider and more various than action. It has its nourishment, art and speculative thought, activities which can be described either as self-justifying or in no need of justification. What a work of art does is to make us see or comprehend something singular, not judge or generalize. This act of comprehension accompanied by voluptuousness is the only valid end, and sole sufficient justification, of a work of art.

• •

Perhaps the best way of clarifying the nature of our experience of works of art, and the relation between art and the rest of human feeling and doing, is to invoke the notion of will. It is a useful notion because will is not just a particular posture of consciousness, energized consciousness. It is also an attitude toward the world, of a subject toward the world.

The complex kind of willing that is embodied, and communicated, in a work of art both abolishes the world and encounters it in an extraordinary intense and specialized way. This double aspect of the will in art is succinctly expressed by Bayer when he says: "Each work of art gives us the schematized and disengaged memory of a volition." Insofar as it is schematized, disengaged, a memory, the willing involved in art sets itself at a distance from the world.

All of which harkens back to Nietzsche's famous statement in *The Birth of Tragedy*: "Art is not an imitation of nature but its metaphysical supplement, raised up beside it in order to overcome it."

• •

All works of art are founded on a certain distance from the lived reality which is represented. This "distance" is, by definition, inhuman or impersonal to a certain degree; for in order to appear to us as art, the work must restrict sentimental intervention and emotional participation, which are functions of "closeness." It is the degree and manipulating of this distance, the conventions of distance, which constitute the style of the work. In the final analysis, "style" *is* art. And art is nothing more or less than various modes of stylized, dehumanized representation.

But this view—expounded by Ortega y Gasset, among others—can easily be misinterpreted, since it seems to suggest that art, so far as it approaches its own norm, is a kind of irrelevant, impotent toy. Ortega himself greatly contributes to such a misinterpretation by omitting the various dialectics between self and world involved in the experiencing of works of art. Ortega focuses too exclusively on the notion of the work of art as a certain kind of object, with its own, spiritually aristocratic, standards for being savored. A work of art is first of all an object, not an imitation; and it is true that all great art is founded on distance, on artificiality, on style, on what Ortega calls dehumanization. But the notion of distance (and of dehumanization, as well) is misleading, unless one adds that the movement is not just away from but toward the world. The overcoming or transcending of the world in art is also a way of encountering the world, and of training or educating the will to be in the world. It would seem that Ortega and even Robbe-Grillet, a more recent exponent of the same position, are still not wholly free of the spell of the notion of "content." For, in order to limit the human content of art, and to fend off tired ideologies like humanism or socialist realism which would put art in the service of some moral or social idea, they feel required to ignore or scant the function of art. But art does not become function-less when it is seen to be, in the last analysis, content-less. For all the persuasiveness of Ortega's and Robbe-Grillet's defense of the formal nature of art, the specter of banished "content" continues to lurk around the edges of their argument, giving to "form" a defiantly anemic, salutarily eviscerated look.

The argument will never be complete until "form" or "style" can be thought of without that banished specter, without a feeling of loss. Valéry's daring inversion—"Literature. What is 'form' for anyone else is 'content' for me"—scarcely does the trick. It is hard to think oneself out of a distinction so habitual and apparently self-evident. One can do so only by adopting a different, more organic, theoretical vantage point—such as the notion of will. What is wanted of such a vantage point is that it do justice to the twin aspects of art: as object and as function, as artifice and as living form of consciousness, as the overcoming or supplementing of reality and as the making explicit of forms of encountering reality, as autonomous individual creation and as dependent historical phenomenon.

• •

Art is the objectifying of the will in a thing or performance, and the provoking or arousing of the will. From the point of view of the artist, it is the objectifying of a volition; from the point of view of the spectator, it is the creation of an imaginary décor for the will.

Indeed, the entire history of the various arts could be rewritten as the history of different attitudes toward the will. Nietzsche and Spengler wrote pioneer studies on this theme. A valuable recent attempt is to be found in a book by Jean Starobinski, *The Invention of Liberty*, mainly devoted to 18th century painting and architecture. Starobinski examines the art of this period in terms of the new ideas of self-mastery and of mastery of the world, as embodying new relations between the self and the world. Art is seen as the naming of emotions. Emotions, longings, aspirations, by thus being named, are virtually invented and certainly promulgated by art: for example, the "sentimental solitude" provoked by the gardens that were laid out in the 18th century and by much-admired ruins.

Thus, it should be clear that the account of the autonomy of art I have been outlining, in which I have characterized art as an imaginary landscape or décor of the will, not only does not preclude but rather invites the examination of works of art as historically specifiable phenomena.

The intricate stylistic convolutions of modern art, for example, are clearly a function of the unprecedented technical extension of the human will by technology, and the devastating commitment of human will to a novel form of social and psychological order, one based on incessant change. But it also remains to be said that the very possibility of the explosion of technology, of the contemporary disruptions of self and society, depends on the attitudes toward the will which are partly invented and disseminated by works of art at a certain historical moment, and then come to appear as a "realistic" reading of a perennial human nature.

• •

Style is the principle of decision in a work of art, the signature of the artist's will. And as the human will is capable of an indefinite number of stances, there are an indefinite number of possible styles for works of art.

Seen from the outside, that is, historically, stylistic decisions can always be correlated with some historical development—like the invention of writing or of movable type, the invention or transformation of musical instruments, the availability of new materials to the sculptor or architect. But this approach, however sound and valuable, of necessity sees matters grossly; it treats of "periods" and "traditions" and "schools."

Seen from the inside, that is, when one examines an individual work of art and tries to account for its value and effect, every stylistic decision contains an element of arbitrariness, however much it may seem justifiable *propter hoc*. If art is the supreme game which the will plays with itself, "style" consists of the set of rules by which this game is played. And the rules are always, finally, an artificial and arbitrary limit, whether they are rules of form (like *terza rima* or the twelve-tone row or frontality) or the presence of a certain "content." The role of the arbitrary and unjustifiable in art has never been sufficiently acknowledged. Ever since the enterprise of criticism began with Aristotle's *Poetics*, critics have been beguiled into emphasizing the necessary in art. (When Aristotle said that poetry was more philosophical than history, he was justified insofar as he wanted to rescue poetry, that is, the arts, from being conceived as a type of factual, particular, descriptive statement. But what he said was misleading insofar as it suggests that art supplies something like what philosophy gives us: an argument. The metaphor of the work of art as an "argument," with premises and entailments, has informed most criticism since.) Usually critics who want to praise a work of art feel compelled to demonstrate that each part is justified, that it could not be other than it is. And every artist, when it comes to his own work, remembering the role of chance, fatigue, external distractions, knows what the critic says to be a lie, knows that it could well have been otherwise. The sense of inevitability that a great work of art projects is not made up of the inevitability or necessity of its parts, but of the whole.

• •

In other words, what is inevitable in a work of art is the style. To the extent that a work seems right, just, unimaginable otherwise (without loss or damage), what we are responding to is a quality of its style. The most attractive works of art are those which give us the illusion that the artist had no alternatives, so wholly centered is he *in* his style. Compare that which is forced, labored, synthetic in the construction of *Madame Bovary* and of *Ulysses* with the ease and harmony of such equally ambitious works as *Les Liaisons Dangereuses* and Kafka's *Metamorphosis*. The first two books I have mentioned are great indeed. But the greatest art seems secreted, not constructed.

For an artist's style to have this quality of authority, assurance, seamlessness, inevitability does not, of course, alone put his work at the very highest level of achievement. Radiguet's two novels have it as well as Bach.

• •

The difference that I have drawn between "style" and "styliza-tion" might be analogous to the difference between will and willfulness.

• •

An artist's style is, from a technical point of view, nothing other than the particular idiom in which he deploys the forms of his art. It is for this reason that the problems raised by the concept of "style" overlap with those raised by the concept of "form," and their solutions will have much in common.

For instance, one function of style is identical with, because it is simply a more individual specification of, that important function of form pointed out by Coleridge and Valéry: to preserve the works of the mind against oblivion. This function is easily demonstrated in the rhythmical, sometimes rhyming, character of all primitive, oral literatures. Rhythm and rhyme, and the more complex formal resources of poetry such as meter, symmetry of figures, antitheses, are the means that words afford for creating a memory of themselves before material signs (writing) are invented; hence everything that an archaic culture wishes to commit to memory is put in poetic form. "The form of a work," as Valéry puts it, "is the sum of its perceptible characteristics, whose physical action compels recogni-tion and tends to resist all those varying causes of dissolution which threaten the expressions of thought, whether it be inattention, for-getfulness, or even the objections that may arise against it in the mind."

Thus, form—in its specific idiom, style—is a plan of sensory im-printing, the vehicle for the transaction between immediate sensu-ous impression and memory (be it individual or cultural). This mnemonic function explains why every style depends on, and can be analyzed in terms of, some principle of repetition or redundancy.

It also explains the difficulties of the contemporary period of the arts. Today styles do not develop slowly and succeed each other gradually, over long periods of time which allow the audience for art to assimilate fully the principles of repetition on which the work

II

The artist
as exemplary
sufferer

CESARE PAVESE began
writing around 1930, and the novels which have been translated
and published here—*The House on the Hill, The Moon and the
Bonfires, Among Women Only,* and *The Devil in the Hills*—were
all written in the years 1947-49, so that a reader confined to English
translations can't generalize about his work as a whole. From these
four novels alone, however, it appears that his main virtues as a
novelist are delicacy, economy, and control. The style is flat, dry,
unemotional. One remarks the coolness of Pavese's fiction, though
the subject-matter is often violent. This is because the real subject
is never the violent happening (e.g. the suicide in *Among Women
Only;* the war in *The Devil in the Hills*) but, rather, the cautious
subjectivity of the narrator. The typical effort of a Pavese hero is
lucidity; the typical problem is that of lapsed communication. The
novels are about crises of conscience, and the refusal to allow crises

of conscience. A certain atrophy of the emotions, an enervation of sentiment and bodily vitality, is presupposed. The anguish of prematurely disillusioned, highly civilized people alternating between irony and melancholic experiments with their own emotions is indeed familiar. But unlike other explorations of this vein of modern sensibility—for example, much of French fiction and poetry of the last eighty years—Pavese's novels are unsensational and chaste. The main action always takes place off-stage, or in the past; and erotic scenes are curiously avoided.

As if to compensate for the detached relations which his characters have with each other, Pavese typically attributes to them a deep involvement with a place—usually either the cityscape of Turin, where Pavese went to the university and lived most of his adult life, or the surrounding Piedmont countryside, where he was born and spent his childhood. This sense of place, and the desire to find and recover the meaning of a place, does not, however, give Pavese's work any of the characteristics of regional fiction, and this may in part account for the failure of his novels to arouse much enthusiasm among an English-speaking audience, nothing like that aroused by the work of Silone or Moravia, though he is a much more gifted and original writer than either of these. Pavese's sense of place and of people is not what one expects of an Italian writer. But then Pavese was a Northern Italian; Northern Italy is not the Italy of the foreign dream, and Turin is a large industrial city lacking in the historical resonance and incarnate sensuality which attracts foreigners to Italy. One finds no monuments, no local color, no ethnic charm in Pavese's Turin and Piedmont. The place is there, but as the unattainable, the anonymous, the inhuman.

Pavese's sense of the relation of people to place (the way in which people are transfixed by the impersonal force of a place) will be familiar to anyone who has seen the films of Alain Resnais and especially of Michelangelo Antonioni—Le Amiche (which was adapted from Pavese's best novel, Among Women Only), L'Avventura, and La Notte. But the virtues of Pavese's fiction are not popular virtues, any more than are the virtues of, say, Antonioni's films. (Those who don't take to Antonioni's films call them "literary" and "too subjective.") Like Antonioni's films, Pavese's novels are refined, elliptical (though never obscure), quiet, anti-dramatic, self-contained. Pavese is not a major writer, as Antonioni is a major film-maker. But he does deserve a good deal more attention in England and America than he has gotten thus far.*

Recently Pavese's diaries from the years 1935 to 1950, when he committed suicide at the age of forty-two, have been issued in English.† They can be read without any acquaintance with Pavese's novels, as an example of a peculiarly modern literary genre—the writer's "diary" or "notebooks" or "journal."

Why do we read a writer's journal? Because it illuminates his books? Often it does not. More likely, simply because of the rawness of the journal form, even when it is written with an eye to future publication. Here we read the writer in the first person; we encounter the ego behind the masks of ego in an author's works. No degree of intimacy in a novel can supply this, even when the author writes in the first person or uses a third person which transpar-

---

* The same is true of another Italian, Tommaso Landolfi, with a large body of stories and novels, born the same year as Pavese (1908) but still living and writing. Landolfi, who is thus far represented in English by only one volume, a selection of nine of his short stories, entitled *Gogol's Wife and Other Stories*, is a very different and, at his best, more forceful writer than Pavese. His morbid wit, austere intellectuality, and rather surrealistic notions of disaster put him closer to writers like Borges and Isak Dinesen. But he and Pavese have something in common which makes the work of both unlike the fiction mainly being written today in England and America, and apparently uninteresting to the audience for that fiction. What they share is the project of a basically neutral, reserved kind of writing. In such writing, the act of relating a story is seen primarily as an act of intelligence. To narrate is palpably to employ one's intelligence; the unity of the narration characteristic of European and Latin American fiction is the unity of the narrator's intelligence. But the writing of fiction common in America today has little use for this patient, dogged, unshowy use of intelligence. American writers mostly want the facts to declare, to interpret themselves. If there is a narrative voice, it is likely to be immaculately mindless—or else strainingly clever and bouncy. Thus, most American writing is grossly rhetorical (that is, there is an overproduction of means in relation to ends), in contrast to the classical mode of European writing, which achieves its effects with an anti-rhetorical style—a style that holds back, that aims ultimately at neutral transparency. Both Pavese and Landolfi belong squarely in this anti-rhetorical tradition.

† *The Burning Brand: Diaries 1935-1950* by Cesare Pavese. Translated by A. E. Murch (with Jeanne Molli). New York, Walker & Co.

ently points to himself. Most of Pavese's novels, including the four translated into English, are narrated in the first person. Yet we know that the "I" in Pavese's novels is not identical with Pavese himself, no more than is the "Marcel" who tells *Remembrance of Things Past* identical with Proust, nor the "K." of *The Trial* and *The Castle* identical with Kafka. We are not satisfied. It is the author naked which the modern audience demands, as ages of religious faith demanded a human sacrifice.

The journal gives us the workshop of the writer's soul. And why are we interested in the soul of the writer? Not because we are so interested in writers as such. But because of the insatiable modern preoccuption with psychology, the latest and most powerful legacy of the Christian tradition of introspection, opened up by Paul and Augustine, which equates the discovery of the self with the discovery of the suffering self. For the modern consciousness, the artist (replacing the saint) is the exemplary sufferer. And among artists, the writer, the man of words, is the person to whom we look to be able best to express his suffering.

The writer is the exemplary sufferer because he has found both the deepest level of suffering and also a professional means to sublimate (in the literal, not the Freudian, sense of sublimate) his suffering. As a man, he suffers; as a writer, he transforms his suffering into art. The writer is the man who discovers the use of suffering in the economy of art—as the saints discovered the utility and necessity of suffering in the economy of salvation.

The unity of Pavese's diaries is to be found in his reflections on how to use, how to act on, his suffering. Literature is one use. Isolation is another, both as a technique for the inciting and perfecting of his art, and as a value in itself. And suicide is the third, ultimate use of suffering—conceived of not as an end to suffering, but as the ultimate way of acting on suffering.

Thus we have the following remarkable sequence of thought, in a diary entry of 1938. Pavese writes: "Literature is a defense against the attacks of life. It says to life: 'You can't deceive me. I know your habits, foresee and enjoy watching your reactions, and steal your secrets by involving you in cunning obstructions that halt your normal flow.' . . . The other defense against things in general is silence as we muster strength for a fresh leap forward. But we must impose that silence on ourselves, not have it imposed on us, not even by death. To choose a hardship for ourselves is our only defense against that hardship . . . Those who by their very nature can suffer completely, utterly, have an advantage. This is how we can disarm the power of suffering, make it our own creation, our own choice; submit to it. A justification for suicide."

The modern form of the writer's journal shows a curious evolution if we examine some of its principal exemplars: Stendhal, Baudelaire, Gide, Kafka, and now Pavese. The uninhibited display of egotism devolves into the heroic quest for the cancellation of the self. Pavese has none of Gide's Protestant sense of his life as a work of art, his respect for his own ambition, his confidence in his own feelings, his love for himself. Nor does he have Kafka's exquisite commitment without mockery to his own anguish. Pavese, who used the "I" so freely in his novels, usually speaks of himself as "you" in his diaries. He does not describe himself, but addresses himself. He is the ironic, exhortatory, reproachful spectator of himself. The ultimate consequence of such a bracketed view of the self would seem to have been, inevitably, suicide.

The diaries are in effect a long series of self-assessments and self-interrogations. They record nothing of daily life or observed incidents; nor is there any description of family, friends, lovers, colleagues or reaction to public events (as in Gide's *Journals*). All that satisfies the more conventional expectation of the contents of a writer's journal (as in Coleridge's *Notebooks*, and again in Gide's *Journals*) are the numerous reflections on the general problems of style and literary composition, and the copious notes on the writer's reading. Pavese was very much a "good European," though he never travelled outside Italy; the diaries attest that he was at home in all of European literature and thought, and in American writing (in which he was especially interested) as well. Pavese was not simply a novelist but a *uomo di cultura*: poet, novelist, short story writer, literary critic, translator, and editor with one of Italy's leading publishers (Einaudi). Much space in the diaries is taken up by this writer-as-man-of-letters. There are sensitive and subtle comments on a lifetime of immensely varied reading that ranged from

the Rig-Veda, Euripides, and Defoe to Corneille, Vico, Kierkegaard, and Hemingway. But it is not this aspect of the diaries which
I am considering here, for it is not this which constitutes the specific interest that writers' journals hold for a modern audience.
It should however be noted that when Pavese discusses his own
writing, it is not as the writer of it but rather as a reader or critic.
There is no discussion of work-in-progress, or plans and sketches for
stories, novels, and poems to be written. The only work discussed
is what has been finished. Another notable omission in the diaries
is any reflection of Pavese's involvement in politics—neither his
anti-fascist activities, for which he was imprisoned for ten months
in 1935, nor his long, ambivalent, and finally disillusioned association with the Communist Party.

It might be said that there are two personae in the diary. Pavese
the man, and Pavese the critic and reader. Or: Pavese thinking
prospectively, and Pavese thinking retrospectively. There is the self-
reproachful and self-exhortatory analysis of his feelings and projects; the focus of reflection is on his talents—as a writer, as a lover
of women, and as a prospective suicide. Then there is all the retro-
spective comment: analyses of some of his completed books, and
their place in his work; the notes on his reading. Insofar as the
"present" of Pavese's life enters the diaries at all, it is mainly in the
form of a consideration of his capabilities and prospects.

Apart from writing, there are two prospects to which Pavese continually recurs. One is the prospect of suicide, which tempted
Pavese at least as early as his university years (when two of his close
friends killed themselves) and is a theme to be found on almost
every page of the diaries. The other is the prospect of romantic love
and erotic failure. Pavese shows himself as tormented by a profound
sense of sexual inadequacy, which he bulwarked by all sorts of
theories about sexual technique, the hopelessness of love, and the
sex war. Remarks on the predatoriness, the exploitativeness of
women are interspersed with confessions of his own failure to love,
or to provide sexual satisfaction. Pavese, who never married, records
in the journal the reactions to a number of long affairs and casual
sexual experiences, usually at the point when he is expecting trouble

or after they actually have failed. The women themselves are never described; the events of the relationship are not even alluded to.

The two themes are intimately connected, as Pavese himself experienced. In the closing months of his life, in the midst of an unhappy affair with an American film star, he writes: "One does not kill oneself for love of a woman, but because love—any love—reveals us in our nakedness, our misery, our vulnerability, our nothingness . . . Deep, deep down, did I not clutch at this amazing love affair as it flew . . . to make myself revert to my old thought —my long-standing temptation, to have an excuse for thinking of it again: love and death. This is the hereditary pattern." Or again, in an ironic vein, Pavese remarks: "It is possible not to think about women, just as one does not think about death." Women and death never ceased to fascinate Pavese, and with an equal degree of anxiety and morbidity, since his main problem in both cases was whether he would be equal to the occasion.

What Pavese has to say about love is the familiar other side of romantic idealization. Pavese rediscovers, with Stendhal, that love is an essential fiction; it is not that love sometimes makes mistakes, but that it is, essentially, a mistake. What one takes to be an attachment to another person is unmasked as one more dance of the solitary ego. It is easy to see how this view of love is peculiarly congruent to the modern vocation of the writer. In the Aristotelian tradition of art as imitation, the writer was the medium or vehicle for describing the truth about something outside himself. In the modern tradition (roughly, Rousseau forward) of art as expression, the artist tells the truth about himself. Therefore it was inevitable that a theory of love as an experience or revelation of oneself, deceptively presented as an experience or revelation of the value of a loved person or object, should suggest itself. Love, like art, becomes a medium of self-expression. But because making a woman is not as solitary an act as making a novel or a poem, it is doomed to failure. A prevailing theme of serious literature and cinema today is the failure of love. (When we encounter the opposite statement, as for instance in *Lady Chatterley's Lover* or in Louis Malle's film *The Lovers*, we incline to describe it as a "fairy tale.") Love dies because its birth was an error. However, the error remains a necessary one, so long as one sees the world, in Pavese's words, as a "jungle of self-interest." The isolated ego does not cease to suffer. "Life is pain and the enjoyment of love is an anaesthetic."

A further consequence of this modern belief in the fictional nature of erotic attachment is a new self-conscious aquiescence in the inevitable attractiveness of unrequited love. As love is an emotion felt by the solitary ego and mistakenly projected outward, the impregnability of the beloved's ego exercises a hypnotic attraction for the romantic imagination. The lure of unrequited love lies in the identity of what Pavese calls "perfect behavior" and a strong, absolutely isolated, indifferent ego. "Perfect behavior is born of complete indifference," Pavese writes in his diary in 1940. "Perhaps that is why we always love madly someone who treats us with indifference; she represents 'style,' the fascination of 'class,' all that is desirable."

Many of Pavese's remarks on love seem like a case history supporting the thesis of Denis de Rougemont and other historians of the Western imagination who have traced the evolution of the Western image of sexual love since Tristan and Isolde as a "romantic agony," a death-wish. But the striking rhetorical enmeshment of the terms "writing," "sex," and "suicide" in Pavese's diaries indicates that this sensibility in its modern form is more complex. Rougemont's thesis may throw light on the Western overvaluation of love, but not on the modern pessimism about it: the view that love, and sensual fulfillment, are hopeless projects. Rougemont might well have used Pavese's own words: "Love is the cheapest of religions."

My own view is that the modern cult of love is not part of the story of a Christian heresy (Gnostic, Manichean, Catharist), as Rougemont suggests, but expresses the central and peculiarly modern preoccupation of the loss of feeling. To wish to cultivate "the art of looking at ourselves as though we were characters in one of our novels . . . as the way to put ourselves in a position to think constructively and reap the benefits" reveals Pavese speaking hopefully about a situation of self-alienation which elsewhere in the diaries is a subject of continual sorrow. For "life begins in the body," as Pavese observes in another entry; and he continually gives voice to the reproach which the body makes to the mind. If civilization may be defined as that stage of human life at which, objectively, the body becomes a problem, then our moment of civilization may be described as that stage at which we are subjectively aware of, and feel trapped by, this problem. Now we aspire to the life of the body and we reject the ascetic traditions of Judaism and Christianity, but we are still confined in the generalized sensibility which that religious tradition bequeathed us. Hence we complain; we are resigned and detached; we complain. Pavese's continual prayers for the strength to lead a life of rigorous seclusion and solitude ("The only heroic rule is to be alone, alone, alone") are entirely of a piece with his repeated complaints about his inability to feel. (See, for example, his remarks on his absence of feeling when his best friend, Leone Ginzburg, eminent professor and Resistance leader, was tortured to death by the fascists in 1940.) Here is where the modern cult of love enters: it is the main way in which we test ourselves for strength of feeling, and find ourselves deficient.

Everyone knows that we have a different, much more emphatic view of love between the sexes than the ancient Greeks and the Orientals, and that the modern view of love is an extension of the spirit of Christianity, in however attenuated and secularized a form. But the cult of love is not, as Rougemont claims, a Christian heresy. Christianity is, from its inception (Paul), the romantic religion. The cult of love in the West is an aspect of the cult of suffering—suffering as the supreme token of seriousness (the paradigm of the Cross). We do not find among the ancient Hebrews, Greeks, and the Orientals the same value placed on love because we do not find there the same positive value placed on suffering. Suffering was not the hallmark of seriousness; rather, seriousness was measured by one's ability to evade or transcend the penalty of suffering, by one's ability to achieve tranquillity and equilibrium. In contrast, the sensibility we have inherited identifies spirituality and seriousness with turbulence, suffering, passion. For two thousand years, among Christians and Jews, it has been spiritually fashionable to be in pain. Thus it is not love which we over-

value, but suffering—more precisely, the spiritual merits and benefits of suffering.

The modern contribution to this Christian sensibility has been
to discover the making of works of art and the venture of sexual
love as the two most exquisite sources of suffering. It is this that we
look for in a writer's diary, and which Pavese provides in disquieting
abundance.

[1962]

Simone Weil

THE culture-heroes of our liberal bourgeois civilization are anti-liberal and anti-bourgeois; they are writers who are repetitive, obsessive, and impolite, who impress by force—not simply by their tone of personal authority and by their intellectual ardor, but by the sense of acute personal and intellectual extremity. The bigots, the hysterics, the destroyers of the self—these are the writers who bear witness to the fearful polite time in which we live. Mostly it is a matter of tone: it is hardly possible to give credence to ideas uttered in the impersonal tones of sanity. There are certain eras which are too complex, too deafened by contradictory historical and intellectual experiences, to hear the voice of sanity. Sanity becomes compromise, evasion, a lie. Ours is an age which consciously pursues health, and yet only believes in the reality of sickness. The truths we respect are those born of affliction. We measure truth in terms of the cost to the writer in suffering—rather than by the standard of an objective truth to which a writer's words correspond. Each of our truths must have a martyr.

What revolted the mature Goethe in the young Kleist, who submitted his works to the elder statesman of German letters "on the knees of his heart"—the morbid, the hysterical, the sense of the unhealthy, the enormous indulgence in suffering out of which Kleist's plays and tales were mined—is just what we value today. Today Kleist gives pleasure, most of Goethe is a classroom bore. In the same way, such writers as Kierkegaard, Nietzsche, Dostoevsky, Kafka, Baudelaire, Rimbaud, Genet—and Simone Weil—have their authority with us precisely because of their air of unhealthiness. Their unhealthiness is their soundness, and is what carries conviction.

Perhaps there are certain ages which do not need truth as much as they need a deepening of the sense of reality, a widening of the imagination. I, for one, do not doubt that the sane view of the world is the true one. But is that what is always wanted, truth? The need for truth is not constant; no more than is the need for repose. An idea which is a distortion may have a greater intellectual thrust than the truth; it may better serve the needs of the spirit, which vary. The truth is balance, but the opposite of truth, which is unbalance, may not be a lie.

Thus I do not mean to decry a fashion, but to underscore the motive behind the contemporary taste for the extreme in art and thought. All that is necessary is that we not be hypocritical, that we recognize why we read and admire writers like Simone Weil. I cannot believe that more than a handful of the tens of thousands of readers she has won since the posthumous publication of her books and essays really share her ideas. Nor is it necessary—necessary to share Simone Weil's anguished and unconsummated love affair with the Catholic Church, or accept her gnostic theology of divine absence, or espouse her ideals of body denial, or concur in her violently unfair hatred of Roman civilization and the Jews. Similarly, with Kierkegaard and Nietzsche; most of their modern admirers could not, and do not embrace their ideas. We read writers of such scathing originality for their personal authority, for the example of their seriousness, for their manifest willingness to sacrifice themselves for their truths, and—only piecemeal—for their "views." As the corrupt Alcibiades followed Socrates, unable and unwilling to change his own life, but moved, enriched, and full of love, so the sensitive modern reader pays his respect to a level of spiritual reality which is not, could not, be his own.

Some lives are exemplary, others not; and of exemplary lives, there are those which invite us to imitate them, and those which we regard from a distance with a mixture of revulsion, pity, and reverence. It is, roughly, the difference between the hero and the saint (if one may use the latter term in an aesthetic, rather than a religious sense). Such a life, absurd in its exaggerations and degree of self-mutilation—like Kleist's, like Kierkegaard's—was Simone Weil's. I am thinking of the fanatical asceticism of Simone Weil's life, her contempt for pleasure and for happiness, her noble and ridiculous political gestures, her elaborate self-denials, her tireless courting of affliction; and I do not exclude her homeliness, her physical clumsiness, her migraines, her tuberculosis. No one who loves life would wish to imitate her dedication to martyrdom, or would wish it for his children or for anyone else whom he loves. Yet so far as we love seriousness, as well as life, we are moved by it, nourished by it. In the respect we pay to such lives, we acknowledge the presence of mystery in the world—and mystery is just what the secure possession of the truth, an objective truth, denies. In this sense, all truth is superficial; and some (but not all) distortions of the truth, some (but not all) insanity, some (but not all) unhealthiness, some (but not all) denials of life are truth-giving, sanity-producing, health-creating, and life-enhancing.

[1963]

Camus'
Notebooks

GREAT writers are either husbands or lovers. Some writers supply the solid virtues of a husband: reliability, intelligibility, generosity, decency. There are other writers in whom one prizes the gifts of a lover, gifts of temperament rather than of moral goodness. Notoriously, women tolerate qualities in a lover—moodiness, selfishness, unreliability, brutality —that they would never countenance in a husband, in return for excitement, an infusion of intense feeling. In the same way, readers put up with unintelligibility, obsessiveness, painful truths, lies, bad grammar—if, in compensation, the writer allows them to savor rare emotions and dangerous sensations. And, as in life, so in art both are necessary, husbands and lovers. It's a great pity when one is forced to choose between them.

Again, as in life, so in art: the lover usually has to take second place. In the great periods of literature, husbands have been more numerous than lovers; in all the great periods of literature, that is, except our own. Perversity is the muse of modern literature. Today the house of fiction is full of mad lovers, gleeful rapists, castrated sons—but very few husbands. The husbands have a bad conscience, they would all like to be lovers. Even so husbandly and solid a writer as Thomas Mann was tormented by an ambivalence toward virtue, and was forever carrying on about it in the guise of a conflict between the bourgeois and the artist. But most modern writers don't even acknowledge Mann's problem. Each writer, each literary movement vies with its predecessor in a great display of temperament, obsession, singularity. Modern literature is oversupplied with madmen of genius. No wonder, then, that when an immensely gifted writer, whose talents certainly fall short of genius, arises who boldly assumes the responsibilities of sanity, he should be acclaimed beyond his purely literary merits.

I mean, of course, Albert Camus, the ideal husband of contemporary letters. Being a contemporary, he had to traffic in the madmen's themes: suicide, affectlessness, guilt, absolute terror. But he does so with such an air of reasonableness, mesure, effortlessness, gracious impersonality, as to place him apart from the others. Starting from the premises of a popular nihilism, he moves the reader— solely by the power of his own tranquil voice and tone—to humanist and humanitarian conclusions in no way entailed by his premises. This illogical leaping of the abyss of nihilism is the gift for which readers are grateful to Camus. This is why he evoked feelings of real affection on the part of his readers. Kafka arouses pity and terror, Joyce admiration, Proust and Gide respect, but no modern writer that I can think of, except Camus, has aroused love. His death in 1960 was felt as a personal loss by the whole literate world.

Whenever Camus is spoken of there is a mingling of personal, moral, and literary judgment. No discussion of Camus fails to include, or at least suggest, a tribute to his goodness and attractiveness as a man. To write about Camus is thus to consider what occurs between the image of a writer and his work, which is tantamount to the relation between morality and literature. For it is not only that Camus himself is always thrusting the moral problem upon his readers. (All his stories, plays, and novels relate the career of a responsible sentiment, or the absence of it.) It is because his work, solely as a literary accomplishment, is not major enough to bear the weight of admiration that readers want to give it. One wants Camus to be a truly great writer, not just a very good one. But he is not. It might be useful here to compare Camus with George Orwell and James Baldwin, two other husbandly writers who essay to combine the role of artist with civic conscience. Both Orwell and Baldwin are better writers in their essays than they are in their fiction. This disparity is not to be found in Camus, a far more important writer. But what is true is that Camus' art is always in the service of certain intellectual conceptions which are more fully stated in the essays. Camus' fiction is illustrative, philosophical. It is not so much about its characters—Meursault, Caligula, Jan, Clamence, Dr. Rieux—as it is about the problems of innocence and guilt, responsibility and nihilistic indifference. The three novels, the stories, and the plays have a thin, somewhat skeletal quality which makes them a good deal less than absolutely first-rate, judged by the standards of art. Unlike Kafka, whose most illustrative and symbolic fictions are at the same time autonomous acts of the imagination, Camus' fiction continually betrays its source in an intellectual concern.

What of Camus' essays, political articles, addresses, literary criticism, journalism? It is extremely distinguished work. But was Camus a thinker of importance? The answer is no. Sartre, however distasteful certain of his political sympathies are to his English-speaking audience, brings a powerful and original mind to philosophical, psychological, and literary analysis. Camus, however attractive his political sympathies, does not. The celebrated philosophical essays (*The Myth of Sisyphus, The Rebel*) are the work of an extraordinarily talented and literate epigone. The same is true of Camus as a historian of ideas and as a literary critic. Camus is at his best when he disburdens himself of the baggage of existentialist culture (Nietzsche, Kierkegaard, Dostoevsky, Heidegger, Kafka) and speaks in his own person. This happens in the great essay against capital punishment, "Reflections on the Guillotine," and in the casual writings, like the essay-portraits of Algiers, Oran, and other Mediterranean places.

Neither art nor thought of the highest quality is to be found in Camus. What accounts for the extraordinary appeal of his work is beauty of another order, moral beauty, a quality unsought by most 20th century writers. Other writers have been more engaged, more moralistic. But none have appeared more beautiful, more convincing in their profession of moral interest. Unfortunately, moral beauty in art—like physical beauty in a person—is extremely perishable. It is nowhere so durable as artistic or intellectual beauty. Moral beauty has a tendency to decay very rapidly into sententiousness or untimeliness. This happens with special frequency to the writer, like Camus, who appeals directly to a generation's image of what is exemplary in a man in a given historical situation. Unless he possesses extraordinary reserves of artistic originality, his work is likely to seem suddenly denuded after his death. For a few, this decay overtook Camus within his own lifetime. Sartre, in the famous debate that ended their famous friendship, noted cruelly but truthfully that Camus carried about with him "a portable pedestal." Then came that deadly honor, the Nobel Prize. And shortly before his death, one critic was predicting for Camus the same fate as that of Aristides: that we would tire of hearing him called "the Just."

Perhaps it is always dangerous for a writer to inspire gratitude in his readers, gratitude being one of the most vehement but also the shortest-lived of the sentiments. But one cannot dismiss such unkind remarks simply as the revenge of the grateful. If Camus' moral earnestness at times ceased to enthrall and began to irritate, it is because there was a certain intellectual weakness in it. One sensed in Camus, as one senses in James Baldwin, the presence of an entirely genuine, and historically relevant, passion. But also, as with Baldwin, that passion seemed to transmute itself too readily into stately language, into an inexhaustible self-perpetuating oratory. The moral imperatives—love, moderation—offered to palliate intolerable historical or metaphysical dilemmas were too general, too abstract, too rhetorical.

Camus is the writer who for a whole literate generation was the heroic figure of a man living in a state of permanent spiritual revolution. But he is also the man who advocated that paradox: a civilized nihilism, an absolute revolt that acknowledges limits—and converted the paradox into a recipe for good citizenship. What intricate goodness, after all! In Camus' writing, goodness is forced to search simultaneously for its appropriate act and for its justifying reason. So is revolt. In 1939, in the midst of reflections on the war, which had just begun, the young Camus interrupted himself in his Notebooks to remark: "I am seeking reasons for my revolt which nothing has so far justified." His radical stance preceded the reasons which justified it. More than a decade later, in 1951, Camus published The Rebel. The refutation of revolt in that book was, equally, a gesture of temperament, an act of self-persuasion.

What is remarkable is that, given Camus' refined temperament, it was possible for him to act, to make real historical choices, as wholeheartedly as he did. It should be remembered that Camus had to make no less than three model decisions in his brief life-time—to participate personally in the French Resistance, to disassociate himself from the Communist Party, and to refuse to take sides in the Algerian revolt—and that he acquitted himself admirably, in my opinion, in two out of the three. Camus' problem in the last years of his life was not that he became religious, or that he subsided into bourgeois humanitarian seriousness, or that he lost his socialist nerve. It was, rather, that he was hoist on the petard of his own virtue. A writer who acts as public conscience needs extraordinary nerve and fine instincts, like a boxer. After a time, these instincts inevitably falter. He also needs to be emotionally tough. Camus was not that tough, not tough in the way that Sartre is. I do not underestimate the courage involved in disavowing the pro-Communism of many French intellectuals in the late forties. As a moral judgment, Camus' decision was right then, and since the death of Stalin he has been vindicated many times over in a political sense as well. But moral and political judgment do not always so happily coincide. His agonizing inability to take a stand on the Algerian question—the issue on which he, as both Algerian and Frenchman, was uniquely qualified to speak—was the final and unhappy testament of his moral virtue. Throughout the fifties, Camus declared that his private loyalties and sympathies made it impossible for him to render decisive political judgment. Why is so much demanded of a writer, he asked plaintively. While Camus clung to his silence, both Merleau-Ponty, who had followed Camus out of the *Temps Modernes* group over the issue of Communism, and Sartre himself, gathered influential signatories for two historic manifestoes protesting the continuation of the Algerian War. It is a harsh irony that both Merleau-Ponty, whose general political and moral outlook was so close to that of Camus, and Sartre, whose political integrity Camus had seemed to demolish a decade before, were in a position to lead French intellectuals of conscience to the inevitable stand, the only stand, the one everyone hoped Camus would take.

In a perceptive review of one of Camus' books some years ago, Lionel Abel spoke of him as the man who incarnates the Noble Feeling, as distinct from the Noble Act. This is exactly right, and does not mean that there was some sort of hypocrisy in Camus's morality. It means that action is not Camus' first concern. The ability to act, or to refrain from acting, is secondary to the ability or inability to feel. It is less an intellectual position which Camus elaborated than an exhortation to feel—with all the risks of political impotence that this entailed. Camus' work reveals a temperament in search of a situation, noble feelings in search of noble acts. Indeed, this disjunction is precisely the subject of Camus' fiction and philosophical essays. There one finds the prescription of an attitude (noble, stoical, at the same time detached and compassionate) tacked on to the description of excruciating events. The attitude, the noble feeling, is not genuinely linked to the event. It is a transcendence of the event, more than a response to it or a solution of it. Camus' life and work are not so much about morality as they are about the pathos of moral positions. This pathos is Camus' modernity. And his ability to suffer this pathos in a dignified and virile way is what made his readers love and admire him.

Again one comes back to the man, who was so strongly loved and yet so little known. There is something disembodied in Camus' fiction; and in the voice, cool and serene, of the famous essays. This, despite the unforgettable photographs, with their beautifully informal presence. A cigarette dangles between the lips, whether he wears a trench-coat, a sweater and open shirt, or a business suit.

It is in many ways an almost ideal face: boyish, good-looking but not too good-looking, lean, rough, the expression both intense and modest. One wants to know this man.

In the Notebooks, 1935-1942,* the first of three volumes to be published comprising the notebooks which Camus kept from 1935 until his death, his admirers will naturally hope to find a generous sense of the man and the work which has moved them. I am sorry to have to say, first of all, that the translation by Philip Thody is poor work. It is repeatedly inaccurate, sometimes to the point of seriously misconstruing Camus' sense. It is heavy-handed, and quite fails to find the equivalent in English to Camus' compressed, off-hand, and very eloquent style. The book also has an obtrusive academic apparatus which may not annoy some readers; it did annoy me. (For an idea of how Camus should sound in English, curious readers might look up the accurate and sensitive translation by Anthony Hartley of sections of the Notebooks which appeared in Encounter two years ago.) Yet no translation, whether faithful or tone-deaf, can make the Notebooks less interesting than they are, or more interesting either. These are not great literary journals, like those of Kafka and Gide. They do not have the white-hot intellectual brilliance of Kafka's Diaries. They lack the cultural sophistication, the artistic diligence, the human density of Gide's Journals. They are comparable, say to the Diaries of Cesare Pavese, except that they lack the element of personal exposure, of psychological intimacy.

Camus' Notebooks contain an assortment of things. They are literary work-books, quarries for his writings, in which phrases, scraps of overheard conversation, ideas for stories, and sometimes whole paragraphs later incorporated into the novels and essays, were first jotted down. These sections of the Notebooks are sketchy stuff, and for that reason I doubt if they will be terribly exciting even to aficionados of Camus' fiction, despite the zealous annotation and correlation with the published works supplied by Mr. Thody. The Notebooks also contain a miscellany of reading

* Notebooks, 1935-1942, by Albert Camus. Translated from the French by Philip Thody. New York, Knopf.

notes (Spengler, Renaissance history, etc.) of a rather limited range —the vast reading that went into writing The Rebel is certainly not recorded here—and a number of maxims and reflections on psychological and moral themes. Some of these reflections have a great deal of boldness and finesse. They are worth reading, and they might help dispel one current image of Camus—according to which he was a sort of Raymond Aron, a man deranged by German philosophy belatedly converting to Anglo-Saxon empiricism and common sense under the name of "Mediterranean" virtue. The Notebooks, at least this first volume, exude an endearing atmosphere of domesticated Nietzscheanism. The young Camus writes as a French Nietzsche, melancholy where Nietzsche is savage, stoical where Nietzsche is outraged, impersonal and objective in tone where Nietzsche is personal and subjective to the point of mania. And lastly, the Notebooks are full of personal comments—declarations and resolutions, one might better describe them—of a markedly impersonal nature.

Impersonality is perhaps the most telling thing about Camus' Notebooks; they are so anti-autobiographical. It is hard to remember, when reading the Notebooks, that Camus was a man who had a very interesting life, a life (unlike that of many writers) interesting not only in an interior but also in an outward sense. Scarcely anything of this life is preserved in the Notebooks. There is nothing about his family, to whom he was closely attached. Neither is there any mention of the events which took place in this period: his work with the Théâtre de l'Équipe, his first and second marriages, his membership in the Communist Party, his career as an editor of a left-wing Algerian newspaper.

Of course, a writer's journal must not be judged by the standards of a diary. The notebooks of a writer have a very special function: in them he builds up, piece by piece, the identity of a writer to himself. Typically, writers' notebooks are crammed with statements about the will: the will to write, the will to love, the will to renounce love, the will to go on living. The journal is where a writer is heroic to himself. In it he exists solely as a perceiving, suffering, struggling being. That is why all the personal comments in Camus' Notebooks are of so impersonal a nature, and completely exclude the events and the people in his life. Camus writes about himself only as a solitary—a solitary reader, voyeur, sun-and-sea worshipper, and walker in the world. In this he is being very much the writer. Solitariness is the indispensable metaphor of the modern writer's consciousness, not only to self-declared emotional misfits like Pavese, but even to as sociable and socially conscientious a man as Camus.

Thus the Notebooks, while absorbing reading, do not resolve the question of Camus' permanent stature or deepen our sense of him as a man. Camus was, in the words of Sartre, "the admirable conjunction of a man, of an action, and of a work." Today only the work remains. And whatever that conjunction of man, action, and work inspired in the minds and hearts of his thousands of readers and admirers cannot be wholly reconstituted by experience of the work alone. It would have been an important and happy occurrence if Camus' Notebooks had survived their author to give us more than they do of the man, but unfortunately they do not.

[1963]

Michel Leiris'
Manhood

ARRIVING in translation in the year 1963, Michel Leiris' brilliant autobiographical narrative *L'Age d'Homme*, is at first rather puzzling. *Manhood*, as it is called in English, appears without any covering note.* There is no way for the reader to find out that Leiris, now in his sixties and the author of some twenty books, none of which are yet in English, is an important poet and senior survivor of the Surrealist generation in Paris in the 1920s, and a fairly eminent anthropologist. Nor does the American edition explain that *Manhood* is not recent—that it was in fact written in the early 1930s, first published in 1939, and republished with an important prefatory essay, "Literature Considered as a Bullfight," in 1946, when it had a great *succès de scandale*. Although autobiographies can enthrall even though we have

* *Manhood* by Michel Leiris. Translated from the French by Richard Howard. New York, Grossman.

no prior interest—or reason for becoming interested—in the writer, the fact that Leiris is unknown here complicates matters, because his book is very much part of a life-history as well as a life-work.

In 1929, Leiris suffered a severe mental crisis, which included becoming impotent, and underwent a year or so of psychiatric treatment. In 1930, when he was thirty-four years old, he began *Manhood*. At that time, he was a poet, strongly influenced by Apollinaire and by his friend Max Jacob; he had already published several volumes of poetry, the first of which is *Simulacre* (1925); and in the same year that he began *Manhood*, he wrote a remarkable novel in the Surrealist manner, *Aurora*. But shortly after beginning *Manhood* (it was not finished until 1935), Leiris entered upon a new career—as an anthropologist. He made a field trip to Africa (Dakar and Djibouti) in 1931-33, and upon his return to Paris joined the staff of the Musée de l'Homme, where he remains, in an important curatorial post, to the present day. No trace of this startling shift—from bohemian and poet to scholar and museum bureaucrat—is recorded in the wholly intimate disclosures of *Manhood*. There is nothing in the book of the accomplishments of the poet or the anthropologist. One feels there cannot be; to have recorded them would mar the impression of failure.

Instead of a history of his life, Leiris gives us a catalogue of its limitations. *Manhood* begins not with "I was born in . . ." but with a matter-of-fact description of the author's body. We learn in the first pages of Leiris' incipient baldness, of a chronic inflammation of the eyelids, of his meager sexual capacities, of his tendency to hunch his shoulders when sitting and to scratch his anal region when he is alone, of a traumatic tonsillectomy undergone as a child, of an equally traumatic infection in his penis; and, subsequently, of his hypochondria, of his cowardice in all situations of the slightest danger, of his inability to speak any foreign language fluently, of his pitiful incompetence in physical sports. His character, too, is described under the aspect of limitation: Leiris presents it as "corroded" with morbid and aggressive fantasies concerning the flesh in general and women in particular. *Manhood* is a manual of abjection—anecdotes and fantasies and verbal associations and dreams set down in the tones of a man, partly anesthetized, curiously fingering his own wounds.

One may think of Leiris' book as an especially powerful instance of the venerable preoccupation with sincerity peculiar to French letters. From Montaigne's *Essays* and Rousseau's *Confessions* through Stendhal's journals to the modern confessions of Gide, Jouhandeau, and Genet, the great writers of France have been concerned to a singular extent with the detached presentation of intimate feelings, particularly those connected with sexuality and ambition. In the name of sincerity, both in autobiographical form and in the form of fiction (as in Constant, Laclos, Proust), French writers have been coolly exploring erotic manias, and speculating on techniques of emotional disengagement. It is this long-standing preoccupation with sincerity—over and beyond emotional expressiveness—that gives a severity, a certain classicism even, to most French works of the romantic period. But to see Leiris' book simply in this way does it an injustice. *Manhood* is odder, harsher than such a lineage suggests. Far more than any avowals to be found in the great French autobiographical documents of incestuous feelings, sadism, homosexuality, masochism, and crass promiscuity, what Leiris admits to is obscene and repulsive. It is not especially what Leiris has done that shocks. Action is not his forte, and his vices are those of a fearfully cold sensual temperament—wormy failures and deficiencies more often than lurid acts. It is because Leiris' attitude is unredeemed by the slightest tinge of self-respect. This lack of esteem or respect for himself is obscene. All the other great confessional works of French letters proceed out of self-love, and have the clear purpose of defending and justifying the self. Leiris loathes himself, and can neither defend nor justify. *Manhood* is an exercise in shamelessness—a sequence of self-exposures of a craven, morbid, damaged temperament. It is not incidentally, in the course of his narration, that Leiris reveals what is disgusting about himself. What is disgusting is the *topic* of his book.

One may well ask: who cares? *Manhood* undoubtedly has a certain value as a clinical document; it is full of lore for the professional student of mental aberration. But the book would not be worth attention did it not have value as literature. This, I think, it does—though, like so many modern works of literature, it makes its way as anti-literature. (Indeed, much of the modern movement in the arts presents itself as anti-art.) Paradoxically, it is just its animus to the idea of literature that makes Manhood—a very carefully (though not beautifully) written and subtly executed book—interesting as literature. In the same way, it is precisely through Manhood's unstated rejection of the rationalist project of self-understanding that Leiris makes his contribution to it.

The question that Leiris answers in Manhood in not an intellectual one. It is what we would call a psychological—and the French, a moral—question. Leiris is not trying to understand himself. Neither has he written Manhood to be forgiven, or to be loved. Leiris writes to appall, and thereby to receive from his readers the gift of a strong emotion—the emotion needed to defend himself against the indignation and disgust he expects to arouse in his readers. Literature becomes a mode of psychotechnics. As he explains in the prefatory essay "De la Littérature Considérée comme une Tauromachie," to be a writer, a man of letters, is not enough. It is boring, pallid. It lacks danger. Leiris must feel, as he writes, the equivalent of the bullfighter's knowledge that he risks being gored. Only then is writing worthwhile. But how can the writer achieve this invigorating sense of mortal danger? Leiris' answer is: through self-exposure, through not defending himself; not through fabricating works of art, objectifications of himself, but through laying himself—his own person—on the line of fire. But we, the readers, the spectators of this bloody act, know that when it is performed well (think of how the bullfight is discussed as a preeminently aesthetic, ceremonial act) it becomes, whatever the disavowals of literature—literature.

A writer who subscribes to a program similar to Leiris' for creating literature inadvertently, out of self-laceration and self-exposure, is Norman Mailer. For some years now Mailer has conceived of writing as a blood sport (more often in the image of boxing than bullfighting), and insisted that the better writer is the man who dares more, who risks more. For this reason, Mailer has used himself increasingly as the subject of his essays and quasi-fiction. But there are big differences between Mailer and Leiris, and they are revealing. In Mailer, this enthusiasm for danger appears much of the time in a base form—as megalomania, and a tiresome competitiveness with other writers. In Leiris' writings, there is no awareness of a literary scene, of other writers, fellow-toreros competing for the most ravishing danger. (On the contrary, Leiris, who has known practically everybody, painters as well as writers, is extremely deferential when he discusses the work and person of his friends.) Mailer in his writings is ultimately more concerned with success than with danger; danger is only a means to success. Leiris in his writings is not concerned with success at all. Mailer records in his recent essays and public appearances his perfecting of himself as a virile instrument of letters; he is perpetually in training, getting ready to launch himself from his own missile pad into a high, beautiful orbit; even his failures may yet be turned to successes. Leiris records the defeats of his own virility; completely incompetent in the arts of the body, he is perpetually in training to extinguish himself; even his successes look to him like failures. Perhaps the essential contrast between the optimistic, populist temperament of most American writers and the drastically alienated posture of the best European writers can be seen here. Leiris is a much more subjective, less ideological writer than Mailer. Mailer shows us how his private travails and weaknesses produce the strength of his public work—and wants to engage the reader in this process of transformation. But Leiris doesn't see any continuity between his public self, distinguished as that may be, and his private weaknesses. While Mailer's motives for self-exposure may be described as spiritual (not to mention worldly) ambitiousness—a desire to prove himself through repeated ordeals—Leiris' motives are more desperate: he wishes to prove, not that he is heroic, but that he is at all. Leiris loathes his physical cowardice and ineptness. Yet far from wishing to exonerate himself for his ugly failings, what he seems to wish is to convince himself that this unsatisfactory body —and this unseemly character—really exist. Haunted by a sense of the unreality of the world, and ultimately of himself, Leiris searches for a strong, unequivocal feeling. But, like a regular textbook romantic, the only emotion Leiris acknowledges is the one which involves a risk of death. "With a bitterness that I never suspected before, I have just realized that all I need in order to save myself is a certain fervor," he writes in *Manhood*, "but that this world lacks anything for which I would give my life." All emotions are mortal to Leiris, or they are nothing. What is real is defined as that which involves the risk of death. One knows from his books that Leiris has made several serious attempts at suicide; it might be said that, for him, life becomes real only when placed under the threa⁺ of suicide. The same is true of the vocation of literature. In a view like Leiris', literature has value only as a means of enhancing virility, or as a means of suicide.

Needless to say, it does neither. Literature usually begets literature. Whatever the therapeutic value of his self-exposure in *Manhood*, Leiris' mode of operating upon himself did not end with this book. His literary work since the war does not show a resolution of the problems set forth in *Manhood*, only further types of complication. Under the general title *La Règle du Jeu* (The Rules of the Game), Leiris has been writing essays on sense memories of his childhood, private images of death, sexual fantasies, the associative meanings of certain words—more discursive and more complex autobiographical forays than *Manhood*. Two of the projected three volumes have appeared: *Biffures* (Deletions) in 1948, and *Fourbis* (Odds and Ends) in 1961. The mocking titles tell the story. In *Fourbis*, one finds again the old complaint: "If there is nothing in love—or taste—for which I am ready to face death, I am only stirring up empty space and everything cancels itself out, myself included." The same theme is continued in his recent *Vivantes Cendres. Innomées* (Living Ashes, Unnamed), a cycle of poems which are a "journal" of Leiris' attempted suicide in 1958, and illustrated with line drawings by his friend Giacometti. For, it seems, the greatest problem Leiris faces is the chronic thinness of his emotions. The life which he dissects in all his books is polarized between what he calls his "huge capacity for boredom, from which everything else proceeds," and a staggering burden of morbid fantasies, memories of childhood injuries, fear of punishment, and failure ever to be at home in his own body. By writing about his weaknesses Leiris courts the punishment which he dreads, hoping that he will rouse in himself an unprecedented courage. One has the impression of a man flogging himself just in order to make his lungs consent to draw air.

The tone of *Manhood*, however, is anything but vehement. Leiris speaks somewhere in the book of preferring English clothes, of affecting a sober and correct style "actually a little stiff and even funereal—which corresponds so well, I believe, to my temperament." This is not a bad description of the style of his book. The extreme coldness of his sexual disposition, he explains, entails a profound distaste for the feminine, the liquid, the emotional; a lifelong fantasy is that of his own body becoming petrified, crystalline, mineralized. Everything that is impersonal and cold fascinates Leiris. For example, he is attracted to prostitution because of its character as a ritual; and "brothels are like museums," he explains. It seems his choice of the profession of anthropology also owes to the same taste: he is attracted by the extreme *formalism* of primitive societies. This is evident in the book which Leiris wrote about his two-year field trip, *L'Afrique Fantôme* (1934), as well as in several excellent anthropological monographs. Leiris' love of formalism, reflected in the cool underplayed style of *Manhood*, explains a seeming paradox. For it is surely remarkable that the man who has dedicated himself to ruthless self-exposure has written a brilliant monograph on the use of masks in African religious rituals ("Possession and Its Theatrical Aspects among the Ethiopians of Gondar," 1958), that the man who has carried the notion of candor to its most painful limits has also concerned himself professionally with the idea of secret languages ("The Secret Language of the Dogons of Sanga," 1948).

This coolness of tone—combined with a great intelligence and subtlety about motives—makes *Manhood* an attractive book in a fairly familiar sense. To its other qualities, though, we may react with impatience, for they violate many preconceptions. Apart from the brilliant prefatory essay, *Manhood* meanders, circles, and doubles back; there is no reason for it to end where it does; such types of insight are interminable. The book has no movement or direction and provides no consummation or climax. *Manhood* is another of those very modern books which are fully intelligible only as part of the project of a life: we are to take the book as an action, giving on to other actions. This type of literature, item by item, rather than retrospectively viewed as part of a body of work, is often hermetic and opaque, sometimes boring. Now, it is not hard to make out a defense for hermeticism and opaqueness as a possible condition for literary works of an extreme density. But what about boredom? Can that ever be justified? I think it can, sometimes. (Is it the obligation of great art to be continually interesting? I think not.) We should acknowledge certain uses of boredom as one of the most creative stylistic features of modern literature—as the conventionally ugly and messy have already become essential resources of modern painting, and silence (since Webern) a positive, structural element in contemporary music.

[1964]

The paradox is irresoluble: the less one culture communicates with another, the less likely they are to be corrupted, one by the other; but on the other hand, the less likely it is, in such conditions, that the respective emissaries of these cultures will be able to seize the richness and significance of their diversity. The alternative is inescapable: either I am a traveller in ancient times, and faced with a prodigious spectacle which would be almost entirely unintelligible to me and might, indeed, provoke me to mockery or disgust; or I am a traveller of my own day, hastening in search of a vanished reality. In either case I am the loser . . . for today, as I go groaning among the shadows, I miss, inevitably, the spectacle that is now taking shape.

from Tristes Tropiques

The anthropologist
as hero

MOST serious thought in our time struggles with the feeling of homelessness. The felt unreliability of human experience brought about by the inhuman acceleration of historical change has led every sensitive modern mind to the recording of some kind of nausea, of intellectual vertigo. And the only way to cure this spiritual nausea seems to be, at least initially, to exacerbate it. Modern thought is pledged to a kind of applied Hegelianism: seeking its Self in its Other. Europe seeks itself in the exotic—in Asia, in the Middle East, among pre-literate peoples, in a mythic America; a fatigued rationality seeks itself in the impersonal energies of sexual ecstasy or drugs; consciousness seeks its meaning in unconsciousness; humanistic problems seek their oblivion in scientific "value neutrality" and quantification. The "other" is experienced as a harsh purification of "self." But at the same time the "self" is busily colonizing all strange domains of expe-

rience. Modern sensibility moves between two seemingly contradictory but actually related impulses: surrender to the exotic, the
strange, the other; and the domestication of the exotic, chiefly
through science.

Although philosophers have contributed to the statement and
understanding of this intellectual homelessness—and, in my opinion, only those modern philosophers who do so have an urgent
claim on our interest—it is mainly poets, novelists, a few painters
who have *lived* this tortured spiritual impulse, in willed derangement and in self-imposed exile and in compulsive travel. But there
are other professions whose conditions of life have been made to
bear witness to this vertiginous modern attraction to the alien.
Conrad in his fiction, and T. E. Lawrence, Saint-Exupéry, Mon-
therlant among others in their lives as well as their writing, created
the métier of the adventurer as a spiritual vocation. Thirty-five
years ago, Malraux chose the profession of the archaeologist, and
went to Asia. And, more recently, Claude Lévi-Strauss has invented the profession of the anthropologist as a total occupation,
one involving a spiritual commitment like that of the creative artist
or the adventurer or the psychoanalyst.

Unlike the writers mentioned above, Lévi-Strauss is not a man of
letters. Most of his writings are scholarly, and he has always been
associated with the academic world. At present, since 1960, he holds
a very grand academic post, the newly created chair of social anthropology at the Collège de France, and heads a large and richly
endowed research institute. But his academic eminence and ability
to dispense patronage are scarcely adequate measures of the formidable position he occupies in French intellectual life today. In
France, where there is more awareness of the adventure, the *risk*
involved in intelligence, a man can be both a specialist and the
subject of general and intelligent interest and controversy. Hardly a
month passes in France without a major article in some serious
literary journal, or an important public lecture, extolling or attacking the ideas and influence of Lévi-Strauss. Apart from the tireless
Sartre and the virtually silent Malraux, he is the most interesting
intellectual "figure" in France today.

So far, Lévi-Strauss is hardly known in this country. A collection

of previously scattered essays on the methods and concepts of anthropology, brought out in 1958 and entitled *Anthropologie Struc-
turale*, and his *Le Totémisme Aujourd'hui* (1962) have been translated in the last year. Still to appear are another collection of essays, more philosophical in character, entitled *La Pensée Sauvage*
(1962); a book published by UNESCO in 1952 called *Race et Histoire*; and the brilliant work on the kinship systems of primitives,
Les Structures Élémentaires de la Parenté (1949).* Some of these
writings presuppose more familiarity with anthropological literature
and with the concepts of linguistics, sociology, and psychology than
the ordinary cultivated reader has. But it would be a great pity if
Lévi-Strauss' work, when it is all translated, were to find no more
than a specialist audience in this country. For Lévi-Strauss has assembled, from the vantage point of anthropology, one of the few
interesting and possible intellectual positions—in the most general
sense of that phrase. And one of his books is a masterpiece. I mean
the incomparable *Tristes Tropiques*, a book that became a best-
seller when published in France in 1955, but when translated into
English and brought out here in 1961 was shamefully ignored.
Tristes Tropiques is one of the great books of our century. It is
rigorous, subtle, and bold in thought. It is beautifully written. And,
like all great books, it bears an absolutely personal stamp; it speaks
with a human voice.

Ostensibly *Tristes Tropiques* is the record, or memoir rather,
written over fifteen years after the event, of the author's experience
in the "field." Anthropologists are fond of likening field research to
the puberty ordeal which confers status upon members of certain
primitive societies. Lévi-Strauss' ordeal was in Brazil, before the
Second World War. Born in 1908 and of the intellectual generation and circle which included Sartre, Beauvoir, Merleau-Ponty,
and Paul Nizan, he studied philosophy in the late twenties, and,
like them, taught for a while in a provincial lycée. Dissatisfied with
philosophy he soon gave up his teaching post, returned to Paris to
study law, then began the study of anthropology, and in 1935 went
to São Paulo as Professor of Anthropology. From 1935 to 1939,

* In 1965, Lévi-Strauss published *Le Cru et le Cuit*, a lengthy study of the
"mythologies" of food preparation among primitive peoples.

during the long university vacations from November to March and
for one period of more than a year, Lévi-Strauss lived among In-
dian tribes in the interior of Brazil. *Tristes Tropiques* offers a
record of his encounters with these tribes—the nomadic, mis-
sionary-murdering Nambikwara, the Tupi-Kawahib whom no
white man had ever seen before, the materially splendid Bororo,
the ceremonious Caduveo who produce huge amounts of abstract
painting and sculpture. But the greatness of *Tristes Tropiques* lies
not simply in this sensitive reportage, but in the way Lévi-Strauss
uses his experience—to reflect on the nature of landscape, on the
meaning of physical hardship, on the city in the Old World and
the New, on the idea of travel, on sunsets, on modernity, on the
connection between literacy and power. The key to the book is
Chapter Six, "How I Became an Anthropologist," where Lévi-
Strauss finds in the history of his own choice a case study of the
unique spiritual hazards to which the anthropologist subjects himself. *Tristes Tropiques* is an intensely personal book. Like Montaigne's *Essays* and Freud's *Interpretation of Dreams*, it is an intellectual autobiography, an exemplary personal history in which a
whole view of the human situation, an entire sensibility, is elaborated.

The profoundly intelligent sympathy which informs *Tristes Tropiques* makes other memoirs about life among pre-literate peoples seem ill-at-ease, defensive, provincial. Yet sympathy is modulated throughout by a hard-won impassivity. In her autobiography
Simone de Beauvoir recalls Lévi-Strauss as a young philosophy
student-teacher expounding "in his detached voice, and with a
deadpan expression . . . the folly of the passions." Not for
nothing is *Tristes Tropiques* prefaced by a motto from Lucretius'
De Rerum Natura. Lévi-Strauss' aim is very much like that of
Lucretius, the Graecophile Roman who urged the study of the natural sciences as a mode of ethical psychotherapy. The aim of Lucretius was not independent scientific knowledge, but the reduction of emotional anxiety. Lucretius saw man as torn between
the pleasure of sex and the pain of emotional loss, tormented by
superstitions inspired by religion, haunted by the fear of bodily
decay and death. He recommended scientific knowledge, which

teaches intelligent detachment, equanimity. Scientific knowledge is, for Lucretius, a mode of psychological gracefulness. It is a way of learning to let go.

Lévi-Strauss sees man with a Lucretian pessimism, and a Lucretian feeling for knowledge as both consolation and necessary disenchantment. But for him the demon is history—not the body or the appetites. The past, with its mysteriously harmonious structures, is broken and crumbling before our eyes. Hence, the tropics are tristes. There were nearly twenty thousand of the naked, indigent, nomadic, handsome Nambikwaras in 1915, when they were first visited by white missionaries; when Lévi-Strauss arrived in 1938 there were no more than two thousand of them; today they are miserable, ugly, syphilitic, and almost extinct. Hopefully, anthropology brings a reduction of historical anxiety. It is interesting that Lévi-Strauss describes himself as an ardent student of Marx since the age of seventeen ("Rarely do I tackle a problem in sociology or ethnology without having first set my mind in motion by reperusal of a page or two from the 18th Brumaire of Louis Bonaparte or the Critique of Political Economy") and that many of Lévi-Strauss' students are reported to be former Marxists, come as it were to lay their piety at the altar of the past since it cannot be offered to the future. Anthropology is necrology. "Let's go and study the primitives," say Lévi-Strauss and his pupils, "before they disappear."

It is strange to think of these ex-Marxists—philosophical optimists if ever such have existed—submitting to the melancholy spectacle of the crumbling prehistoric past. They have moved not only from optimism to pessimism, but from certainty to systematic doubt. For, according to Lévi-Strauss, research in the field, "where every ethnological career begins, is the mother and nursemaid of doubt, the philosophical attitude par excellence." In Lévi-Strauss' program for the practicing anthropologist in Structural Anthropology, the Cartesian method of doubt is installed as a permanent agnosticism. "This 'anthropological doubt' consists not merely in knowing that one knows nothing but in resolutely exposing what one knows, even one's own ignorance, to the insults and denials inflicted on one's dearest ideas and habits by those ideas and habits which may contradict them to the highest degree."

To be an anthropologist is thus to adopt a very ingenious stance vis-à-vis one's own doubts, one's own intellectual uncertainties. Lévi-Strauss makes it clear that for him this is an eminently *philosophical* stance. At the same time, anthropology reconciles a number of divergent personal claims. It is one of the rare intellectual vocations which do not demand a sacrifice of one's manhood. Courage, love of adventure, and physical hardiness—as well as brains—are called upon. It also offers a solution to that distressing by-product of intelligence, alienation. Anthropology conquers the estranging function of the intellect by institutionalizing it. For the anthropologist, the world is professionally divided into "home" and "out there," the domestic and the exotic, the urban academic world and the tropics. The anthropologist is not simply a neutral observer. He is a man in control of, and even consciously exploiting, his own intellectual alienation. A *technique de dépaysement*, Lévi-Strauss calls his profession in *Structural Anthropology*. He takes for granted the philistine formulas of modern scientific "value neutrality." What he does is to offer an exquisite, aristocratic version of this neutrality. The anthropologist in the field becomes the very model of the 20th century consciousness: a "critic at home" but a "conformist elsewhere." Lévi-Strauss acknowledges that this paradoxical spiritual state makes it impossible for the anthropologist to be a citizen. The anthropologist, so far as his own country is concerned, is sterilized politically. He cannot seek power, he can only be a critical dissenting voice. Lévi-Strauss himself, although in the most generic and very French way a man of the Left (he signed the famous Manifesto of the 121, which recommended civil disobedience in France in protest against the Algerian War), is by French standards an apolitical man. Anthropology, in Lévi-Strauss' conception, is a technique of political disengagement; and the anthropologist's vocation requires the assumption of a profound detachment. "Never can he feel himself 'at home' anywhere; he will always be, psychologically speaking, an amputee."

Certainly the earliest visitors to pre-literate peoples were far from being detached. The original field workers in what was then called ethnology were missionaries, bent on redeeming the savage from his follies and making him over into a civilized Christian. To cover the bosoms of the women, put pants on the men, and send them all to Sunday school to mumble the gospel was the aim of an army of stony-eyed spinsters from Yorkshire and rawboned farmers' sons from the American Midwest. Then there were the secular humanists—impartial, respectful, hands-off observers who did not come to sell Christ to the savages but to preach "reason," "tolerance," and "cultural pluralism" to the bourgeois literary public back home. And back home there were the great consumers of anthropological data, building rationalist world views, like Frazer and Spencer and Robertson Smith and Freud. But always anthropology has struggled with an intense, fascinated repulsion towards its subject. The horror of the primitive (naïvely expressed by Frazer and Lévy-Bruhl) is never far from the anthropologist's consciousness. Lévi-Strauss marks the furthest reach of the conquering of the aversion. The anthropologist in the manner of Lévi-Strauss is a new breed altogether. He is not, like recent generations of American anthropologists, simply a modest data-collecting "observer." Nor does he have any axe—Christian, rationalist, Freudian, or otherwise—to grind. Essentially he is engaged in saving his own soul, by a curious and ambitious act of intellectual catharsis.

The anthropologist—and herein lies his essential difference, according to Lévi-Strauss, from the sociologist—is an eye-witness. "It is sheer illusion that anthropology can be taught purely theoretically." (One wonders why a Max Weber writing about ancient Judaism or Confucian China is permissible, if a Frazer describing scapegoat rituals among the Tagbanua tribe in the Philippines is not.) Why? Because anthropology, for Lévi-Strauss, is an intensely personal kind of intellectual discipline, like psychoanalysis. A spell in the field is the exact equivalent of the training analysis undergone by candidate psychoanalysts. The purpose of field work, Lévi-Strauss writes, is to "create that psychological revolution which marks the decisive turning point in the training of the anthropologist." And no written tests, but only the judgment of "experienced members of the profession" who have undergone the same psychological ordeal, can determine "if and when" a candidate anthropologist "has, as a result of field work, accomplished that inner revolution that will really make him into a new man."

However, it must be emphasized that this literary-sounding conception of the anthropologist's calling—the twice-born spiritual adventure, pledged to a systematic déracinement—is complemented in most of Lévi-Strauss' writings by an insistence on the most unliterary techniques of analysis and research. His important essay on myth in Structural Anthropology outlines a technique for analyzing and recording the elements of myths so that these can be processed by a computer. European contributions to what in America are called the "social sciences" are in exceedingly low repute in this country, for their insufficient empirical documentation, for their "humanist" weakness for covert culture criticism, for their refusal to embrace the techniques of quantification as an essential tool of research. Lévi-Strauss' essays in Structural Anthropology certainly escape these strictures. Indeed, far from disdaining the American fondness for precise quantitative measurement of traditional problems, Lévi-Strauss finds it not sophisticated or methodologically rigorous enough. Somewhat at the expense of the French school (Durkheim, Mauss, and their followers) to whom he is closely allied, Lévi-Strauss pays lavish tribute throughout the essays in Structural Anthropology to the work of American anthropologists—particularly Lowie, Boas, and Kroeber.* But his nearest affinity is to the more avant-garde methodologies of economics, neurology,

---

* Lévi-Strauss relates in Tristes Tropiques that although he had long been familiar with the writings of the French anthropologists and sociologists, it was a reading of Lowie's Primitive Society in 1934 or 1935 which effected his conversion from philosophy to anthropology. "Thus began my long intimacy with Anglo-American anthropology . . . I started as an avowed anti-Durkheimian and the enemy of any attempt to put sociology to metaphysical uses."

Nevertheless, Lévi-Strauss has made it clear that he considers himself the true legate of the Durkheim-Mauss tradition, and recently has not hesitated to situate his work in relation to the philosophical problems posed by Marx, Freud, and Sartre. And, on the level of technical analysis, he is fully aware of his debt to the French writers, particularly by way of the Essai sur Quelques Formes Primitives de Classification (1901–2) by Durkheim and Mauss, and Mauss' Essai sur le Don (1924). From the first essay, Lévi-Strauss derives the starting point of the studies of taxonomy and the "concrete science" of primitives in La Pensée Sauvage. From the second essay, in which Mauss puts forth the proposition that kinship relations, relations of economic and ceremonial exchange, and linguistic relations are fundamentally of the same order, Lévi-Strauss derives the approach most fully exemplified in Les Structures Élémentaires de la Parenté. To Durkheim and Mauss, he repeatedly says, he owes the decisive insight that "la pensée dite primitive était une pensée quantifiée."

linguistics, and game theory. For Lévi-Strauss, there is no doubt that anthropology must be a science, rather than a humanistic study. The question is only how. "For centuries," he writes, "the humanities and the social sciences have resigned themselves to contemplate the world of the natural and exact sciences as a kind of paradise which they will never enter." But recently, a doorway to paradise has been opened by the linguists, like Roman Jakobson and his school. Linguists now know how to reformulate their problems so that they can "have a machine built by an engineer and make a kind of experiment, completely similar to a natural-science experiment," which will tell them "if the hypothesis is worthwhile or not." Linguists—as well as economists and game theorists—have shown the anthropologist "a way to get out of the confusion resulting from too much acquaintance and familiarity with concrete data."

Thus the man who submits himself to the exotic to confirm his own inner alienation as an urban intellectual ends by aiming to vanquish his subject by translating it into a purely formal code. The ambivalence toward the exotic, the primitive, is not overcome after all, but only given a complex restatement. The anthropologist, as a man, is engaged in saving his own soul. But he is also committed to recording and understanding his subject by a very high-powered mode of formal analysis—what Lévi-Strauss calls "structural" anthropology—which obliterates all traces of his personal experience and truly effaces the human features of his subject, a given primitive society.

In La Pensée Sauvage, Lévi-Strauss calls his thought "anecdotique et géometrique." The essays in Structural Anthropology show mostly the geometrical side of his thought; they are applications of a rigorous formalism to traditional themes—kinship systems, totemism, puberty rites, the relation between myth and ritual, and so forth. A great cleansing operation is in process, and the broom that sweeps everything clean is the notion of "structure." Lévi-Strauss strongly dissociates himself from what he calls the "naturalistic" trend of British anthropology, represented by such leading figures as Malinowski and Radcliffe-Brown. British anthropologists have been the most consistent proponents of "functional analysis," which interprets the variety of custom as different strategies for producing universal social ends. Thus, Malinowski thought that empirical observation of a single primitive society would make it possible to understand the "universal motivations" present in all societies. According to Lévi-Strauss, this is nonsense. Anthropology cannot aim to understand anything more than its own proper subject. Nothing can be inferred from anthropological material for psychology or sociology, for anthropology cannot possibly get complete knowledge of the societies it studies. Anthropology (the comparative study of "structures" rather than "functions") can neither be a descriptive nor an inductive science; it occupies itself with only the formal features which differentiate one society from another. It has properly no interest in the biological basis, psychological content, or social function of institutions and customs. Thus, while Malinowski and Radcliffe-Brown argue, for example, that biological ties are the origin of and the model for every kinship tie, "structuralists" like Lévi-Strauss, following Kroeber and Lowie, emphasize the artificiality of kinship rules. They would discuss kinship in terms of notions which admit of mathematical treatment. Lévi-Strauss and the structuralists, in short, would view society like a game, which there is no one right way to play; different societies assign different moves to the players. The anthropologist can regard a ritual or a taboo simply as a set of rules, paying little attention to "the nature of the partners (either individuals or groups) whose play is being patterned after these rules." Lévi-Strauss' favorite metaphor or model for analyzing primitive institutions and beliefs is a language. And the analogy between anthropology and linguistics is the leading theme of the essays in *Structural Anthropology*. All behavior, according to Lévi-Strauss, is a language, a vocabulary and grammar of order; anthropology proves nothing about human nature except the need for order itself. There is no universal truth about the relations between, say, religion and social structure. There are only models showing the variability of one in relation to the other.

To the general reader, perhaps the most striking example of Lévi-Strauss' theoretical agnosticism is his view of myth. He treats myth as a purely formal mental operation, without any psychological content or any necessary connection with rite. Specific narratives are

exposed as logical designs for the description and possibly the soft-
ening of the rules of the social game when they give rise to a tension or contradiction. For Lévi-Strauss, the logic of mythic thought
is fully as rigorous as that of modern science. The only difference is
that this logic is applied to different problems. Contrary to Mircea
Eliade, his most distinguished opponent in the theory of primitive
religion, Lévi-Strauss argues that the activity of the mind in impos-
ing form on content is fundamentally the same for all minds, archaic
and modern. Lévi-Strauss sees no difference in quality between the
scientific thinking of modern "historical" societies and the mythic
thinking of prehistoric communities.

The demonic character which history and the notion of historical consciousness has for Lévi-Strauss is best exposed in his brilliant
and savage attack on Sartre, the last chapter of *La Pensée Sauvage*. I am not persuaded by Lévi-Strauss' arguments against Sartre.
But I should say that he is, since the death of Merleau-Ponty, the
most interesting and challenging critic of Sartrean existentialism
and phenomenology.

Sartre, not only in his ideas but in his entire sensibility, is the antithesis of Lévi-Strauss. With his philosophical and political dogma-
tisms, his inexhaustible ingenuity and complexity, Sartre always has
the manners (which are often bad manners) of the enthusiast. It is
entirely apt that the writer who has aroused Sartre's greatest enthusiasm is Jean Genet, a baroque and didactic and insolent writer
whose ego effaces all objective narrative; whose characters are
stages in a masturbatory revel; who is the master of games and
artifices, of a rich, overrich style stuffed with metaphors and con-
ceits. But there is another tradition in French thought and sensibility—the cult of aloofness, *l'esprit géometrique*. This tradition is
represented, among the new novelists, by Nathalie Sarraute, Alain
Robbe-Grillet, and Michel Butor, so different from Genet in their
search for an infinite precision, their narrow dehydrated subject-
matter and cool microscopic styles, and, among film-makers, by
Alain Resnais. The formula for this tradition—in which I would
locate Lévi-Strauss, as I would put Sartre with Genet—is the mixture of pathos and coldness.

Like the formalists of the "new novel" and film, Lévi-Strauss'
emphasis on "structure," his extreme formalism and intellectual
agnosticism, are played off against an immense but thoroughly sub-
dued pathos. Sometimes the result is a masterpiece like *Tristes
Tropiques*. The very title is an understatement. The tropics are not
merely sad. They are in agony. The horror of the rape, the final
and irrevocable destruction of pre-literate peoples taking place
throughout the world today—which is the true subject of Lévi-
Strauss' book—is told at a certain distance, the distance of a personal experience of fifteen years ago, and with a sureness of feeling
and fact that allows the readers' emotions more rather than less
freedom. But in the rest of his books, the lucid and anguished observer has been taken in hand, purged, by the severity of theory.

Exactly in the same spirit as Robbe-Grillet disavows the traditional empirical content of the novel (psychology, social observation), Lévi-Strauss applies the methods of "structural analysis" to
traditional materials of empirical anthropology. Customs, rites,
myths, and taboo are a language. As in language, where the sounds
which make up words are, taken in themselves, meaningless, so the
parts of a custom or a rite or a myth (according to Lévi-Strauss)
are meaningless in themselves. When analyzing the Oedipus myth,
he insists that the parts of the myth (the lost child, the old man at
the crossroad, the marriage with the mother, the blinding, etc.)
mean nothing. Only when put together in the total context do the
parts have a meaning—the meaning that a logical model has. This
degree of intellectual agnosticism is surely extraordinary. And one
does not have to espouse a Freudian or a sociological interpretation
of the elements of myth to contest it.

Any serious critique of Lévi-Strauss, however, must deal with the
fact that, ultimately, his extreme formalism is a moral choice, and
(more surprisingly) a vision of social perfection. Radically anti-
historicist, he refuses to differentiate between "primitive" and
"historical" societies. Primitives have a history; but it is unknown
to us. And historical consciousness (which they do not have), he
argues in the attack on Sartre, is not a privileged mode of consciousness. There are only what he revealingly calls "hot" and
"cold" societies. The hot societies are the modern ones, driven by

the demons of historical progress. The cold societies are the primitive ones, static, crystalline, harmonious. Utopia, for Lévi-Strauss, would be a great lowering of the historical temperature. In his inaugural lecture at the Collège de France, Lévi-Strauss outlined a post-Marxist vision of freedom in which man would finally be freed from the obligation to progress, and from "the age-old curse which forced it to enslave men in order to make progress possible." Then:

history would henceforth be quite alone, and society, placed outside and above history, would once again be able to assume that regular and quasi-crystalline structure which, the best-preserved primitive societies teach us, is not contradictory to humanity. It is in this admittedly Utopian view that social anthropology would find its highest justification, since the forms of life and thought which it studies would no longer be of mere historic and comparative interest. They would correspond to a permanent possibility of man, over which social anthropology would have a mission to stand watch, especially in man's darkest hours.

The anthropologist is thus not only the mourner of the cold world of the primitives, but its custodian as well. Lamenting among the shadows, struggling to distinguish the archaic from the pseudo-archaic, he acts out a heroic, diligent, and complex modern pessimism.

[1963]

The literary criticism
of Georg Lukács

THE Hungarian philosopher and literary critic Georg Lukács is the senior figure living today within the borders of the Communist world who speaks a Marxism that it is possible for intelligent non-Marxists to take seriously.

I do not believe (as many do) that Lukács is the figure who speaks the most interesting or plausible form of Marxism today, much less that he is (as he has been called) "the greatest Marxist since Marx." But there can be no doubt that he has a special eminence and claim to our attention. Not only is he the mentor of new intellectual stirrings in Eastern Europe and Russia; outside of Marxist circles as well, Lukács has counted for a long time. His early writings, for instance, are the source of many of the ideas of Karl Mannheim (on the sociology of art, culture, and knowledge), and through Mannheim upon all of modern sociology; he has also had a great influence on Sartre, and through him on French existentialism.

He was born Georg von Lukács, of a wealthy, recently ennobled Jewish banking family, in Hungary in 1885. From the start, his intellectual career was an extraordinary one. While still in his teens he wrote, gave public lectures, founded a theater, and launched a liberal journal. When he came to Germany to study at the Universities of Berlin and Heidelberg, he astonished his great teachers, Max Weber and Georg Simmel, by his brilliance. His main interest was literature, but he was interested in everything else as well. His doctoral dissertation, in 1907, was *The Metaphysics of Tragedy*. His first major work, in 1908, was *The Development of Modern Drama*. In 1910, he published a collection of literary and philosophical essays, *Soul and Form*; in 1916, *The Theory of the Novel*. Some time during the First World War he moved from neo-Kantianism, his earliest philosophical view, to the philosophy of Hegel, and thence to Marxism. He joined the Communist Party in 1918 (dropping the *von* before his name).

From here on, Lukács' career is a stunning testament to the difficulties of a free intellectual committed to a view which has taken on more and more the character of a closed system, and, in addition, living in a society which listens to what intellectuals say and write with the utmost gravity. For, from the beginning, Lukács' interpretation of Marxist theory was free-wheeling, speculative.

Shortly after joining the Party, Lukács, for the first of two times in his life, took part in a revolution. Returning to Hungary, he became Minister of Education in the brief Communist dictatorship of Béla Kun in 1919. After the Kun regime was overthrown, he escaped to Vienna, where he lived for the next ten years. His most important book of this period was a philosophical discussion of Marxist theory, the now almost legendary *History and Class Consciousness* (1923)—of all his works, perhaps the one most esteemed by non-Marxists, and for which he immediately came under strong and unremitting attack from within the Communist movement.

The controversy over this book marked the defeat of Lukács in his battle with Kun for leadership of the Hungarian Communist Party, a battle which was fought in those years of exile in Vienna.

After being attacked throughout the Communist world by every-one from Lenin, Bukharin, and Zinoviev on down, he was expelled from the central committee of the Hungarian party, and deprived of the editorship of his magazine *Kommunismus*. But throughout this decade Lukács defended his books, standing firm and retract-ing nothing.

Then, in 1930, after a year in Berlin, he went to Moscow for a year to do research on the staff of the famous Marx-Engels Insti-tute (whose brilliant director, N. Ryazanoff, was to disappear in the purges of the late thirties). What was happening, subjectively, to Lukács at this time is not known. The facts are that, after return-ing to Berlin in 1931, he went back to Moscow in 1933, when Hitler came to power; and the same year publicly repudiated in the most abject terms the *History and Class Consciousness* and all his previous writings as infected by "bourgeois idealism."

Lukács lived on as a refugee in Moscow for twelve years; even after his recantation, and numerous attempts to bring his work more into line with Communist orthodoxy, he remained in dis-favor. Nevertheless, unlike Ryazanoff, he survived the terrible purges. One of his finest books, *The Young Hegel*, dates from this period (it was written in 1938, but not published until a decade later), as well as a vile simplistic tract against modern philosophy, *The Destruction of Reason* (1945). The contrast between these two books is typical of the vast fluctuations of quality in Lukács' later work.

In 1945, when the war was over and a Communist government assumed power in Hungary, Lukács returned permanently to his native country to teach at the University of Budapest. Among the books he wrote in the succeeding decade are *Goethe and His Time* (1947) and *Thomas Mann* (1949). Then, at the age of seventy-one, came a second and incredibly moving venture into revolutionary politics, when Lukács emerged as one of the leaders of the revolution of 1956, and was named a minister in Imre Nagy's government. Deported to Rumania and put under house arrest after the suppression of the revolution, he was permitted to return to Budapest four months later to resume teaching and to continue publishing both at home and in Western Europe. Only Lukács' age and his immense international prestige, one supposes, saved him from the fate of Imre Nagy. At any rate, among all the leaders of the revolution, he alone was never put on trial nor has he publicly recanted.

Immediately after the revolution he published *Realism in Our Time* (1956), and last year brought out the first part, consisting of two huge volumes, of his long-awaited *Aesthetics*. He continues to be attacked by cultural bureaucrats and older Communist critics, though much more in, say, East Germany than at home, under the increasingly liberal regime of Kadar. His early writings (which he still strenuously repudiates) are increasingly studied in England and Western Europe and Latin America—he is widely translated in French and Spanish—in the light of the new interest in the early writings of Marx; while for many of the new generation of intellectuals in Eastern Europe, it is the later work which is the touchstone for the cautious but inexorable overthrow of the ideas and practices of Stalinism.

Obviously, Lukács has a great talent for personal and political survival—that is, for being many things to many different men. He has, in effect, accomplished the difficult feat of being both marginal and central in a society which makes the position of the marginal intellectual almost intolerable. To do this, however, he has had to spend a great deal of his life in one or another form of exile. Of the external exile, I have already spoken. But there is also a kind of internal exile, evident in his choice of subjects to write about. The writers Lukács is most devoted to are Goethe, Balzac, Scott, Tolstoy. By virtue of his age, and the possession of a sensibility formed before the advent of the canon of Communist culture, Lukács has been able to protect himself by (intellectually) emigrating out of the present. The only modern writers who receive his unqualified approval are those who, essentially, continue the 19th century tradition of the novel—Mann, Galsworthy, Gorky, and Roger Martin du Gard.

But this commitment to 19th century literature and philosophy is not just an aesthetic choice (as, indeed, there can be no purely aesthetic choices in a Marxist—or a Christian, or a Platonic—view of art). The standard by which Lukács judges the present is a moral one, and it is notable that this standard is drawn from the past. The wholeness of the vision of the past is what Lukács means when he speaks of "realism."

Another way Lukács has partly emigrated from the present is in his choice of the language in which to write. Only his first two books are in Hungarian. The rest—some thirty books and fifty essays—are in German; and to continue writing in German in the Hungary of today is decidedly a polemical act. By concentrating on 19th century literature and stubbornly retaining German as the language in which he writes, Lukács has continued to propose, as a Communist, European and humanist—as opposed to nationalist and doctrinaire—values; living as he does in a Communist and provincial country, he has remained a genuinely European intellectual figure. Needless to say, knowledge of him here is long overdue.

It is perhaps unfortunate, though, that the two works which hereby introduce Lukács to an American public are both works of literary criticism, and both of the "late" rather than "early" Lukács.* *Studies in European Realism*, a collection of eight essays dealing mainly with Balzac, Stendhal, Tolstoy, Zola, and Gorky, was written in Russia during the late thirties, at the time of the purges, and bears the scars of that awful period in the form of several passages of a crude political nature; Lukács published it in 1948. *Realism in Our Time* is a shorter work, written in the fifties, less academic in style and more sprightly and rapid in argument; in the three essays, Lukács reviews the alternatives for literature today and rejects both "modernism" and "socialist realism" in favor of what he calls "critical realism"—essentially the tradition of the 19th century novel.

I say this choice of books may be unfortunate because, while here is a quite accessible Lukács, not hard to read, as he is in his

* *Studies in European Realism*, translated by Edith Bone. New York, Grosset & Dunlap. *Realism in Our Time*, translated by John and Necke Mander. New York, Harper. (*Essays on Thomas Mann* was translated and published in England in 1964. *The Historical Novel*, written in 1936, has also recently been translated.)

philosophical writings, we are forced to react to him as a literary critic alone. What is Lukács' intrinsic value and quality as a literary critic? Sir Herbert Read has praised him lavishly; Thomas Mann called him "the most important literary critic of today"; George Steiner regards him as "the only major German literary critic of our epoch" and claims that "among critics, only Sainte-Beuve and Edmund Wilson have matched the breadth of Lukács' response" to literature; and Alfred Kazin clearly regards him as a very able, sound, and important guide to the great tradition of the 19th century novel. But do the present books support these claims? I think not. Indeed, I rather suspect that the current vogue for Lukács—promoted by such effusions as the essays of George Steiner and Alfred Kazin offered as prefaces to the present translations—is motivated more by cultural good will than by strictly literary criteria.

It is easy to sympathize with Lukács' boosters. I, too, am inclined to give Lukács all the benefit of the doubt, if only in protest against the sterilities of the Cold War which have made it impossible to discuss Marxism seriously for the last decade or more. But we may be generous toward the "late" Lukács only at the price of not taking him altogether seriously, of subtly patronizing him by treating his moral fervor aesthetically, as style rather than idea. My own inclination is to take him at his word. Then, what about the fact that Lukács rejects Dostoevsky, Proust, Kafka, Beckett, almost all modern literature? It is scarcely adequate to remark, as Steiner does in his introduction, that "Lukács is a radical moralist . . . like [the] Victorian critics. . . . In this great Marxist, there is an old-style Puritan."

This type of shallow, knowing comment, by which notorious radicalisms are domesticated, amounts to a surrender of judgment. It is cute or appealing to discover that Lukács—like Marx, like Freud—is morally conventional, even positively prudish, only if one has started with a cliché about an intellectual bogey-man. The point is: Lukács does treat literature as a branch of moral argument. Is the way he does it plausible, powerful? Does it allow for sensitive and discriminating and true literary judgments? I, for one, find Lukács' writings of the 1930s, 1940s, and 1950s to be seriously marred, not by his Marxism but by the coarseness of his argument.

Any critic is entitled to wrong judgments, of course. But certain lapses of judgment indicate the radical failure of an entire sensibility. And a writer who—as Lukács does—dismisses Nietzsche as merely a forerunner of Nazism, who criticizes Conrad for not "portraying the totality of life" (Conrad "is really a short-story writer rather than a novelist"), is not just making isolated mistakes of judgment, but proposing standards that ought not to be assented to.

Nor can I agree, as Kazin in his introduction seems to suggest, that, regardless of where Lukács went wrong, where he is right he is sound. Admirable as the 19th century realist tradition in the novel may be, the standards of admiration which Lukács proposes are unnecessarily coarse. For everything depends on Lukács' view that "the business of the critic is the relation between ideology (in the sense of *Weltanschauung*) and artistic creation." Lukács is committed to a version of the mimetic theory of art which is simply far too crude. A book is a "portrayal"; it "depicts," it "paints a picture"; the artist is a "spokesman." The great realist tradition of the novel does not need to be defended in these terms.

Both of the present books, "late" writings, lack intellectual subtlety. Of the two, *Realism in Our Time* is by far the better. The first essay in particular, "The Ideology of Modernism," is a powerful, in many ways brilliant, attack. Lukács' thesis is that modernist literature (he sweeps Kafka, Joyce, Moravia, Benn, Beckett, and a dozen others into this net) is really allegorical in character; he goes on to develop the connection between allegory and the refusal of historical consciousness. The next essay, "Franz Kafka or Thomas Mann?" is a cruder, and less interesting, restatement of the same thesis. The final essay, "Critical Realism and Socialist Realism," refutes from a Marxist point of view the base doctrines of art which were part of the Stalin era.

But even this book disappoints in many ways. The notion about allegory in the first essay is based on ideas of the late Walter Benjamin, and the quotations from Benjamin's essay on allegory leap off the page as examples of a type of writing and reasoning much finer than that of Lukács. Ironically, Benjamin, who died in 1940, is one of the critics influenced by the "early" Lukács. But, irony aside, the truth is that Benjamin is a great critic (it is he who deserves the title "the only major German literary critic of our epoch"), and the "late" Lukács is not. Benjamin shows us what Lukács as a literary critic might have been.

Writers like Sartre, in France, and the German school of neo-Marxist critics whose most illustrious members, besides Benjamin, are Theodore Adorno and Herbert Marcuse, have developed the Marxist (more accurately, the radical Hegelian) position as a mode of philosophical and cultural analysis capable, among other things, of doing justice to at least certain aspects of modern literature. It is against these writers that Lukács must be compared, and found wanting. I am sympathetic to the reasons and experiences which underlie Lukács' reactionary aesthetic sensibility, and respectful even of his chronic moralizing and the burden of ideology which he valiantly carries, in part, to assist in the taming of its philistinism. But as I cannot accept either the intellectual premises of Lukács' taste or its consequences, his sweeping strictures against the greatest works of contemporary literature, neither can I pretend that, for me, these do not vitiate his entire later critical work.

For his new American audience, the best service to Lukács would be to translate the earlier books, *Soul and Form* (which includes his thesis on tragedy), *The Theory of the Novel*, and, of course, *History and Class Consciousness*. Besides this, the best service to the vitality and scope inherent in the Marxist position on art would be to translate the German and French critics I have mentioned—above all, Benjamin. Only when all the important writings of this group are taken together can we properly evaluate Marxism as an important position vis-à-vis art and culture.

[1964]

POSTSCRIPT:

Karl Mannheim, in his review (published in 1920) of Lukács' *Theory of the Novel*, described it as "an attempt at interpreting aesthetic phenomena, particularly the novel, from a higher point of view, that of the philosophy of history." For Mannheim, "Lukács' book moves in the right direction." Putting aside judgments of right and wrong, such a direction is clearly a limiting one, I should say. More precisely, both the strength and the limitation of the Marxist approach to art arise from its commitment to a "higher point of view." There is no question in the writings of the critics I have cited (the early Lukács, Benjamin, Adorno, etc.) of a narrow forcing of art per se into the service of a particular moral or historical tendency. But none of these critics, even at their best, are free of certain notions which in the end serve to perpetuate an ideology that, for all its attractiveness when considered as a catalogue of ethical duties, has failed to comprehend in other than a dogmatic and disapproving way the texture and qualities, the peculiar vantage point, of contemporary society. I mean "humanism." Despite their commitment to the notion of historical progress, the neo-Marxist critics have shown themselves to be singularly insensitive to most of the interesting and creative features of contemporary culture in non-socialist countries. In their general lack of interest in avant-garde art, in their blanket indictment of contemporary styles of art and life of very different quality and import (as "alienated," "dehumanized," "mechanized"), they reveal themselves as little different in spirit from the great conservative critics of modernity who wrote in the 19th century such as Arnold, Ruskin, and Burckhardt. It is odd, and disquieting, that such strongly apolitical critics as Marshall McLuhan have got so much better grasp on the texture of contemporary reality.

The variety of particular judgments made by the neo-Marxist critics may seem to indicate less unanimity of sensibility than I have argued. But when one notes the recurrence of the same terms of praise throughout, the differences seem slight. True, Schoenberg is defended by Adorno in his Philosophy of New Music—but in the name of "progress." (Adorno complements his defense of Schoenberg with an attack on Stravinsky, whom he unfairly identifies with just one period, the neo-classical. For raiding the past, for making musical pastiches—an analogous case could be made against Picasso—Stravinsky is labeled as a "reactionary," in the end, a "fascist.") However, Kafka is attacked by Lukács for the qualities which, *mutatis mutandis,* in the history of music, would have made him in Adorno's terms a "progressive." Kafka is a reactionary because of the allegorical, that is, the dehistoricized, texture of his writings, while Mann is a progressive because of his realism, that is, his sense of history. But I imagine that Mann's writings—old-fashioned in their form, riddled with parody and irony—could, if the discussion were set up differently, be labeled as reactionary. In the one case, "reaction" is identified with an inauthentic relation to the past; in the other, with abstractness. Using either standard—despite the exceptions allowed by individual taste—these critics must be generally inhospitable to or obtuse about modern art. Mostly, they don't get any nearer to it than they have to. The only contemporary novelist the French neo-Marxist critic Lucien Goldmann has written on at any length is André Malraux. Even the extraordinary Benjamin, who wrote with equal brilliance on Goethe, Leskov, and Baudelaire, did not deal with any 20th century writers. And the cinema, the only wholly new major art form of our century, to which he did devote the better part of an important essay, was singularly misunderstood and unappreciated by Benjamin. (He thought the movies embodied the abolition of tradition and historical consciousness, and therefore—once again!—fascism.)

What all the culture critics who descend from Hegel and Marx have been unwilling to admit is the notion of art as autonomous (not merely historically interpretable) form. And since the peculiar spirit which animates the modern movements in the arts is based on, precisely, the rediscovery of the power (including the emotional power) of the formal properties of art, these critics are poorly situated to come to sympathetic terms with modern works of art, except through their "content." Even form is viewed by the historicist critics as a kind of content. This is very clear in *The Theory of the Novel,* where Lukács' analysis of the various literary genres—epic, lyric, novel—proceeds by an explication of the attitude toward social change incarnated in the form. A similar prejudice is less explicit, but equally pervasive, in the writings of many American literary critics—who get their Hegelianism partly from Marx but mainly from sociology.

There is certainly much that is valuable in the historicist approach. But if form may be understood as a certain kind of content, it is equally true (and perhaps more important to say now) that all content may be considered as a device of form. Only when the historicist critics and all their progeny are able to accommodate into their views a large measure of devotion to works of art as, above all, works of art (rather than as sociological, cultural, moral, or political documents) will they be open to more than a few of the many great works of art which are of the 20th century, and will they develop—this is mandatory for any responsible critic today— an intelligent involvement with the problems and objectives of "modernism" in the arts.

[1965]

Sartre's
Saint Genet

Saint Genet is a cancer of a book, grotesquely verbose, its cargo of brilliant ideas borne aloft by a tone of viscous solemnity and by ghastly repetitiveness. One knows that the book began as an introductory essay to the collected edition of Genet's works published by Gallimard—some fifty pages, perhaps—and grew to its present length, whereupon it was issued in 1952 as a separate volume, the first, of the Collected Genet.* To read it, familiarity with Genet's writings in prose, most as yet untranslated, is surely essential. Even more important, the reader must come equipped with sympathy for Sartre's way of explicating a text. Sartre breaks every rule of decorum established for the critic; this is criticism by immersion, without guidelines. The book simply plunges into Genet; there is little discernible organiza-

* *Saint Genet*, by Jean-Paul Sartre. Translated by Bernard Frechtman. New York, George Braziller.

tion to Sartre's argument; nothing is made easy or clear. One should perhaps be grateful that Sartre stops after six hundred and twenty-five pages. The indefatigable act of literary and philosophical disembowelment which he practices on Genet could just as well have gone on for a thousand pages. Yet, Sartre's exasperating book is worth all one's effort of attention. *Saint Genet* is not one of the truly great, mad books; it is too long and too academic in vocabulary for that. But it is crammed with stunning and profound ideas.

What made the book grow and grow is that Sartre, the philosopher, could not help (however reverentially) upstaging Genet, the poet. What began as an act of critical homage and recipe for the bourgeois literary public's "good use of Genet" turned into something more ambitious. Sartre's enterprise is really to exhibit his own philosophical style—compounded of the phenomenological tradition from Descartes through Husserl and Heidegger, plus a liberal admixture of Freud and revisionist Marxism—while writing about a specific figure. In this instance, the person whose acts are made to yield the value of Sartre's philosophical vocabulary is Genet. In a previous effort at "existential psychoanalysis," published in 1947 and kept to a more digestible length, it was Baudelaire. In this earlier essay, Sartre was much more concerned with specifically psychological issues, such as Baudelaire's relation to his mother and his mistresses. The present study of Genet is more philosophical because, to put it bluntly, Sartre admires Genet in a way that he does not admire Baudelaire. It would seem that, for Sartre, Genet deserves something more than perceptive psychologizing. He merits philosophical diagnosis.

And a philosophical dilemma accounts for the length—and the breathlessness—of the book. All thought, as Sartre knows, universalizes. Sartre wants to be concrete. He wants to reveal Genet, not simply to exercise his own tireless intellectual facility. But he cannot. His enterprise is fundamentally impossible. He cannot catch the real Genet; he is always slipping back into the categories of Foundling, Thief, Homosexual, Free Lucid Individual, Writer. Somewhere Sartre knows this, and it torments him. The length, and the inexorable tone, of *Saint Genet* are really the product of intellectual agony.

The agony comes from the philosopher's commitment to impose meaning upon action. Freedom, the key notion of existentialism, reveals itself in *Saint Genet*, even more clearly than in *Being and Nothingness*, as a compulsion to assign meaning, a refusal to let the world alone. According to Sartre's phenomenology of action, to act is to change the world. Man, haunted by the world, acts. He acts in order to modify the world in view of an end, an ideal. An act is therefore intentional, not accidental, and an accident is not to be counted as an act. Neither the gestures of personality nor the works of the artist are simply to be experienced. They must be understood, they must be interpreted as modifications of the world. Thus, throughout *Saint Genet*, Sartre continually moralizes. He moralizes upon the acts of Genet. And since Sartre's book was written at a time when Genet was chiefly a writer of prose narratives (among the plays, only the first two, *The Maids* and *Deathwatch*, had been written), and since these narratives are all autobiographical and written in the first person, Sartre need not separate the personal from the literary act. Although Sartre occasionally refers to things which he knows through his own friendship with Genet, it is almost entirely the man revealed by his books of whom Sartre speaks. It is a monstrous figure, real and surreal at the same time, all of whose acts are seen by Sartre as meaningful, intentional. This is what gives *Saint Genet* a quality that is clotted and ghostly. The name "Genet" repeated thousands of times throughout the book never seems to be the name of a real person. It is the name given to an infinitely complex process of philosophical transfiguration.

Given all these ulterior intellectual motives, it is surprising how well Sartre's enterprise serves Genet. This is because Genet himself, in his writings, is notably and explicitly involved in the enterprise of self-transfiguration. Crime, sexual and social degradation, above all murder, are understood by Genet as occasions for glory. It did not require much ingenuity on Sartre's part to propose that Genet's writings are an extended treatise on abjection—conceived as a spiritual method. The "sanctity" of Genet, created by an onanistic meditation upon his own degradation and the imaginative annihilation of the world, is the explicit subject of his prose works.

What remained for Sartre was to draw out the implications of what is explicit in Genet. Genet may never have read Descartes, Hegel, or Husserl. But Sartre is right, entirely right, in finding a relation in Genet to the ideas of Descartes, Hegel, and Husserl. As Sartre brilliantly observes: "Abjection is a methodical conversion, like Cartesian doubt and Husserlian epoché: it establishes the world as a closed system which consciousness regards from without, in the manner of the divine understanding. The superiority of this method to the other two lies in its being lived in pain and pride. It therefore does not lead to the transcendental and universal consciousness of Husserl, the formal and abstract thinking of the Stoics, or the substantial cogito of Descartes, but to an individual existence at its highest degree of tension and lucidity."

As I have said, the only work of Sartre's comparable to *Saint Genet* is the dazzling essay on Baudelaire. Baudelaire is analyzed as a man in revolt whose life is continually lived in bad faith. His freedom is not creative, rebellious though it may have been, because it never finds its own set of values. Throughout his life the profligate Baudelaire needed bourgeois morality to condemn him. Genet is a true revolutionist. In Genet, freedom is won for freedom's sake. Genet's triumph, his "sanctity," is that he broke through the social framework against unbelievable odds to found his own morality. Sartre shows us Genet making a lucid, coherent system out of *le mal*. Unlike Baudelaire, Genet is free of self-deception.

Saint Genet is a book about the dialectic of freedom, and is, formally at least, set in the Hegelian mold. What Sartre wants to show is how Genet, by means of action and reflection, has spent his whole life attaining the lucid free act. Cast from his birth in the role of the Other, the outcast, Genet chose himself. This original choice is asserted through three different metamorphoses—the criminal, the aesthete, the writer. Each one is necessary to fulfill freedom's demand for a push beyond the self. Each new level of freedom carries with it a new knowledge of the self. Thus the whole discussion of Genet may be read as a dark travesty on Hegel's analysis of the relations between self and other. Sartre speaks of the works of Genet as being, each one of them, small editions of

The Phenomenology of Mind. Absurd as it sounds, Sartre is correct. But it is also true that all of Sartre's writings as well are versions, editions, commentaries, satires on Hegel's great book. This is the bizarre point of connection between Sartre and Genet; two more different human beings it would be hard to imagine.

In Genet, Sartre has found his ideal subject. To be sure, he has drowned in him. Nevertheless, Saint Genet is a marvellous book, full of truths about moral language and moral choice. (Take, as only one instance, the insight that "evil is the systematic substitution of the abstract for the concrete.") And the analyses of Genet's narratives and plays are consistently perceptive. On Genet's most daring book, Funeral Rites, Sartre is particularly striking. And he is certainly capable of appraisal, as well as explication, as in the entirely just comment that "The style of Our Lady of the Flowers, which is a dream poem, a poem of futility, is very slightly marred by a kind of onanistic complacency. It does not have the spirited tone of the works that follow." Sartre does say many foolish, superfluous things in Saint Genet. But everything true and interesting that can be said about Genet is in this book as well.

It is also a crucial book for the understanding of Sartre at his best. After Being and Nothingness, Sartre stood at the crossroads. He could move from philosophy and psychology to an ethics. Or he could move from philosophy and psychology to a politics, a theory of group action and history. As everyone knows, and many deplore, Sartre chose the second path; and the result is the Critique of Dialectical Reason, published in 1960. Saint Genet is his complex gesture in the direction he did not go.

Of all the philosophers in the Hegelian tradition (and I include Heidegger), Sartre is the man who has understood the dialectic between self and other in Hegel's Phenomenology in the most interesting and usable fashion. But Sartre is not simply Hegel with knowledge of the flesh, any more than he deserves to be written off as a French disciple of Heidegger. Sartre's great book, Being and Nothingness, is heavily indebted to the language and problems of Hegel, Husserl, and Heidegger, to be sure. But it has a fundamentally different intention from theirs. Sartre's work is not contemplative, but is moved by a great psychological urgency. His pre-war novel, *Nausea*, really supplies the key to all his work. Here is stated the fundamental problem of the assimilability of the world in its repulsive, slimy, vacuous, or obtrusively substantial thereness —the problem which moves all of Sartre's writings. *Being and Nothingness* is an attempt to develop a language to cope with, to record the gestures of, a consciousness tormented by disgust. This disgust, this experience of the superfluity of things and of moral values, is simultaneously a psychological crisis and a metaphysical problem.

Sartre's solution is nothing if not impertinent. Corresponding to the primitive rite of anthropophagy, the eating of human beings, is the philosophical rite of cosmophagy, the eating of the world. The hallmark of the philosophical tradition to which Sartre is heir starts with consciousness as the sole given. Sartre's solution to the anguish of consciousness confronted by the brute reality of things is cosmophagy, the devouring of the world by consciousness. More exactly, consciousness is understood as both world-constituting and world-devouring. All relations—especially, in the most brilliant passages in *Being and Nothingness*, the erotic—are analyzed as gestures of consciousness, appropriations of the other in the interminable self-definition of the self.

In *Being and Nothingness*, Sartre reveals himself as a psychologist of the first rank—worthy to rank with Dostoevsky, Nietzsche, and Freud. And the focus of the Baudelaire essay is the analysis of Baudelaire's work and biography, treated as texts equivalent from a symptomatic point of view, disclosing fundamental psychological gestures. What makes *Saint Genet* even more interesting than the Baudelaire essay (though, at the same time, more unmanageable as well) is that, through thinking about Genet, Sartre has gone beyond the notion of action as a mode of psychological self-conservation. Through Genet, Sartre has glimpsed something of the autonomy of the aesthetic. More exactly, he has redemonstrated the connection between the aesthetic dimension and freedom, rather differently argued by Kant. The artist who is the subject of *Saint Genet* is not psychologized away. Genet's works are interpreted in terms of a saving ritual, a ceremony of consciousness. That this ceremony is essentially onanistic, is curiously apt. According to

European philosophy since Descartes, world-creating has been the principal activity of consciousness. Now, a disciple of Descartes has interpreted world-creating as a form of world-procreating, as masturbation.

Sartre correctly describes Genet's spiritually most ambitious book, *Funeral Rites*, as "a tremendous effort of transubstantiation." Genet relates how he transformed the whole world into the corpse of his dead lover, Jean Decarnin, and this young corpse into his own penis. "The Marquis de Sade dreamt of extinguishing the fires of Etna with his sperm," Sartre observes. "Genet's arrogant madness goes further: he jerks off the Universe." Jerking off the universe is perhaps what all philosophy, all abstract thought is about: an intense, and not very sociable pleasure, which has to be repeated again and again. It is a rather good description, anyway, of Sartre's own phenomenology of consciousness. And, certainly, it is a perfectly fair description of what Genet is about.

[1963]

**Nathalie Sarraute
and the novel**

A N E W mode of didacticism has conquered the arts, is indeed the "modern" element in art. Its central dogma is the idea that art must evolve. Its result is the work whose main intention is to advance the history of the genre, to break ground in matters of technique. The paramilitary imagery of avant-garde and arrière-garde perfectly expresses the new didacticism. Art is the army by which human sensibility advances implacably into the future, with the aid of ever newer and more formidable techniques. This mainly negative relation of individual talent to tradition, which gives rise to the rapid and built-in obsolescence of each new item of technique, and each new use of materials, has vanquished the conception of art as giving familiar pleasure, and produced a body of work which is principally didactic and admonitory. As everyone knows by now, the point of Duchamp's "Nude Descending a Staircase" is not so much to represent anything, much less a nude, descending a staircase, as to teach a lesson on how natural forms may be broken into a series of kinetic planes. The point of the prose works of Stein and Beckett is to show how diction, punctuation, syntax, and narrative order can be recast to express continuous impersonal states of consciousness. The point of the music of Webern and Boulez is to show how, for example, the rhythmical function of silence and the structural role of tone colors can be developed.

The victory of the modern didacticism has been most complete in music and painting, where the most respected works are those which give little pleasure on first hearing and seeing (except to a small and highly trained audience) but make important advances in the technical revolutions which have taken place in these arts. Compared with music and painting, the novel, like the cinema, lags well to the rear of the battlefield. A body of "difficult" novels comparable to Abstract Expressionist painting and *musique concrète* has not overrun the territory of critically respectable fiction. On the contrary, most of the novel's few brave ventures to the front line of modernism get marooned there. After a few years they seem merely idiosyncratic, for no troops follow the brave CO and back him up. Novels which, in the order of difficulty and of merit, are comparable to the music of Gian-Carlo Menotti and the painting of Bernard Buffet, are garnished with the highest critical acclaim. The ease of access and lack of rigor that causes embarrassment in music and painting are no embarrassment in the novel, which remains intransigently *arrière-garde*.

Yet, middle-class art form or no, there is no genre in greater need of sustained reexamination and renovation. The novel is (along with opera) the archetypal art form of the 19th century, perfectly expressing that period's wholly mundane conception of reality, its lack of really ambitious spirituality, its discovery of the "interesting" (that is, of the commonplace, the inessential, the accidental, the minute, the transient), its affirmation of what E. M. Cioran calls "destiny in lower case." The novel, as all the critics who praise it never tire of reminding us and upbraiding contemporary writers who deviate, is about man-in-society; it brings alive a chunk of the world and sets its "characters" within that world. Of course, one can treat the novel as the successor to the epic and the picaresque tale. But everyone knows that this inheritance is superficial. What animates the novel is something wholly missing from these older narrative forms: the discovery of psychology, the transposition of motives into "experiences." This passion for the documentation of "experience," for facts, made the novel the most open of all art forms. Every art form works with some implicit standard of what is elevated and what is vulgar—except the novel. It could accommodate any level of language, any plot, any ideas, any information. And this, of course, was its eventual undoing as a serious art form. Sooner or later discriminating readers could no longer be expected to become interested in one more leisurely "story," in half a dozen more private lives laid open for their inspection. (They found the movies doing this, with more freedom and with more vigor.) While music and the plastic arts and poetry painfully dug themselves out of the inadequate dogmas of 19th century "realism," by a passionate commitment to the idea of progress in art and a hectic quest for new idioms and new materials, the novel has proved unable to assimilate whatever of genuine quality and spiritual ambition has been performed in its name in the 20th century. It has sunk to the level of an art form deeply, if not irrevocably, compromised by philistinism.

When one thinks of giants like Proust, Joyce, the Gide of *Lafcadio*, Kafka, the Hesse of *Steppenwolf*, Genet, or lesser but nonetheless masterly writers such as Machado de Assis, Svevo, Woolf, Stein, the early Nathanael West, Céline, Nabokov, the early Pasternak, the Djuna Barnes of *Nightwood*, Beckett (to mention only some), one thinks of writers who close off rather than inaugurate, who cannot be learned from, so much as imitated, and whom one imitates at the peril of merely repeating what they have done. One hesitates to blame or praise critics for anything that happens in an art form, whether for good or bad. Yet it is hard not to conclude that what the novel has lacked, and what it must have if it is to continue as a generally (as opposed to sporadically) serious art form, is any sustained distance from its 19th century premises. (The great flowering of literary criticism in England and America in the last thirty years, which began with the criticism of poetry and then passed on to the novel, precisely does not contain such a reevaluation. It is a philosophically naïve criticism, unquestioning and uncritical of the prestige of "realism.")

This coming-of-age of the novel will entail a commitment to all sorts of questionable notions, like the idea of "progress" in the arts and the defiantly aggressive ideology expressed in the metaphor of the avant-garde. It will restrict the novel's audience because it will demand accepting new pleasures—such as the pleasure of solving a problem—to be gotten from prose fiction and learning how to get them. (It may mean, for example, that we shall have to read aloud as well as with the eye, and it will certainly mean that we must expect to read a novel a number of times to understand it fully or to feel ourselves competent to judge it. We have already accepted this idea of repeated looking or hearing or reading with serious contemporary poetry, painting, sculpture, and music.) And it will make self-conscious aestheticians, didactic explorers, of all who wish seriously to practice the form. (All "modern" artists are aestheticians.) This surrender of the novel's commitment to facileness, to easy availability and the perpetuation of an outmoded aesthetic, will undoubtedly give rise to a great many boring and pretentious books; and one may well come to wish the old unselfconsciousness back again. But the price must be paid. Readers must be made to see, by a new generation of critics who may well have to force this ungainly period of the novel down their throats by all sorts of seductive and partly fraudulent rhetoric, the necessity of this move. And the sooner the better.

For until we have a continuous serious "modern" tradition of the novel, venturesome novelists will work in a vacuum. (Whether critics will decide not to call these prose fictions novels any more doesn't matter. Nomenclature has not proved an obstacle in painting or music or poetry, although it has in sculpture, so that we now tend to drop that word in favor of words like "construction" and "assemblage.") We shall continue to have monstrous hulks, like abandoned tanks, lying about the landscape. An example, perhaps the greatest example, is *Finnegans Wake*—still largely unread and unreadable, left to the care of academic exegetes who may decipher the book for us, but cannot tell us why it should be read or what we can learn from it. That Joyce expected his readers to devote their whole lives to his book may seem an outrageous demand; but it is a logical one, considering the singularity of his work. And the fate of Joyce's last book presages the obtuse reception of a number of its less mammoth but equally plotless successors in English—the books of Stein, Beckett, and Burroughs come to mind. No wonder these stand out, as stark isolated forays, on an eerily pacified battleground.

Lately, however, the situation appears to be changing. A whole school—should I say a battalion?—of important and challenging novels is being produced in France. There are actually two waves here. The earlier was led by Maurice Blanchot, Georges Bataille, and Pierre Klossowski; most of these books were written in the 1940s and are as yet untranslated into English. Better known, and mostly translated, are a "second wave" of books written in the 1950s, by (among others) Michel Butor, Alain Robbe-Grillet, Claude Simon, and Nathalie Sarraute. All these writers—and they differ greatly from each other, in intention and achievement—have this in common: they reject the idea of the "novel" whose task is to tell a story and delineate characters according to the conventions of 19th century realism, and all they abjure is summed up in the notion of "psychology." Whether they try to transcend psychology by Heidegger's phenomenology (a powerful influence) or undercut it by behavioristic, external description, the results are at least negatively similar, and constitute the first body of work on the form of the novel which gives promise of telling us something useful about the new forms which fiction may take.

But perhaps the more valuable achievement to come out of France for the novel has been a whole body of criticism inspired by the new novelists (and, in some cases, written by them) which amounts to a most impressive attempt to think systematically about the genre. This criticism—I am thinking of essays by Maurice Blanchot, Roland Barthes, E. M. Cioran, Alain Robbe-Grillet, Nathalie Sarraute, Michel Butor, Michel Foucault, and others —is, by far, the most interesting literary criticism today. And nothing prevents novelists in the English-speaking world from drawing sustenance from the brilliant reexamination of the premises of the novel expounded by these critics, but doing work in the novel very different from that of the French novelists. The reason these essays may prove more valuable than the novels is that they propose standards that are ampler and more ambitious than anything yet achieved by any writer. (Robbe-Grillet, for example, admits that his novels are inadequate illustrations of the diagnoses and recommendations put forth in his essays.)

This is, to me, the importance of the appearance in English of *The Age of Suspicion*, a collection of Nathalie Sarraute's essays in which, ostensibly, the theory behind her novels is fully set forth.* Whether or not one enjoys or admires Sarraute's novels (I really like only *Portrait of a Man Unknown* and *The Planetarium*), whether or not she really practices what she preaches (in a crucial respect, I think she does not), the essays broach a number of criticisms of the traditional novel which seem to me a good beginning for the theoretical reconsideration long overdue on this side of the Atlantic.

Perhaps the best approach to Sarraute's polemic for an English-speaking reader would be to compare it with two other manifestoes on what the novel should be, Virginia Woolf's "Mr. Bennett and Mrs. Brown" and Mary McCarthy's "The Fact in Fiction." Sarraute scorns as "naïve" Virginia Woolf's dismissal of naturalism and objective realism, her call to the modern novelist to examine "the dark places of psychology." But Sarraute is equally hard on the position represented by Mary McCarthy's essay, which may be read as a rebuttal of Virginia Woolf, calling as it does for a return to the old novelistic virtues of setting forth a real world, giving a sense of verisimilitude, and constructing memorable characters.

Sarraute's case against realism is a convincing one. Reality is not that unequivocal; life is not that lifelike. The immediate cozy recognition that the lifelike in most novels induces is, and should be, suspect. (Truly, as Sarraute says, the genius of the age is suspicion. Or, if not its genius, at least its besetting vice.) I wholeheartedly sympathize with what she objects to in the old-fashioned novel:

* *The Age of Suspicion* by Nathalie Sarraute. Translated by Maria Jolas. New York, Braziller.

Vanity Fair and Buddenbrooks, when I reread them recently, however marvellous they still seemed, also made me wince. I could not stand the omnipotent author showing me that's how life is, making me compassionate and tearful; with his obstreperous irony, his confidential air of perfectly knowing his characters and leading me, the reader, to feel I knew them too. I no longer trust novels which fully satisfy my passion to understand. Sarraute is right, too, that the novel's traditional machinery for furnishing a scene, and describing and moving about characters, does not justify itself. Who really cares about the furniture of so-and-so's room, or whether he lit a cigarette or wore a dark gray suit or uncovered the typewriter after sitting down and before inserting a sheet of paper in the typewriter? Great movies have shown that the cinema can invest pure physical action—whether fleeting and small-scale like the wig-changing in L'Avventura, or important like the advance through the forest in The Big Parade—with more immediate magic than words ever can, and more economically, too.

More complex and problematic, however, is Sarraute's insistence that psychological analysis in the novel is equally obsolete and misguided. "The word 'psychology,'" Sarraute says, "is one that no present-day writer can hear spoken with regard to himself without averting his gaze and blushing." By psychology in the novel, she means Woolf, Joyce, Proust: novels which explore a substratum of hidden thoughts and feelings beneath action, the depiction of which replaces the concern with character and plot. All Joyce brought up from these depths, she remarks, was an uninterrupted flow of words. And Proust, too, failed. In the end Proust's elaborate psychological dissections recompose themselves into realistic characters, in which the practiced reader "immediately recognizes a rich man of the world in love with a kept woman, a prominent, awkward, gullible doctor, a parvenu bourgeoise or a snobbish 'great lady,' all of which will soon take their places in the vast collection of fictitious characters that people his imaginary museum."

Actually Sarraute's novels are not so unlike Joyce's (and Woolf's) as she thinks, and her rejection of psychology is far from total. What she wants herself is precisely the psychological, but (and this is the basis of her complaint against Proust) without the possibility of any conversion back into "character" and "plot." She is against psychological dissection, for that assumes there is a body to dissect. She is against a provisional psychology, against psychology as a new means to the old end. The use of the psychological microscope must not be intermittent, a device merely in the furthering of the plot. This means a radical recasting of the novel. Not only must the novelist not tell a story; he must not distract the reader with gross events like a murder or a great love. The more minute, the less sensational the event the better. (Thus *Martereau* consists of the ruminations of a nameless young man, an interior decorator, about the artistic aunt and rich businessman uncle with whom he lives, and about an older, not-so-well-off man named Martereau, concerning why and in what circumstances he feels comfortable with them, and why and when he feels he is succumbing to the force of their personalities and the objects with which they surround themselves. The aunt and uncle's project of buying a house in the country provide the only "action" of the book, and if for a time it is suspected that Martereau has defrauded the uncle in the matter of the house, you can bet that in the end all suspicions are allayed. In *The Planetarium* something does happen. A social-climbing young man, shamelessly trying to gain admittance to the circle of a rich, vain, and very famous woman writer, actually does manage to dispossess his doting, gullible aunt from her five-room apartment.) But Sarraute's characters do not really ever act. They scheme, they throb, they shudder—under the impact of the minutiae of daily life. These preliminaries and gropings toward action are the real subject of her novels. Since analysis is out—that is, the speaking, interpreting author is out—Sarraute's novels are logically written only in the first person, even when the interior musings use "she" and "he."

What Sarraute proposes is a novel written in continuous monologue, in which dialogue between characters is a functional extension of monologue, "real" speech a continuation of silent speech. This kind of dialogue she calls "sub-conversation." It is comparable to theatrical dialogue in that the author does not intervene or interpret, but unlike theatrical dialogue it is not broken up or assigned to clearly separable characters. (She has some particularly sharp and mocking words to say about the creaky *he said's, she replied's, so-and-so declared's* with which most novels are strewn.) Dialogue must "become vibrant and swollen with those tiny inner movements that propel and extend it." The novel must disavow the means of classical psychology—introspection—and proceed instead by immersion. It must plunge the reader "into the stream of those subterranean dramas of which Proust only had time to obtain a rapid aerial view, and concerning which he observed and reproduced nothing but the broad motionless outlines." The novel must record without comment the direct and purely sensory contact with things and persons which the "I" of the novelist experiences. Abstaining from all creating of likenesses (Sarraute hands that over to the cinema), the novel must preserve and promote "that element of indetermination, of opacity and mystery that one's own actions always have for the one who lives them."

There is something exhilarating in Sarraute's program for the novel, which insists on an unlimited respect for the complexity of human feelings and sensations. But there is, for me, a certain softness in her argument, based as it is on a diagnosis of psychology that is both excessively doctrinaire in its remedy and equivocal. A view which regards "the efforts of Henry James or Proust to take apart the delicate wheelworks of our inner mechanisms" as wielding a pick and shovel has dazzling standards of psychological refinement indeed. Who would contradict Sarraute when she characterizes the feelings as an immense mobile mass in which almost anything can be found; or when she says that no theory, least of all a cipher like psychoanalysis, can give an account of all its movements? But Sarraute is only attacking psychology in the novel on behalf of a better, closer technique of psychological description.

Her views of the complexity of feeling and sensation are one thing, her program for the novel another. True, all accounts of motivation simplify. But, admitting that, there still remain many choices available to the novelist besides seeking a more refined and microscopic way of representing motives. Certain kinds of overviews, for example—which scant the minutiae of feeling altogether—are, I am sure, at least as valid a solution to the problem Sarraute raises as the technique of dialogue and narration which she takes as the logical consequence of her critique. Character may be (as Sarraute insists) an ocean, a confluence of tides and streams and eddies, but I do not see the privileged value of immersion. Skin-diving has its place, but so has oceanic cartography, what Sarraute contemptuously dismisses as "the aerial view." Man is a creature who is designed to live on the surface; he lives in the depths—whether terrestrial, oceanic, or psychological—at his peril. I do not share her contempt for the novelist's effort to transmute the watery shapeless depths of experience into solid stuff, to impose outlines, to give fixed shape and sensuous body to the world. That it's boring to do it in the old ways goes without saying. But I cannot agree that it should not be done at all.

Sarraute invites the writer to resist the desire to amuse his contemporaries, to reform them, to instruct them, or to fight for their emancipation; and simply, without trimming or smoothing or overcoming contradictions, to present "reality" (the word is Sarraute's) as he sees it, with as great a sincerity and sharpness of vision as he is capable. I will not here dispute the question of whether the novel should amuse, reform, or instruct (why should it not, so long as it justifies itself as a work of art?) but only point out what a tendentious definition of reality she proposes. Reality, for Sarraute, means a reality that is rid of the "preconceived ideas and ready-made images that encase it." It is opposed to "the surface reality that everyone can easily see and which, for want of anything better, everyone uses." According to Sarraute, for a writer to be in contact with reality he must "attain something that is thus far unknown, which, it seems to him, he is the first to have seen."

But what is the point of this multiplication of realities? For truly, it is the plural rather than the singular that Sarraute should have used. If each writer must "bring to light this fragment of reality that is his own"—and all the whales and sharks have been catalogued; it is new species of plankton she is after—then the writer not only is a maker of fragments, but is condemned to being an exponent only of what is original in his own subjectivity. When he comes to the literary arena bearing his jar of tiny, and as yet uncatalogued, marine specimens, are we to welcome him in the name of science? (The writer as marine biologist.) Of sport? (The writer as deep-sea diver.) Why does he deserve an audience? How many fragments of reality do readers of novels need?

By invoking the notion of reality at all, Sarraute has, in fact, narrowed and compromised her argument when she need not have done so. The metaphor of the work of art as a representation of reality should be retired for a while; it has done good service throughout the history of the analysis of works of art, but now it can scarcely fail to skirt the important issues. In Sarraute's exposition, it has the unfortunate result of giving further life to the tedious alternatives of subjectivity versus objectivity, the original versus what is preconceived and ready-made. There is no reason why the novelist cannot make new arrangements and transformations of what everybody has seen, and restrict himself precisely to preconceived ideas and ready-made images.

Sarraute's allegiance to this rather vacuous notion of reality (a reality lying in the depths rather than the surface) is also responsible for the unnecessarily grim tone of some of her admonitions. Her chilly dismissal of the possibility of the writer's providing "aesthetic enjoyment" to his readers is mere rhetoric, and does serious injustice to the position she, in part, ably represents. The writer, she says, must renounce "all desire to write 'beautifully' for the pleasure of doing so, to give aesthetic enjoyment to himself or to his readers." Style is "capable of beauty only in the sense that any athlete's gesture is beautiful; the better it is adapted to its purpose, the greater the beauty." The purpose, remember, is the recording of the writer's unique apprehension of an unknown reality. But there is absolutely no reason to equate "aesthetic enjoyment," which every work of art is by definition designed to supply, with the notion of a frivolous, decorative, merely "beautiful" style. . . . It really is science, or better yet sport, that Sarraute has in mind as model for the novel. The final justification for the novelist's quest as Sarraute characterizes it—what for her frees the novel from all moral and social purposes—is that the novelist is after truth (or a fragment of it), like the scientist, and after functional exercise, like the athlete. And there is nothing, in principle, so objectionable about these models, except their meaning for her. For all the basic soundness of Sarraute's critique of the old-fashioned novel, she still has the novelist chasing after "truth" and "reality."

Sarraute's manifesto must thus be finally judged to do less justice to the position she is defending than that position deserves. A more rigorous and searching account of this position may be found in Robbe-Grillet's essays "On Several Dated Notions" and "Nature, Humanism, and Tragedy." These appeared in 1957 and 1958, respectively, while Sarraute's were published between 1950 and 1955, and collected in book form in 1956; and Robbe-Grillet has cited Sarraute in a way that might lead one to think that he is a later exponent of the same position. But Robbe-Grillet's complex criticism of the notions of tragedy and of humanism, the unremitting clarity with which he demolishes the old shibboleth of form versus content (his willingness, for example, to declare that the novel, so far as it belongs in the domain of art, has no content), the compatibility of his aesthetic with technical innovations in the novel quite different from those he has chosen, put his arguments on a far higher level than those of Sarraute. Robbe-Grillet's essays are truly radical and, if one grants but a single of his assumptions, carry one all the way to conviction. Sarraute's essays, useful as they may be to introduce the literate English-speaking public to the important critique of the traditional novel which has been launched in France, in the end hedge and compromise.

Undoubtedly, many people will feel that the prospects for the novel laid out by the French critics are rather bleak; and wish that the armies of art would go on fighting on other battlefronts and leave the novel alone. (In the same mood, some of us wish we were endowed with a good deal less of the excruciating psychological self-consciousness that is the burden of educated people in our time.) But the novel as a form of art has nothing to lose, and everything to gain, by joining the revolution that has already swept over most of the other arts. It is time that the novel became what it is not, in England and America with rare and unrelated exceptions: a form of art which people with serious and sophisticated taste in the other arts can take seriously.

[1963; revised 1965]

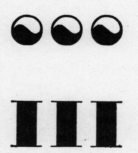

III

Ionesco

IT IS fitting that a playwright whose best works apotheosize the platitude has compiled a book on the theater crammed with platitudes.* I quote, at random:

Didacticism is above all an attitude of mind and an expression of the will to dominate.

A work of art really is above all an adventure of the mind.

Some have said that Boris Vian's The Empire Builders was inspired by my own Amédée. Actually, no one is inspired by anyone except by his own self and his own anguish.

I detect a crisis of thought, which is manifested by a crisis of language; words no longer meaning anything.

No society has even been able to abolish human sadness; no polit-

* *Notes and Counter Notes: Writings on the Theatre* by Eugène Ionesco. Translated by Donald Watson. New York, Grove.

ical system can deliver us from the pain of living, from our fear of death, our thirst for the absolute.

What is one to make of a view at once so lofty and so banal? As if this were not enough, Ionesco's essays are laden with superfluous self-explication and unctuous vanity. Again, at random:

I can affirm that neither the public nor the critics have influenced me.

Perhaps I am socially minded in spite of myself.

With me every play springs from a kind of self-analysis.

I am not an ideologue, for I am straightforward and objective.

The world ought not to interest me so much. In reality, I am obsessed with it.

Etcetera, etcetera. Ionesco's essays on the theater offer a good deal of such, presumably unconscious, humor.

There are, to be sure, some ideas in *Notes and Counter Notes* worth taking seriously, none of them original with Ionesco. One is the idea of the theater as an instrument which, by dislocating the real, freshens the sense of reality. Such a function for the theater plainly calls not only for a new dramaturgy, but for a new body of plays. "No more masterpieces," Artaud demanded in *The Theatre and Its Double*, the most daring and profound manifesto of the modern theater. Like Artaud, Ionesco scorns the "literary" theater of the past: he likes to read Shakespeare and Kleist but not to see them performed, while Corneille, Molière, Ibsen, Strindberg, Pirandello, Giraudoux and company bore him either way. If the old-fashioned theater pieces must be done at all, Ionesco suggests (as did Artaud) a certain trick. One should play "against" the text: by grafting a serious, formal production onto a text that is absurd, wild, comic, or by treating a solemn text in the spirit of buffoonery. Along with the rejection of the literary theater—the theater of plot and individual character—Ionesco calls for the scrupulous avoidance of all psychology, for psychology means "realism," and realism is dull and confines the imagination. His rejection of psychology permits the revival of a device common to all non-realistic

theatrical traditions (it is equivalent to frontality in naïve painting), in which the characters turn to face the audience (rather
than each other), stating their names, identities, habits, tastes, acts
... All this, of course, is very familiar: the canonical modern
style in the theater. Most of the interesting ideas in *Notes and
Counter Notes* are watered-down Artaud; or rather Artaud spruced
up and made charming, ingratiating; Artaud without his hatreds,
Artaud without his madness. Ionesco comes closest to being original in certain remarks about humor, which he understands as poor
mad Artaud did not at all. Artaud's notion of a Theater of Cruelty
emphasized the darker registers of fantasy: frenzied spectacle, melodramatic deeds, bloody apparitions, screams, transports. Ionesco,
noting that any tragedy becomes comic simply if it is speeded up,
has devoted himself to the violently comic. Instead of the cave or
the palace or the temple or the heath, he sets most of his plays in
the living room. His comic terrain is the banality and oppressive-
ness of the "home"—be it the bachelor's furnished room, the
scholar's study, the married couple's parlor. Underneath the forms
of conventional life, Ionesco would demonstrate, lies madness, the
obliteration of personality.

But Ionesco's plays, it seems to me, need little explanation. If an
account of his work is desired, Richard N. Coe's excellent short
book on Ionesco, published in 1961 in the English *Writers and
Critics* series, offers a far more coherent and compact defense of the
plays than anything in *Notes and Counter Notes*. The interest of
Ionesco on Ionesco is not for its author's theory of theater, but for
what the book suggests about the puzzling thinness—puzzling considering their richness of theme—of Ionesco's plays. The tone of
the book tells a great deal. For behind the relentless egotism of Ionesco's writings on the theater—the allusions to unending battles
with obtuse critics and a bovine public—is an insistent, plaintive
uneasiness. Ionesco protests, incessantly, that he has been misunderstood. Therefore, everything he says at one point in *Notes and
Counter Notes*, he takes back on another page. (Though these
writings span the years 1951–61, there is no development in the
argument.) His plays are avant-garde theater; there is no such thing
as avant-garde theater. He is writing social criticism; he is not writ-

ing social criticism. He is a humanist; he is morally and emotionally estranged from humanity. Throughout, he writes as a man sure—whatever you say of him, whatever he says of himself—that his true gifts are misunderstood.

What is Ionesco's accomplishment? Judging by the most exacting standards, he has written one really remarkable and beautiful play, *Jack, or the Submission* (1950); one brilliant lesser work, *The Bald Soprano*, his first play (written 1948-49); and several effective short plays which are pungent reprises of the same material, *The Lesson* (1950), *The Chairs* (1951), and *The New Tenant* (1953). All these plays—Ionesco is a prolific writer—are "early" Ionesco. The later works are marred by a diffuseness in the dramatic purpose and an increasing, unwieldy self-consciousness. The diffuseness can be clearly seen in *Victims of Duty* (1952), a work with some powerful sections but unhappily overexplicit. Or one can compare his best play, *Jack*, with a short sequel using the same characters, *The Future Is in Eggs* (1951). *Jack* abounds with splendid harsh fantasy, ingenious and logical; it alone, of all Ionesco's plays, gives us something up to the standard of Artaud: the Theater of Cruelty as Comedy. But in *The Future Is in Eggs*, Ionesco has embarked upon the disastrous course of his later writings, railing against "views" and tediously attributing to his characters a concern with the state of the theater, the nature of language, and so forth. Ionesco is an artist of considerable gifts who has been victimized by "ideas." His work has become water-logged with them; his talents have coarsened. In *Notes and Counter Notes* we have a chunk of that endless labor of self-explication and self-vindication as a playwright and thinker which occupies the whole of his play, *Improvisation*, which dictates the intrusive remarks on playwriting in *Victims of Duty* and *Amédée*, which inspires the oversimplified critique of modern society in *The Killer* and *Rhinoceros*.

Ionesco's original artistic impulse was his discovery of the poetry of banality. His first play, *The Bald Soprano*, was written almost by accident, he says, after he discovered the Smiths and the Martins *en famille* in the Assimil phrase book he bought when he decided to study English. And all the subsequent plays of Ionesco contin-

ued at least to open with a volleying back and forth of clichés. By
extension, the discovery of the poetry of cliché led to the discovery
of the poetry of meaninglessness—the convertibility of all words
into one another. (Thus, the litany of "*chat*" at the end of *Jack*.)
It has been said that Ionesco's early plays are "about" meaninglessness, or "about" non-communication. But this misses the important fact that in much of modern art one can no longer really speak
of subject-matter in the old sense. Rather, the subject-matter is the
technique. What Ionesco did—no mean feat—was to appropriate
for the theater one of the great technical discoveries of modern
poetry: that all language can be considered from the outside, as by
a stranger. Ionesco disclosed the *dramatic* resources of this attitude,
long known but hitherto confined to modern poetry. His early
plays are not "about" meaninglessness. They are attempts to use
meaninglessness theatrically.

Ionesco's discovery of the cliché meant that he declined to see
language as an instrument of communication or self-expression,
but rather as an exotic substance secreted—in a sort of trance—by
interchangeable persons. His next discovery, also long familiar in
modern poetry, was that he could treat language as a palpable
thing. (Thus, the teacher kills the student in *The Lesson* with the
word "knife.") The key device for making language into a thing is
repetition. This verbal repetition is dramatized further by another
persistent motif of Ionesco's plays: the cancerous, irrational multiplication of material things. (Thus: the egg in *The Future Is in
Eggs*; the chairs in *The Chairs*; the furniture in *The New Tenant*;
the boxes in *The Killer*; the cups in *Victims of Duty*; the noses and
fingers of Roberta II in *Jack*; the corpse in *Amédée, or How to Get
Rid of It*.) These repeating words, these demonically proliferating
things, can only be exorcised as in a dream, by being obliterated.
Logically, poetically—and not because of any "ideas" Ionesco has
about the nature of individual and society—his plays must end
either in a *da capo* repetition, or in incredible violence. Some
typical endings are: massacre of the audience (the proposed end of
The Bald Soprano), suicide (*The Chairs*), entombment and silence (*The New Tenant*), unintelligibility and animal moans
(*Jack*), monstrous physical coercion (*Victims of Duty*), the col-

lapse of the stage (*The Future Is in Eggs*). In Ionesco's plays, the recurrent nightmare is of a wholly clogged, overrun world. (The nightmare is explicit with respect to the furniture in *The New Tenant*, the rhinoceroses in *Rhinoceros*.) The plays therefore must end in either chaos or non-being, destruction or silence.

These discoveries of the poetry of cliché and of language-as-thing gave Ionesco some remarkable theatrical material. But then ideas were born, a theory about the meaning of this theater of meaninglessness took up residence in Ionesco's work. The most fashionable modern experiences were invoked. Ionesco and his defenders claimed that he had begun with his experience of the meaninglessness of contemporary existence, and developed his theater of cliché to express this. It seems more likely that he began with the discovery of the poetry of banality, and then, alas, called on a theory to bulwark it. This theory amounts to the hardiest clichés of the criticism of "mass society," all scrambled together—alienation, standardization, dehumanization. To sum up this dreadfully familiar discontent, Ionesco's favorite word of abuse is "bourgeois," or sometimes "petty bourgeois." Ionesco's bourgeois has little in common with that favorite target of Leftist rhetoric, although perhaps he has adopted it from that source. For Ionesco, "bourgeois" means everything he doesn't like: it means "realism" in the theater (something like the way Brecht used "Aristotelian"); it means ideology; it means conformism. Of course, none of this would have mattered were it merely a question of Ionesco's pronouncements on his work. What mattered is that increasingly it began to infect his work. More and more, Ionesco tended to "indicate" shamelessly what he was doing. (One cringes when, at the end of *The Lesson*, the professor dons a swastika armband as he prepares to dispose of the corpse of his student.) Ionesco began with a fantasy, the vision of a world inhabited by language puppets. He was not criticizing anything, much less discovering what in an early essay he called "The Tragedy of Language." He was just discovering one way in which language could be used. Only afterward was a set of crude, simplistic attitudes extracted from this artistic discovery— attitudes about the contemporary standardization and dehumanization of man, all laid at the feet of a stuffed ogre called the "bourgeois," "Society," etc. The time then came for the affirmation of individual man against this ogre. Thus Ionesco's work passed through an unfortunate and familiar double phase: first, works of anti-theater, parody; then, the socially constructive plays. These later plays are thin stuff. And the weakest in all his oeuvre are the Bérenger plays—*The Killer* (1957), *Rhinoceros* (1960), and *The Pedestrian of the Air* (1962)—where Ionesco (as he said) created in Bérenger an alter ego, an Everyman, a beleaguered hero, a character "to rejoin humanity." The difficulty is that affirmation of man cannot simply be willed, either in morals or in art. If it is merely willed, the result is always unconvincing, and usually pretentious.

In this, Ionesco's development is just the reverse of Brecht's. Brecht's early works—*Baal*, *In the Jungle of Cities*—give way to the "positive" plays which are his masterpieces: *The Good Woman of Setzuan*, *The Caucasian Chalk Circle*, *Mother Courage*. But then —quite apart from the theories they espouse—Brecht is simply a much greater writer than Ionesco. To Ionesco, of course, he represents the arch-villain, the arch-bourgeois. He is political. But Ionesco's attacks on Brecht and the Brechtians—and on the idea of a politically committed art—are trivial. Brecht's political attitudes are, at best, the occasion for his humanism. They allow him to focus and expand his drama. The choice Ionesco insists on, between political affirmation and affirmation of man, is spurious, and dangerous besides.

Compared with Brecht, Genet, and Beckett, Ionesco is a minor writer even at his best. His work does not have the same weight, the same full-bloodedness, the same grandeur and relevance. Ionesco's plays, especially the shorter ones (the form for which his gifts are most suited), have their considerable virtues: charm, wit, a nice feeling for the macabre; above all, theatricality. But the recurrent themes—identities slipping out of gear, the monstrous proliferation of things, the gruesomeness of togetherness—are rarely so moving, so appalling, as they might be. Perhaps it is because—with the exception of *Jack*, where Ionesco lets his fantasy have its head —the terrible is always, somehow, circumscribed by the cute. Ionesco's morbid farces are the boulevard comedies of the avant-garde sensibility; as one English critic has pointed out, little really separates Ionesco's whimsy of conformity from Feydeau's whimsy of adultery. Both are skillful, cold, self-referring.

To be sure, Ionesco's plays—and writings about the theater—pay strenuous lip service to the emotions. Of *The Bald Soprano*, for instance, Ionesco says that it is about "talking and saying nothing because [of] the absence of any inner life." The Smiths and the Martins represent man totally absorbed in his social context, they "have forgotten the meaning of emotion." But what of the numerous descriptions which Ionesco gives in *Notes and Counter Notes* of his own inability to feel—an inability which he regards as rescuing him from being, rather than turning him into, a mass man? It is not protest against passionlessness which moves Ionesco, but a kind of misanthropy, which he has covered over with fashionable clichés of cultural diagnosis. The sensibility behind this theater is tight, defensive, and riddled with sexual disgust. Disgust is the powerful motor in Ionesco's plays: out of disgust, he makes comedies of the distasteful.

Disgust with the human condition is perfectly valid material for art. But disgust for ideas, expressed by a man with little talent for ideas, is another matter. This is what mars many of Ionesco's plays and makes his collection of writings on the theater irritating rather than amusing. Disgusted with ideas as one more foul human excrescence, Ionesco flails about in this repetitious book, at once assuming and disavowing all positions. The unifying theme of *Notes and Counter Notes* is his desire to maintain a position that is not a position, a view that is no view—in a word, to be intellectually invulnerable. But this is impossible, since initially he experiences an idea only as a cliché: "systems of thought on all sides are nothing more than alibis, something to hide reality (another cliché word) from us." By a sickening glide in the argument, ideas somehow become identified with politics, and all politics identified with a fascistic nightmare world. When Ionesco says, "I believe that what separates us all from one another is simply society itself, or, if you like, politics," he is expressing his anti-intellectualism rather than a position about politics. This can be seen with special clarity in the most interesting section in the book (pp. 87-108), the so-called London Controversy, an exchange of essays and letters with Kenneth Tynan, representing ostensibly a Brechtian point of view, which first appeared in the English weekly *The Observer* in 1958. The high moment of this controversy is a noble and eloquent letter from Orson Welles, who points out that the separation between art and politics cannot emerge, much less prosper, except in a certain kind of society. As Welles wrote, "Whatever is valuable is likely to have a rather shopsoiled name," and all freedoms—including Ionesco's privilege to shrug his shoulders at politics—"were, at one time or another, political achievements." It is not "politics which is the arch-enemy of art; it is neutrality . . . [which is] a political position like any other. . . . If we are doomed indeed, let M. Ionesco go down fighting with the rest of us. He should have the courage of our platitudes."

What is disconcerting about Ionesco's work is, then, the intellectual complacency it sponsors. I have no quarrel with works of art that contain no ideas at all; on the contrary, much of the greatest art is of this kind. Think of the films of Ozu, Jarry's *Ubu Roi*, Nabokov's *Lolita*, Genet's *Our Lady of the Flowers*—to take four modern examples. But the intellectual blankness is one (often very salutary) thing, intellectual surrender is another. In Ionesco's case, the intellect that has surrendered is not interesting, relying as it does on a view of the world that sets up an opposition between the wholly monstrous and the wholly banal. At first we may take pleasure in the monstrousness of the monstrous, but finally we are left with the banality of banality.

[1964]

Reflections on
The Deputy

THE supreme tragic event of modern times is the murder of the six million European Jews. In a time which has not lacked in tragedies, this event most merits that unenviable honor—by reason of its magnitude, unity of theme, historical meaningfulness, and sheer opaqueness. For no one understands this event. The murder of the six million Jews cannot be wholly accounted for either in terms of passions, private or public, or of error, or of madness, or of moral failure, or of overwhelming and irresistible social forces. Some twenty years after, there is more controversy about it than ever. What happened? How did it happen? How could it have been allowed to happen? Who are responsible? This great event is a wound that will not heal; even the balm of intelligibility is denied to us.

Yet, if we did know more, that would not suffice. In saying this event was "tragic," we allow other demands than those for factual historical understanding. By tragic, I mean an event—piteous and terrifying in the extreme—whose causation is supercharged and overdetermined, and which is of an exemplary or edifying nature that imposes a solemn duty upon the survivors to confront and assimilate it. In calling the murder of the six million a tragedy, we acknowedge a motive beyond the intellectual (knowing what happened and how) or the moral (catching the criminals and bringing them to justice) for comprehending it. We acknowledge that the event is, in some sense, incomprehensible. Ultimately, the only response is to continue to hold the event in mind, to remember it. This capacity to assume the burden of memory is not always practical. Sometimes remembering alleviates grief or guilt; sometimes it makes it worse. Often, it may not do any good to remember. But we may feel that it is *right*, or fitting, or proper. This moral function of remembering is something that cuts across the different worlds of knowledge, action and art.

We live in a time in which tragedy is not an art form but a form of history. Dramatists no longer write tragedies. But we do possess works of art (not always recognized as such) which reflect or attempt to resolve the great historical tragedies of our time. Among the unacknowledged art forms which have been devised or perfected in the modern era for this purpose are the psychoanalytic session, the parliamentary debate, the political rally, and the political trial. And as the supreme tragic event of modern times is the murder of the six million European Jews, one of the most interesting and moving works of art of the past ten years is the trial of Adolf Eichmann in Jerusalem in 1961.

As Hannah Arendt and others have pointed out, the juridical basis of the Eichmann trial, the relevance of all the evidence presented and the legitimacy of certain procedures, are open to question on strictly legal grounds. But the truth is that the Eichmann trial not only did not, but could not have conformed to legal standards only. It was not Eichmann alone who was on trial. He stood trial in a double role: as both the particular and the generic; both the man, laden with hideous specific guilt, and the cipher, standing for the whole history of anti-Semitism, which climaxed in this unimaginable martyrdom.

The trial was thus an occasion for attempting to make comprehensible the incomprehensible. To this end, while the impassive bespectacled Eichmann sat in his bullet-proof glass cage—tight-lipped, but for all that like one of the great shrieking but unheard creatures from the paintings of Francis Bacon—a great collective dirge was enacted in the courtroom. Masses of facts about the extermination of the Jews were piled into the record; a great outcry of historical agony was set down. There was, needless to say, no strictly legal way of justifying this. The function of the trial was like that of the tragic drama: above and beyond judgment and punishment, catharsis.

The very modern feeling for due process which the trial appealed to was no doubt genuine, but the ancient connections between the theater and the courtroom went deeper. The trial is preeminently a theatrical form (in fact, the very first account in history of a trial comes from the drama—it is in the third play, *The Eumenides*, of Aeschylus' trilogy, the *Oresteia*). And as the trial is preeminently a theatrical form, the theater is a courtroom. The classical form of the drama is always a contest between protagonist and antagonist; the resolution of the play is the "verdict" on the action. All the great stage tragedies take this form of a trial of the protagonist—the peculiarity of the tragic form of judgment being that it is possible to lose the case (i.e., be condemned, suffer, die) and somehow triumph nonetheless.

The Eichmann trial was such a drama. It was not a tragedy itself, but the attempt, dramatically, to deal with and resolve a tragedy. It was, in the profoundest sense, theater. And, as such, it must be judged by other criteria in addition to those of legality and of morality. Because its purposes were not simply those of a historical inquest into the facts, an attempt to determine guilt and affix punishment, the trial of Eichmann did not always "work." But the problem of the Eichmann trial was not its deficient legality, but the contradiction between its juridical form and its dramatic function. As Harold Rosenberg has pointed out: "The trial undertook the function of tragic poetry, that of making the pathetic and terrifying past live again in the mind. But it had to carry out this function on a world stage ruled by the utilitarian code." There was a fundamental paradox in the Eichmann trial: it was primarily a great act of commitment through memory and the renewal of grief, yet it clothed itself in the forms of legality and scientific objectivity. The trial is a dramatic form which imparts to events a certain provisional neutrality; the outcome remains to be decided; the very word "defendant" implies that a defense is possible. In this sense, though Eichmann, as everyone expected, was condemned to death, the form of the trial favored Eichmann. Perhaps this is why many feel, in retrospect, that the trial was a frustrating experience, an anticlimax.

It remains to be seen whether art of a more easily recognizable type—art which need not pretend to be neutral—can do better. By far the most celebrated of all the works of art which take up the same functions of historical memory served by the Eichmann trial is *The Deputy (Der Stellvertreter)*, the lengthy play by the young German playwright Rolf Hochhuth.* Here we have a work of art as we ordinarily understand it—a work for the familiar theater of 8:30 curtains and intermissions, rather than for the austere public stage of the courtroom. Here there are actors, rather than real murderers and real survivors from hell. Yet it is not false to compare it with the Eichmann trial, because *The Deputy* is first of all a compilation, a record. Eichmann himself and many other real persons of the period are represented in the play; the speeches of the characters are drawn from historical records.

In modern times, this use of the theater as a forum for public, moral judgment has been shunted aside. The theater has largely become a place in which private quarrels and agonies are staged; the verdict which events render upon characters in most modern plays has no relevance beyond the play itself. *The Deputy* breaks with the completely private boundaries of most modern theater. And as it would be obtuse to refuse to evaluate the Eichmann trial as a public work of art, it would be frivolous to judge *The Deputy* simply as a work of art.

Some art—but not all—elects as its central purpose *to tell the truth*; and it must be judged by its fidelity to the truth, and by the

* *The Deputy* by Rolf Hochhuth. Translated by Richard and Clara Winston. New York, Grove.

relevance of the truth which it tells. By these standards, The Deputy is an important play. The case against the Nazi party, the SS, the German business elite, and most of the German people—none of which is slighted by Hochhuth—is too well known to need anyone's assent. But The Deputy also stresses, and this is the controversial part of the play, a strong case for the complicity of the German Catholic Church and of Pope Pius XII. This case I am convinced is true, and well taken. (See the ample documentation which Hochhuth has provided at the end of the play, and the excellent book by Guenter Lewy, The Catholic Church and Nazi Germany.) And the importance, historical and moral, of this difficult truth at the present time cannot be overestimated.

In a preface (unfortunately not translated) to the German edition of the play, the director Erwin Piscator, who gave The Deputy its first production in Berlin, wrote that he saw Hochhuth's play as a successor to the historical dramas of Shakespeare and Schiller and the epic theater of Brecht. All questions of quality aside, these comparisons—with classical historical drama and with epic theater when it deals with historical subjects—are misleading. It is the whole point of Hochhuth's play that he has barely transformed his material. Unlike the plays of Shakespeare or Schiller or Brecht, Hochhuth's play stands or falls by its fidelity to the complete historical truth.

This documentary intention of the play also indicates its limitations. The fact is that as not all works of art aim at educating and directing conscience, not all works of art which successfully perform a moral function greatly satisfy as art. I can think of only one dramatic work of the type of The Deputy, the short film Night and Fog by Alain Resnais, which satisfies equally as a moral act and as a work of art. Night and Fog, also a memorial to the tragedy of the six million, is highly selective, emotionally relentless, historically scrupulous, and—if the word seems not outrageous—beautiful. The Deputy is not a beautiful play. Nor does one necessarily ask that it be. Nevertheless, since one can assume the immense interest and moral importance of the play, the aesthetic questions need to be faced. Whatever The Deputy is as a moral event, it is not playwriting of the highest order.

There is the matter of length, for example. I don't find *The Deputy*'s length objectionable. Probably it is, indeed, one of those works of art—like Dreiser's *An American Tragedy*, the operas of Wagner, the best plays of O'Neill—which positively benefit from their outlandish length. The language, though, is a genuine liability. In this English version, it is flat, neither formal nor truly idiomatic. ("The Legation is extraterritorial—be off with you/ Or I'll send for the police.") Hochhuth may have arranged his lines in free-verse form on the page to emphasize the seriousness of his subject, or to reveal the banality of Nazi rhetoric. But I can't imagine any plausible way of *speaking* these lines that conveys the effect (either one) that the author intended. A greater artistic fault is the thick chunks of documentation with which Hochhuth has loaded the play. *The Deputy* is clogged with undigested exposition. There are, to be sure, a number of extremely powerful scenes, particularly those involving the demonic SS doctor. Yet the fact remains that one of the principal and recurrent—and almost, by nature, undramatic—reasons for characters confronting each other in a scene is *to inform each other of something*. Hundreds of names, facts, statistics, reports of conversations, items of current news have been pumped into the dialogue. If the reading of *The Deputy*—I have not yet seen it performed—is tremendously moving, it is because of the weight of its subject, not because of its style or dramaturgy, both of which are extremely conventional.

I imagine that *The Deputy* could be highly satisfying on the stage. But its theatrical effectiveness depends on the director possessing an unusual kind of moral and aesthetic tact. A good production of *The Deputy*, I would think, must be ingeniously stylized. Yet in summoning the resources of the advanced modern theatre, with its bent toward the ritualistic rather than the realistic, the director must beware of undermining the power of the play, which lies in its factual authority, its evocation of a concrete historicity. This seems to me just what Hochhuth has inadvertently done in the one suggestion he makes for the *The Deputy*'s staging. Listing the characters, Hochhuth has made certain groupings of the shorter roles; all the roles in a single grouping are to be played by the same actor. Thus, the same actor is to play both Pius XII and

Baron Rutta of the Reich's Armament Cartel. Another grouping allows a Father in the Papal Legation, an SS sergeant, and a Jewish Kapo all to be played by a single actor. "For recent history," Hochhuth explains, "has taught us that in the age of universal military conscription it is not necessarily to anyone's credit or blame, or even a question of character, which uniform one wears or whether one stands on the side of the victims or the executioners." I can't believe that Hochhuth really subscribes to this facile, fashionable view of the interchangeability of persons and roles (his whole play precisely contradicts this view) and I should resent seeing it embodied in the staging as Hochhuth suggests. The same objection would not apply, however, to the superficially similar theatrical idea devised by Peter Brook for his production of the play in Paris: that the actors all wear identical blue cotton suits, over which, when identification is needed, are slipped the cardinal's scarlet coat, the priest's soutane, the Nazi officer's swastika armband, and so on.

That Hochhuth's play has been the occasion of riots in Berlin, Paris, London, almost everywhere it has been performed, because it depicts (not just reports) the late Pius XII refusing to use the influence of the Catholic Church and oppose, either openly or through private diplomatic channels, the Nazi policy toward the Jews, is irrefutable indication of the valuable site which The Deputy occupies—between art and life. (In Rome, the play was closed by the police on the day it was to open.)

There is good reason to believe that protests by the Church might have saved many lives. Within Germany, when the Catholic hierarchy strongly opposed Hitler's euthanasia program for elderly and incurably ill Aryans—the trial run for the Final Solution of the Jewish Problem—it was stopped. And the precedent of political neutrality cannot be allowed to stand as the Vatican's excuse, since the Vatican had made forceful pronouncements on such matters of international politics as the Russian invasion of Finland. Most damaging to the case of those who regard the play as a calumny on Pius XII are extant documents which indicate that the Pope, like many conservative European rulers of the time, did approve of Hitler's war against Russia and for that reason hesitated to oppose the German government actively. For the scene that depicts this fact, Hochhuth's play has been slandered by many Catholics as an anti-Catholic tract. But either what Hochhuth reports is true or it is not. And, assuming that Hochhuth has his facts (and his notion of Christian courage) right, a good Catholic is no more bound to defend all the actions of Pius XII than he is to admire the libertine Popes of the Renaissance. Dante, whom no one would accuse of being anti-Catholic, consigned Celestine V to hell. Why may not a modern Christian—Hochhuth is a Lutheran—hold up as a standard to the then incumbent Deputy or Vicar of Christ the behavior of the Berlin provost, Bernard Lichtenberg (who publicly prayed for the Jews from his pulpit and volunteered to accompany the Jews to Dachau), or the Franciscan monk, Father Maximilian Kolbe (who died hideously in Auschwitz)?

In any case, the attack on the Pope is scarcely the only subject of *The Deputy*. The Pope appears in only one scene of the play. The action centers on the two heroes—the Jesuit priest Riccardo Fontana (mainly based on Provost Lichtenberg, with something of Father Kolbe) and the remarkable Kurt Gerstein, who joined the SS in order to gather facts to lay before the Papal Nuncio in Berlin. Hochhuth has not placed Gerstein and Fontana (Lichtenberg) in any "grouping," to be played along with other roles by the same actor. There is nothing interchangeable about these men. Thus, the main point that *The Deputy* makes is not a recriminatory one. It is not only an attack on the hierarchy of the German Catholic Church and on the Pope and his advisors, but a statement that genuine honor and decency—though these may entail martyrdom— are possible, and mandatory for a Christian. Precisely because there were Germans who did choose, Hochhuth is saying, we have a right to accuse the others who refused to choose, to speak out, of an unforgivable cowardice.

[1964]

The death
of tragedy

MODERN discussions of the
possibility of tragedy are not exercises in literary analysis; they are
exercises in cultural diagnostics, more or less disguised. The subject
of literature has pre-empted much of the energy that formerly went
into philosophy, until that subject was purged by the empiricists
and logicians. The modern dilemmas of feeling, action, and belief
are argued out on the field of literary masterpieces. Art is seen as a
mirror of human capacities in a given historical period, as the pre-
eminent form by which a culture defines itself, names itself, dram-
atizes itself. In particular, questions about the death of literary
forms—is the long narrative poem still possible, or is it dead? the
novel? verse drama? tragedy?—are of the greatest moment. The
burial of a literary form is a moral act, a high achievement of the
modern morality of honesty. For, as an act of self-definition, it is
also a self-entombment.

Such burials are customarily accompanied by all the displays of mourning; for we mourn ourselves, when we name the lost potential of sensibility and attitude which the defunct form incarnated. In his *Birth of Tragedy*, which is really about the death of tragedy, Nietzsche blamed the radically new prestige of knowledge and conscious intelligence—which arose in ancient Greece with the figure of Socrates—for the waning of instinct and of the sense of reality which made tragedy impossible. All subsequent discussions of the topic have been similarly elegiac, or at least defensive: either mourning the death of tragedy, or hopefully trying to make "modern" tragedy out of the naturalistic-sentimental theater of Ibsen and Chekhov, of O'Neill, Miller, and Williams. It is one of the singular merits of Lionel Abel's book* that the customary accent of lament is missing. Nobody writes tragedies any more? Very well. Abel invites his readers to leave the funeral parlor and come to a party, a party celebrating the dramatic form which is ours, has been ours in fact for three hundred years: the metaplay.

Indeed there is hardly reason to mourn, since the corpse was only a distant relative. Tragedy, says Abel, is not and never has been the characteristic form of Western theater; most Western dramatists, bent on writing tragedy, have been unable to do so. Why? In a word: self-consciousness. First, the self-consciousness of the dramatist himself, and then that of his protagonists. "The Western playwright is unable to believe in the reality of a character who is lacking in self-consciousness. Lack of self-consciousness is as characteristic of Antigone, Oedipus, and Orestes, as self-consciousness is characteristic of Hamlet, that towering figure of Western metatheatre." Thus, it is the metaplay—plots that depict the self-dramatization of conscious characters, a theater whose leading metaphors state that life is a dream and the world a stage—which has occupied the dramatic imagination of the West to the same degree that the Greek dramatic imagination was occupied with tragedy. Two important historical observations follow from this thesis. One is that tragedy is simply much rarer than has been supposed—the Greek plays, one play of Shakespeare (*Macbeth*),

* *Metatheatre: A New View of Dramatic Form*, by Lionel Abel. New York, Hill & Wang.

and a few plays of Racine. Tragedy is not the characteristic form of
the Elizabethan or Spanish theater. Most Elizabethan serious
drama consists of failed tragedies (*Lear, Doctor Faustus*) or successful metaplays (*Hamlet, The Tempest*). The other point relates
to contemporary drama. In Abel's account, Shakespeare and
Calderón are the two great sources of a tradition which is gloriously
revived in the "modern" theater of Shaw, Pirandello, Beckett, Ionesco, Genet, and Brecht.

As a piece of cultural diagnostics, Abel's book is in the grand
continental tradition of meditation on the tribulations of subjectivity and self-consciousness, inaugurated by the romantic poets and
Hegel and continued by Nietzsche, Spengler, the early Lukács, and
Sartre. Their problems, their terminology loom behind Abel's spare,
untechnical essays. Where the Europeans are heavy, he travels
light, without footnotes; where they write tomes, he has written a
set of blunt essays; and where they are gloomy, he is crisply san-
guine. In short, Abel has expounded a continental argument in the
American manner: he has written the first American-style existentialist tract. His argument is clean-cut, pugnacious, prone to slogans, oversimplified—and, in the main, absolutely right. His book
does not plumb the windy depths (but they are depths) of Lucien
Goldmann's great work on Pascal, Racine, and the idea of tragedy,
Le Dieu Caché, which I would guess Abel has learned from. But its
virtues, not the least of which are directness and brevity, are formidable. To an English-speaking audience unfamiliar with the writing of Lukács, Goldmann, Brecht, Duerrenmatt, *et al.*, the very
problems that Abel raises should come as a revelation. Abel's book
is far more stimulating than George Steiner's *Death of Tragedy* and
Martin Esslin's *The Theater of the Absurd*. Indeed, no recent English or American writer on the theater has done anything as interesting or sophisticated.

As I have suggested, the diagnosis presupposed in *Metatheatre*—
that modern man lives with an increasing burden of subjectivity, at
the expense of his sense of the reality of the world—is not new.
Nor do works for the theater constitute the main texts which dis-
close this attitude and its correlative idea, reason as self-manipulation and role-playing. The two greatest documents of this attitude

are Montaigne's *Essays* and Machiavelli's *The Prince*—both manuals of strategy which assume a gulf between the "public self" (the role) and the "private self" (the true self). The value of Abel's book lies in the forthright application of this diagnosis to the drama. He is quite right, for example, in arguing that most of the plays of Shakespeare which their author, and everyone else since, have called tragedies are not, strictly speaking, tragedies at all. In fact, Abel could have gone even further. Not only are most of the putative tragedies really "metaplays"; so are most of the histories and comedies. The principal plays of Shakespeare are plays about self-consciousness, about characters not *acting* so much as *dramatizing themselves* in roles. Prince Hal is the man of perfected self-consciousness and self-control, triumphing over the man of rash, unself-conscious integrity, Hotspur, and over the sentimental, cowardly, self-conscious man of pleasure, Falstaff. Achilles and Oedipus do not see themselves as, but are, hero and king. But Hamlet and Henry V see themselves as acting parts—the part of the avenger, the part of the heroic and confident king leading his troops to battle. Shakespeare's fondness for the play-within-a-play and for putting his characters into disguise for long stretches of the story clearly partakes of the style of metatheater. From Prospero to the Police Chief in Genet's *The Balcony*, the personages of metatheater are characters in search of an action.

I have said that Abel's main thesis is right. But it is also, with respect to three issues, mistaken or incomplete.

First, his thesis would be more complete, and I think somewhat altered, if Abel had considered what comedy is. Without wanting to suggest that comedy and tragedy divide the dramatic universe between them, I would argue that they are best defined in relation to each other. The omission of comedy is particularly striking when one recalls that counterfeit, deceit, role-playing, manipulation, self-dramatization—basic elements of what Abel calls metatheater—are staples of comedy since Aristophanes. Comic plots are stories either of conscious self-manipulation and role-playing (*Lysistrata, The Golden Ass, Tartuffe*) or else of improbably unself-conscious—underconscious, one might say—characters (*Candide,* Buster Keaton,

Gulliver, Don Quixote) playing strange roles which they assent to with a cheerful dumbness that secures their invulnerability. It might well be argued that the form which Abel calls the metaplay, particularly in its modern versions, represents a fusion of the posthumous spirit of tragedy with the most ancient principles of comedy. Some modern metaplays, such as Ionesco's, are obviously comedies. It is hard, too, to deny that Beckett is writing, in *Waiting for Godot, Krapp's Last Tape*, and *Happy Days*, a kind of *comédie noire*.

Second, Abel considerably oversimplifies, and I think indeed misrepresents, the vision of the world which is necessary for the writing of tragedies. He says: "One cannot create tragedy without accepting some implacable values as true. Now the Western imagination has, on the whole, been liberal and skeptical; it has tended to regard *all* implacable values as false." This statement seems to me wrong and, where it is not wrong, superficial. (Abel is here perhaps too much under the influence of Hegel's analysis of tragedy, and that of Hegel's popularizers.) What are the implacable values of Homer? Honor, status, personal courage—the values of an aristocratic military class? But this is not what the *Iliad* is about. It would be more correct to say, as Simone Weil does, that the *Iliad* —as pure an example of the tragic vision as one can find—is about the emptiness and arbitrariness of the world, the ultimate meaninglessness of all moral values, and the terrifying rule of death and inhuman force. If the fate of Oedipus was represented and experienced as tragic, it is not because he, or his audience, believed in "implacable values," but precisely because a crisis had overtaken those values. It is not the implacability of "values" which is demonstrated by tragedy, but the implacability of the world. The story of Oedipus is tragic insofar as it exhibits the brute opaqueness of the world, the collision of subjective intention with objective fate. After all, in the deepest sense, Oedipus is innocent; he is wronged by the gods, as he himself says in *Oedipus at Colonus*. Tragedy is a vision of nihilism, a heroic or ennobling vision of nihilism.

It is also untrue that Western culture has been on the whole liberal and skeptical. Post-Christian Western culture, yes. Montaigne, Machiavelli, the Enlightenment, the psychiatric culture of personal autonomy and health of the 20th century, yes. But what of the dominant religious traditions of Western culture? Were Paul, Augustine, Dante, Pascal, and Kierkegaard liberal skeptics? Hardly. Therefore one must ask, why was there no Christian tragedy?—a question Abel does not raise in his book, though Christian tragedy would seem to be inevitable if one stops at the assertion that belief in implacable values is the necessary ingredient for making tragedies.

As everyone knows, there was no Christian tragedy, strictly speaking, because the content of Christian values—for it is a question of what values, however implacably held; not any will do—is inimical to the pessimistic vision of tragedy. Hence, Dante's theological poem is a "comedy," as is Milton's. That is, as Christians, Dante and Milton make sense out of the world. In the world envisaged by Judaism and Christianity, there are no free-standing arbitrary events. All events are part of the plan of a just, good, providential deity; every crucifixion must be topped by a resurrection. Every disaster or calamity must be seen either as leading to a greater good or else as just and adequate punishment fully merited by the sufferer. This moral adequacy of the world asserted by Christianity is precisely what tragedy denies. Tragedy says there are disasters which are not fully merited, that there is ultimate injustice in the world. So one might say that the final optimism of the prevailing religious traditions of the West, their will to see meaning in the world, prevented a rebirth of tragedy under Christian auspices—as, in Nietzsche's argument, reason, the fundamentally optimistic spirit of Socrates, killed tragedy in ancient Greece. The liberal, skeptical era of metatheater only inherits this will to make sense from Judaism and Christianity. Despite the exhaustion of religious sentiments, the will to make sense and find meaning prevails, although contracted to the idea of an action as the projection of one's idea of oneself.

The third caveat I would make is to Abel's treatment of the modern metaplays, those plays which have all too often been thrown together under the patronizing label "theater of the absurd." Abel is right to point out that these plays are, formally, in an old tradition. Yet the considerations of form which Abel addresses in his essays must not obscure differences in range and tone, which he slights. Shakespeare and Calderón construct metatheatrical *jeux d'esprit* in the bosom of a world rich in established feelings and a sense of openness. The metatheater of Genet and Beckett reflects the feelings of an era whose greatest artistic pleasure is self-laceration, an era suffocated by the sense of eternal return, an era which experiences innovation as an act of terror. That life is a dream, all the metaplays presuppose. But there are restful dreams, troubled dreams, and nightmares. The modern dream—which the modern metaplays project—is a nightmare, a nightmare of repetition, stalled action, exhausted feeling. There are discontinuities between the modern nightmare and the Renaissance dream which Abel (like, more recently, Jan Kott) neglects, at the price of misreading the texts.

For Brecht, particularly, whom Abel includes among the modern metadramatists, the category is misleading. At times Abel seems to use "naturalistic play" rather than "tragedy" as a foil for metatheater. Brecht's plays are anti-naturalistic, didactic. But unless Abel is willing to call *The Play of Daniel* a metaplay—because it has on-stage musicians, and a narrator who explains everything to the audience, and invites them to see the play as a play, a performance—I cannot see that Brecht fits very well into the category. And much of Abel's discussion of Brecht is unhappily disfigured by callow Cold War platitudes. Abel argues that Brecht's plays must be metaplays because to write tragedies one must believe that "individuals are real" and one must "believe in the importance of moral suffering." (Does Abel mean the moral importance of suffering?) Since Brecht was a Communist, and since Communists do "not believe in the individual or in moral experience" (what does it mean, to "believe" in moral experience? does Abel mean moral principles?), Brecht lacked the essential equipment to write tragedies; therefore, dogmatic as he was, Brecht could only write metatheater—that is, make "all human actions, reactions, and expressions of feeling theatrical." This is nonsense. There is no more moralizing doctrine abroad today than Communism, no more sturdy exponent of "implacable values." What else is meant when Western liberals vulgarly call Communism a "secular religion"? And as for the familiar accusation that Communism does not believe in the individual, this is equally nonsense. It is not so much

Marxist theory as the sensibility and historic traditions of the countries in which Communism has taken power that do not and never have held the so-called Western idea of the individual, which separates off the "private" from the "public" self, seeing the private self as the true self which only lends itself grudgingly to the activities of public life. Neither did the Greeks, the creators of tragedy, possess a notion of the individual in the modern Western sense. There is a deep confusion in Abel's argument—his historical generalizations are mostly superficial—when he tries to make the absence of the individual the criterion of metatheater.

Admittedly Brecht was a sly, ambivalent guardian of Communist "morality." But the secret of his plays is to be sought in his idea of the theater as a moralizing instrument. Hence his use of stage techniques borrowed from the non-naturalistic theater of China and Japan, and his famous theory of stage production and acting—the Alienation Effect—which aims to enforce a detached, intellectual attitude upon the audience. (The Alienation Effect seems to be mainly a method of writing plays and of staging them, nonnaturalistically; its effect as a method of acting, from what I have seen of the Berliner Ensemble, is mainly to moderate, to tone down, the naturalistic style of acting—not fundamentally to contradict it.) By assimilating Brecht to the metadramatists, with whom he surely shares something, Abel obscures the difference between Brecht's didacticism and the studied neutrality—the mutual cancellation of all values—which is represented by the true metadramatists. It is something like the difference between Augustine and Montaigne. Both the Confessions and the Essays are didactic autobiographies; but while the author of the Confessions sees his life as a drama illustrating the linear movement of consciousness from egocentricity to theocentricity, the author of the Essays sees his life as a dispassionate, varied exploration of the innumerable styles of being a self. Brecht has as little in common with Beckett, Genet, and Pirandello as Augustine's exercise in self-analysis has with Montaigne's.

[1963]

Going to
theater, etc.

THE theater has a long history as a public art. But, outside the provinces of socialist realism, there are few plays today dealing with social-and-topical problems. The best modern plays are those devoted to raking up private, rather than public, hells. The public voice in the theater today is crude and raucous, and, all too often, weak-minded.

The most notable example of weak-mindedness around at the moment is Arthur Miller's new play, *After the Fall*, which opened the first season of the Lincoln Center Repertory Theater. Miller's play stands or falls on the authenticity of its moral seriousness, and on its being about "big" issues. But, unfortunately, Miller chose as the method of his play the garrulous monologue of the psychoanalytic confessional, and falteringly designated the audience as the Great Listener. "The action of the play takes place in the mind and memory of Quentin, a contemporary man." The

Everymanish hero (remember Willy Loman) and the timeless, placeless interior setting give the show away: whatever stirring public issues *After the Fall* may confront, they are treated as the furniture of a mind. That places an awful burden on Miller's "Quentin, a contemporary man," who must literally hold the world in his head. To pull that one off, it has to be a very good head, a very interesting and intelligent one. And the head of Miller's hero isn't any of these things. Contemporary man (as Miller represents him) seems stuck in an ungainly project of self-exoneration. Self-exoneration, of course, implies self-exposure; and there is a lot of that in *After the Fall*. Many people are willing to give Miller a good deal of credit for the daring of his self-exposure—as husband, lover, political man, and artist. But self-exposure is commendable in art only when it is of a quality and complexity that allows other people to learn about themselves from it. In this play, Miller's self-exposure is mere self-indulgence.

After the Fall does not present an action, but ideas about action. Its psychological ideas owe more to Franzblau than to Freud. (Quentin's mother wanted him to have beautiful penmanship, to take revenge through her son upon her successful but virtually illiterate businessman husband.) As for its political ideas, where politics has not yet been softened up by psychiatric charity, Miller still writes on the level of a left-wing newspaper cartoon. To pass muster at all, Quentin's young German girl friend—this in the mid-1950s—has to turn out to have been a courier for the 20th of July officers' plot; "they were all hanged." Quentin's political bravery is demonstrated by his triumphantly interrupting the harangue of the chairman of the House Committee on Un-American Activities to ask, "How many Negroes do you allow to vote in your patriotic district?" This intellectual weak-mindedness of *After the Fall* leads, as it always does, to moral dishonesty. *After the Fall* claims to be nothing less than modern man taking inventory of his humanity—asking where he is guilty, where innocent, where responsible. What I find objectionable is not the peculiar conjunction of issues, apparently the exemplary issues of the mid-20th century (Communism, Marilyn Monroe, the Nazi extermination camps), which Quentin, this writer *manqué* pretending throughout the play to be a lawyer, has recapitulated in his own person. I object to the fact that in *After the Fall* all these issues are on the same level—not unexpectedly, since they are all in the mind of Quentin. The shapely corpse of Maggie-Marilyn Monroe sprawls on the stage throughout long stretches of the play in which she has no part. In the same spirit a raggedy oblong made of plaster and barbed wire—it represents the concentration camps, I hasten to explain—remains suspended high at the back of the stage, occasionally lit by a spot when Quentin's monologue swings back to Nazis, etc. *After the Fall's* quasi-psychiatric approach to guilt and responsibility elevates personal tragedies, and demeans public ones —to the same dead level. Somehow—staggering impertinence!—it all seems pretty much the same: whether Quentin is responsible for the deterioration and suicide of Maggie, and whether he (modern man) is responsible for the unimaginable atrocities of the concentration camps.

Putting the story inside Quentin's head has, in effect, allowed Miller to short-circuit any serious exploration of his material, though he obviously thought this device would "deepen" his story. Real events become the ornaments and intermittent fevers of consciousness. The play is peculiarly loose-jointed, repetitive, indirect. The "scenes" go on and off—jumping back and forth, to and from Quentin's first marriage, his second marriage (to Maggie), his indecisive courtship of his German wife-to-be, his childhood, the quarrels of his hysterical, oppressive parents, his agonizing decision to defend an ex-Communist law-school teacher and friend against a friend who has "named names." All "scenes" are fragments, pushed out of Quentin's mind when they become too painful. Only deaths, inevitably offstage, seem to move Quentin's life along: the Jews (the word "Jews" is never mentioned) died long ago; his mother dies; Maggie kills herself with an overdose of barbiturates; the law professor throws himself under a subway train. Throughout the play, Quentin seems much more a sufferer than an active agent in his own life—yet this is precisely what Miller never acknowledges, never lets Quentin see as his problem. Instead, he continually exonerates Quentin (and, by implication, the audience) in the most conventional way. For all troubling decisions, and all excruciating memories, Miller issues Quentin the same moral solvent, the same consolation. I (we) am (are) *both* guilty and innocent, both responsible and not responsible. Maggie was right when she denounced Quentin as cold and unforgiving; but Quentin was justified in giving up on the insatiable, deranged, self-destructive Maggie. The professor who refused to "name names" before the House Un-American Activities Committee was right; but the colleague who did testify cooperatively had a certain nobility, too. And (choicest of all), as Quentin realizes while touring Dachau with his Good German girl friend, any one of us could have been a victim there; but we could as well have been one of the murderers, too.

The circumstances and production of the play are marked by certain perverse strokes of realism that underscore the bad faith, the have-it-both-ways temper of the play. That vast sloping stage painted slate gray and empty of props, the mind of contemporary man, is so pointedly bare that one can't help jumping when Quentin, sitting much of the time stage-front on a box-like form and chain smoking, suddenly deposits the ashes in some mysterious pocket ashtray in the abutment. One is jarred again at the sight of Barbara Loden made up like Marilyn Monroe, displaying the mannerisms of Monroe and bearing a certain physical resemblance to Monroe (though lacking the fullness of figure needed to complete the illusion). But perhaps the most appalling combination of reality and play lies in the fact that *After the Fall* is directed by Elia Kazan, well known to be the model for the colleague who named names before the Committee. As I recalled the story of the turbulent relations between Miller and Kazan, I felt the same queasiness as when I first saw *Sunset Boulevard*, with its dizzying parody of and daring references to the real career and former relationships of Gloria Swanson, the old movie queen making a comeback, and Erich Von Stroheim, the forgotten great director. Whatever bravery *After the Fall* possesses is neither intellectual nor moral; it is the bravery of a species of personal perversity. But it is far inferior to *Sunset Boulevard*: it does not acknowledge its morbidity, its qualities of personal exorcism. *After the Fall* insists, as it were, to the bitter end, on being serious, on dealing with big social and moral themes; and as such, it must be judged sadly wanting, in both intelligence and moral honesty.

Since it insists on being serious, I suspect that After the Fall will seem just as belabored, trite, and dated in a few years as O'Neill's Marco Millions, the second play in the Lincoln Center Repertory, does now. Both plays are disfigured by a distressing (though, one imagines, unconscious) complicity with what they profess to attack. The attack which Marco Millions launched upon the philistine values of American business civilization itself reeks of philistinism; After the Fall is a long sermon in favor of being tough with oneself, but the argument is soft as mush. It is indeed difficult to choose between the two plays, or their productions. I don't know which is more heavy-handed: Marco Polo's Babbittish exuberance over the wonders of Cathay ("Sure is a nice little palace you got here, Khan"—Americans are crude and materialistic, see?) or the weird declamations, at times archly poetic and stilted, at times WEVD soap opera, of Miller's hero Quentin (Americans are tormented and complex, see?). I don't know which I found more monotonous, less ingratiating as an acting performance—Jason Robard Jr.'s depleted, gauche Quentin or Hal Holbrook's hysterically boyish Marco Polo. I could hardly tell Zohra Lampert when she was the Bronxy chick who keeps running into Quentin's head to slobber all over him for giving her the courage to have a nose job from Zohra Lampert when she was supposed to be that elegant lovelorn flower of the Orient, Princess Kukachin, in Marco Millions. True, Elia Kazan's staging of After the Fall was stark and moderne and repetitive, while José Quintero's staging of Marco Millions was tricky and pretty and had the advantage of Beni Montresor's lovely costumes, though the stage was so badly lit you couldn't be sure of what you saw. But the differences in the productions seemed trivial, when you consider that Kazan had toiled over a bad play, and Quintero over a play so juvenile that no production, however good, could redeem it. The Lincoln Center Repertory group (our National Theater?) is a stunning disappointment. It's hard to believe that all its vaunted freedom from Broadway commercialism has begotten are passably acted productions of this wretched play by Miller, a play by

O'Neill so bad it isn't even of historical interest, and a fatuous comedy by S. N. Behrman that makes *After the Fall* and *Marco Millions* look like works of genius.

If *After the Fall* fails as a serious play because of its intellectual softness, Rolf Hochhuth's *The Deputy* fails because of its intellectual simplicity and artistic naïveté. But this is failure of another order. *The Deputy* has been put into awkward English and, clearly, Hochhuth couldn't care less about the truth of Aristotle's observation that poetry is more philosophical than historical; Hochhuth's characters are little more than mouthpieces for the exposition of historical facts, exhibits of the collision of moral principles. But after the way in which Miller turns all events into their subjective reverberations, the artistic weakness of *The Deputy* seems almost condonable. *The Deputy* has all the directness toward its subject that Arthur Miller's play lacks. Its virtue is precisely that it refuses to be subtle about the murder of the six million Jews.

But the production by Herman Shumlin is as far from Hochhuth's play (as written) as that play (as written) is from being a great play. Hochhuth's crude but powerful six to eight hour documentary in play form has been put through Shumlin's Broadway Blendor and emerges as a two hour and fifteen minute comic strip, and a dull one to boot—the story of a handsome, well-born hero, a couple of villains, and a few fence-sitters, titled The Story of Father Fontana, or Will the Pope Speak?

I'm not of course insisting that the whole six to eight hours must be played. The play as written is repetitive. But a theater public that is willing to sit through four or five hours of O'Neill could surely be persuaded to sit through—say—four hours of Hochhuth's play. And it is not hard to imagine a four-hour version that would do justice to the narrative. From the present Broadway version, one would never guess that the noble SS Lieutenant Kurt Gerstein (a true person) is as important a character and as much the hero of *The Deputy* as the Jesuit Father Fontana (a composite figure based on two heroic priests of the period). Neither Eichmann, nor the notorious Professor Hirt, nor the Krupp industrialist—all important characters in Hochhuth's play as he wrote it—

appears at all in the Broadway version. (Among the dropped scenes, one particularly misses Act I, Scene 2, the party given by Eichmann.) By concentrating exclusively on the story of Fontana's vain appeals to the Pope, Shumlin has gone far toward burying the historical memories which Hochhuth's play aims to keep alive. But this drastic simplification of Hochhuth's historical argument is not even the worst offense of Shumlin's version. The worst offense is the refusal to dramatize anything really painful to watch. Certain scenes in The Deputy are excruciating to read. None of this—the terror and torture, the gruesome boasts and banter, even the recitals of unimaginable statistics—has been retained. The entire horror of the murder of the six million has been reduced to one scene of police interrogation of some Jewish converts to Catholicism, plus a single image repeated three times in the course of the play: a line of bent, ragged figures shuffles across the dark rear of the stage; midstage stands an SS man, his back to the audience, yelling something that sounds like "Move along now!" A conventional image; an entirely palatable image; an image which neither stirs, nor disgusts, nor terrifies. Even Fontana's long monologue, the speechifying scene on the freightcar headed for Auschwitz— the seventh of the eight scenes in Shumlin's emasculated version —was cut just before opening night. Now the play moves directly from the confrontation between the Pope and Father Fontana at the Vatican to the final scene in Auschwitz, of which all that's left is the amateurish philosophical debate between the demonic SS doctor and Fontana, who has donned the yellow star and elected martyrdom in the gas chambers. The reunion of Gerstein and Fontana, their appalling discovery that Jacobson has been captured, the torture of Carlotta, the death of Fontana—all are omitted.

Although the decisive damage is already done by the version which Shumlin has carved from the play, it should be noted that the production is in most ways inadequate as well. Rouben Ter-Arutunian's slim allusive sets belong to another director; they are lost on a production utterly lacking in the slightest subtlety or stylization. The actors are no more but no less inept and unskillful than the average Broadway cast. As usual, there is the same overstatement of emotions, the same monotony of movement, the same mélange of accents, the same flatness of style that makes for the low level of American acting. The leads, who are English, seem more gifted—though their performances are thin. Emlyn Williams plays Pope Pius XII with a hesitant stiffness of movement and speech, presumably designed to indicate Papal solemnity, which aroused my suspicion that he was indeed the late Pope, exhumed for the occasion, and in an understandably fragile condition. At the least, he looked suspiciously like the life-size statue of Pius XII behind glass near the entrance of Saint Patrick's Cathedral. Jeremy Brett, who plays Father Fontana, has an agreeable presence and lovely diction, though he floundered badly when he had to convey real despair or terror.

These recent plays—and some others, like *Dylan*, which it would be a mercy to pass over in silence—illustrate once again that the American theater is ruled by an extraordinary, irrepressible zest for intellectual simplification. Every idea is reducible to a cliché, and the function of a cliché is to castrate an idea. Now, intellectual simplification has its uses, its value. It is, for example, absolutely indispensable to comedy. But it is inimical to the serious. At present, the seriousness of the American theater is worse than frivolity.

The hope for intelligence in the theater is not through conventional "seriousness," whether in the form of analysis (bad example: *After the Fall*), or the documentary (weak example: *The Deputy*). It is rather, I think, through comedy. The figure in the modern theater who best understood this was Brecht. But comedy, too, has its enormous perils. The danger here is not so much intellectual simplification as failure of tone and taste. It may be that not all subjects can be given a comic treatment.

This question of the adequacy of tone and taste to serious subject-matter is, of course, not confined to the theater alone. There is an excellent illustration of the advantages of comedy, and of its peculiar dilemmas—if I may pass to the movies for a moment—in two films recently showing in New York, Charlie Chaplin's *The Great Dictator* and Stanley Kubrick's *Doctor Strangelove: Or How I Learned to Stop Worrying and Love The Bomb*. The virtues and failures of both films seem to me oddly comparable, and instructive.

In the case of *The Great Dictator*, the problem is easily discernible. The entire conception of the comedy is totally, painfully, insultingly inadequate to the reality it purports to represent. The Jews are Jews, and they live in what Chaplin calls the Ghetto. But their oppressors don't display the swastika but the emblem of the double cross; and the dictator is not Adolf Hitler but a balletic buffoon with a mustache named Adenoid Hynkel. Oppression in *The Great Dictator* is uniformed bullies throwing so many tomatoes at Paulette Goddard that she has to wash her laundry all over again. It is impossible to see *The Great Dictator* in 1964 without thinking of the hideous reality behind the movie, and one is depressed by the shallowness of Chaplin's political vision. One cringes at that embarrassing final speech, when the Little Jewish Barber steps up to the podium in place of Der Phooey to call for "progress," "liberty," "brotherhood," "one world," even "science." And to watch Paulette Goddard looking up at the dawn and smiling through her tears—in 1940!

The problem of *Doctor Strangelove* is more complex, though it may well be that in twenty years it will seem as simple as *The Great Dictator*. If the positive assertions at the close of *The Great Dictator* seem facile and insulting to its subject, so may the display of negative thinking of *Doctor Strangelove* soon (if it does not already) seem equally facile. But this does not explain its appeal now. Liberal intellectuals who saw *Doctor Strangelove* during its many preview showings last October and November marvelled at its political daring, and feared that the film would run into terrible difficulties (mobs of American Legion types storming the theaters, etc.). As it turned out, everybody, from *The New Yorker* to the *Daily News*, has had kind words for *Doctor Strangelove*; there are no pickets; and the film is breaking records at the box-office. Intellectuals and adolescents both love it. But the sixteen-year-olds who are lining up to see it understand the film, and its real virtues, better than the intellectuals, who vastly overpraise it. For *Doctor Strangelove* is not, in fact, a political film at all. It uses the OK targets of left-liberals (the defense establishment, Texas, chewing gum, mechanization, American vulgarity) and treats them from an entirely post-political, *Mad Magazine* point of view. *Doctor Strangelove* is really a very cheerful film. Certainly, its fullbloodedness contrasts favorably with what is (in retrospect) the effeteness of Chaplin's film. The end of *Doctor Strangelove*, with its matter-of-fact image of apocalypse and flip soundtrack ("We'll Meet Again"), reassures in a curious way, for nihilism is our contemporary form of moral uplift. As *The Great Dictator* was Popular Front optimism for the masses, so *Doctor Strangelove* is nihilism for the masses, a philistine nihilism.

What is good in *The Great Dictator* are the solitary autistic acts of grace, like Hynkel playing with the balloon-globe; and the "little man" humor, as in the sequence where the Jews draw lots for a suicidal mission out of slices of a pie, and Chaplin ends up with all the tokens in his slice. These are the perennial elements of comedy, as developed by Chaplin, over which has been pasted this unsatisfactory political cartoon. Similarly, what is good in *Doctor Strangelove* has to do with another perennial source of comedy, mental aberration. The best things in the film are the fantasies of contamination expounded by the psychotic Gen. Jack D. Ripper (played with excruciating brilliance by Sterling Hayden), the super-American clichés and body movements of Gen. Buck Turgidson, a Ring Lardneresque businessman-military type (put together by George C. Scott), and the euphoric satanism of Doctor Strangelove himself, the Nazi scientist with the right arm that hates him (Peter Sellers). The specialty of silent-film comedy (and *The Great Dictator* is still, essentially, a silent film) is the purely visual crossing of grace, folly, and pathos. *Doctor Strangelove* works another classic vein of comedy, as much verbal as visual—the idea of humors. (Hence the joke names of characters in *Doctor Strangelove*, exactly as in Ben Jonson.) But notice that both films rely on the same device for distancing the audience's feelings: employing the same actor to play several key roles. Chaplin plays both the Little Jewish Barber and the dictator Hynkel. Sellers plays the relatively sane British officer, the weak American president, and the Nazi scientist; he was originally supposed to take a fourth role as well—that of the Texan, played in the film by Slim Pickens, who commands the plane which drops the H-Bomb that sets off the Russian Doomsday Machine. Without this device of the same actor playing morally opposed roles, and so subliminally undermining the reality of the entire plot, the precarious ascendancy of comic detachment over the morally ugly or the terrifying in both films would be lost.

Doctor Strangelove fails most obviously in scale. Much (though not all) of its comedy seems to me repetitive, juvenile, hamhanded. And when comedy fails, seriousness begins to leak back in. One begins to ask serious questions about the misanthropy which is the only perspective from which the topic of mass annihilation is comic. . . . For me, the only successful spectacle shown this winter dealing with public issues was a work which was both a pure documentary *and* a comedy—Daniel Talbot and Emile de Antonio's editing into a ninety-minute film of the TV kinescopes of the 1954 Army-McCarthy hearings. Viewed in 1964, the hearings make a quite different impression. All the good guys come off badly—Army Secretary Stevens, Senator Symington, lawyer Welch, and the rest, looked like dopes, stuffed shirts, ninnies, prigs, or opportunists—while the film irresistibly encourages us to relish the villains aesthetically. Roy Cohen, with his swarthy face, slickeddown hair, and double-breasted, pin-stripe suit, looked like a period punk from a Warner Brothers' crime movie of the early thirties; McCarthy, ushaven, fidgety, giggling, looked and acted like W. C. Fields in his most alcoholic, vicious, and inaudible roles. In that it aestheticized a weighty public event, *Point of Order* was the real *comédie noire* of the season, as well as the best political drama.

[Spring 1964]

2

The currency of exchange for most social and moral attitudes is that ancient device of the drama: personifications, masks. Both for play and for edification, the mind sets up these figures, simple and definite, whose identity is easily stated, who arouse quick loves and hates. Masks are a peculiarly effective, shorthand way of defining virtue and vice.

Once a grotesque, a figure of folly—childlike, lawless, lascivious

—"the Negro" is fast becoming the American theater's leading mask of virtue. For definiteness of outline, being black, he even surpasses "the Jew," who has an ambiguous physical identity. (It was part of the lore of the advanced position on Jewishness that Jews didn't have to look like "Jews." But Negroes always look like "Negroes," unless, of course, they are unauthentic.) And for sheer pain and victimage, the Negro is far ahead of any other contender in America. In just a few short years, the old liberalism, whose archetypal figure was the Jew, has been challenged by the new militancy, whose hero is the Negro. But while the temper which gives rise to the new militancy—and to "the Negro" as hero—may indeed scorn the ideas of liberalism, one feature of the liberal sensibility hangs on. We still tend to choose our images of virtue from among our victims.

In the theater, as among educated Americans generally, liberalism has suffered an ambiguous rout. That large streak of moralism, of preachiness in such plays as *Waiting for Lefty, Watch on the Rhine, Tomorrow the World, Deep Are the Roots, The Crucible* —the classics of Broadway liberalism—would be unacceptable now. But what was wrong with these plays, from the most contemporary point of view, is not that they aimed to convert their audiences, rather than simply entertaining them. It was, rather, that they were too optimistic. They thought problems could be solved. James Baldwin's *Blues for Mister Charlie* is a sermon, too. To make it official, Baldwin has said that the play is loosely inspired by the Emmett Till case, and one may read, on the theater program under the director's name, that the play is "dedicated to the memory of Medgar Evers, and his widow and his children, and to the memory of the dead children of Birmingham." But it is a sermon of a new type. In *Blues for Mister Charlie*, Broadway liberalism has been vanquished by Broadway racism. Liberalism preached politics, that is, solutions. Racism regards politics as superficial (and seeks some deeper level); it emphasizes what is unalterable. Across a virtually impassable gulf, the new mask of "the Negro," manly, toughened, but ever vulnerable, faces his antipode, another new mask, "the white" (sub-genus: "the white liberal")—who is pasty-faced, graceless, lying, sexually dull, murderous.

No one in his right mind would wish the old masks back. But

this does not make the new masks wholly convincing. And whoever accepts them should notice that the new mask of "the Negro" has become visible only at the price of emphasizing the fatality of racial antagonisms. If D. W. Griffith could call his famous white supremacist film about the origins of the Ku Klux Klan *The Birth of a Nation*, then James Baldwin could, with more justice to the overt political message of his *Blues for Mister Charlie* ("Mister Charlie" is Negro slang for "white man"), have as well called his play "The Death of a Nation." Baldwin's play, which takes place in a small Southern town, opens with the death of its brash, tormented Negro jazz musician hero, Richard, and ends with the acquittal of his white murderer, a resentful inarticulate young buck named Lyle, and the moral collapse of the local liberal, Parnell. There is the same insistence on the painful ending, even more starkly presented, in LeRoi Jones' one-act play *Dutchman*, now running off-Broadway. In *Dutchman*, a young Negro sitting on the subway reading and minding his own business is first accosted, then elaborately teased and taunted to the point of rage, then suddenly knifed by a twitchy young hustler; while his body is being disposed of by the other passengers, whites, the girl turns her attention to a new young Negro who has just boarded the train. In the new post-liberal morality plays, it is essential that virtue be defeated. Both *Blues for Mister Charlie* and *Dutchman* turn on a shocking murder—even though, in the case of *Dutchman*, the murder is simply not credible in terms of the more or less realistic action that has gone before, and seems crude (dramatically), tacked on, willed. Only murder releases one from the mandate to be moderate. It is essential, dramatically, that the white man win. Murder justifies the author's rage, and disarms the white audience, who have to learn what's coming to them.

For it is indeed an extraordinary sermon that is being preached. Baldwin is not interested in dramatizing the incontestable fact that white Americans have brutally mistreated Negro Americans. What is being demonstrated is not the social guilt of the whites, but their inferiority as human beings. This means, above all, their sexual inferiority. While Richard jeers about his unsatisfying experiences with white women up North, it turns out that the only passions—

in one instance carnal, in the other romantic—ever felt by the two white men who figure importantly in the play, Lyle and Parnell, have been with Negro women. Thus, the oppression by whites of Negroes becomes a classic case of resentment as described by Nietzsche. It is eerie to sit in the ANTA Theatre on 52nd Street and hear that audience—sizably Negro, but still preponderantly white—cheer and laugh and break into applause at every line cursing white America. After all, it's not some exotic Other from across the seas who is being abused—like the rapacious Jew or the treacherous Italian of the Elizabethan drama. It is the majority of the members of the audience themselves. Social guilt would not be enough to explain this remarkable acquiescence of the majority in their own condemnation. Baldwin's plays, like his essays and novels, have undoubtedly touched a nerve other than political. Only by tapping the sexual insecurity that grips most educated white Americans could Baldwin's virulent rhetoric have seemed so reasonable.

But after applause and cheers, what? The masks which the Elizabethan theater proposed were exotic, fantastic, playful. Shakespeare's audience did not come streaming out of the Globe Theatre to butcher a Jew or string up a Florentine. The morality of *The Merchant of Venice* is not incendiary, but merely simplifying. But the masks which *Blues for Mister Charlie* holds up for our scorn are our reality. And Baldwin's rhetoric *is* incendiary, though let loose in a carefully fireproofed situation. The result is not any idea of action—but a vicarious pleasure in the rage vented on the stage, with no doubt an undertow of anxiety.

Considered as art, *Blues for Mister Charlie* runs aground for some of the same reasons it stalls as propaganda. Baldwin might have done something much better with the agitprop scheme of his play (noble, handsome Negro student youth pitted against stupid, vicious town whites), for to that in itself I have no objection. Some of the greatest art arises out of moral simplification. But this play gets bogged down in repetitions, incoherence, and in all sorts of loose ends of plot and motive. For example: it is hard to believe that in a town beset by civil rights agitation and with a race murder on its hands, the white liberal, Parnell, could move so freely, with

so little recrimination, from one community to another. Again: it is
not credible that Lyle, who is Parnell's close friend, and his wife
aren't bewildered and irate when Parnell secures Lyle's arraign-
ment on the charge of murder. Perhaps this remarkable equanimity
owes to the place of love in Baldwin's rhetoric. Love is always on
the horizon, a universal solvent almost in the manner of Paddy
Chayefsky. Again: from what we are shown of the romance struck
up between Richard and Juanita—which begins only a few days
before Richard is killed—it is unconvincing that Juanita should
proclaim that what she has learned from Richard is how to love.
(The truth seems rather that Richard was just beginning to learn
to love, for the first time, from her.) More important: the whole
confrontation between Richard and Lyle, with its explicit tones of
masculine sexual rivalry, seems inadequately motivated. Richard
simply has not enough reason, except that the author wants to say
these things, to introduce the theme of sexual envy on all the occasions that he does. And quite apart from any consideration of the
sentiments expressed, it is grotesque, humanly and dramatically,
for Richard's dying words, as he crawls at Lyle's feet with three
bullets in his gut, to be: "White man! I don't want nothing from
you. You ain't got nothing to give me! You can't talk because nobody won't talk to you. You can't dance because you've got nobody
to dance with . . . Okay. Okay. Okay. Keep your old lady home,
you hear? Don't let her near no nigger. She might get to like it.
You might get to like it, too."

Perhaps the origin of what seems forced, hysterical, unconvincing in *Blues for Mister Charlie*—and in *Dutchman*—is a rather
complex displacement of the play's true subject. Race conflict is
what the plays are supposed to be about. Yet also, in both plays,
the racial problem is drawn mainly in terms of sexual attitudes.
Baldwin has been very plain about the reason for this. White
America, he charges, has robbed the Negro of his masculinity.
What whites withhold from Negroes, and what Negroes aspire to,
is sexual recognition. The withholding of this recognition—and its
converse, treating the Negro as a mere object of lust—is the heart
of the Negro's pain. As stated in Baldwin's essays, the argument
strikes home. (And it doesn't hinder one's considering other conse-

quences, political and economic, of the Negro's oppression.) But what one reads in Baldwin's last novel, or sees on the stage in *Blues for Mister Charlie*, is considerably less persuasive. In Baldwin's novel and play, it seems to me, the racial situation has become a kind of code, or metaphor for sexual conflict. But a sexual problem cannot be wholly masked as a racial problem. Different tonalities, different specifics of emotion are involved.

The truth is that *Blues for Mister Charlie* isn't really about what it claims to be about. It is supposed to be about racial strife. But it is really about the anguish of tabooed sexual longings, about the crisis of identity which comes from confronting these longings, and about the rage and destructiveness (often, self-destructiveness) by which one tries to surmount this crisis. It has, in short, a psychological subject. The surface may be Odets, but the interior is pure Tennessee Williams. What Baldwin has done is to take the leading theme of the serious theater of the fifties—sexual anguish—and work it up as a political play. Buried in *Blues for Mister Charlie* is the plot of several successes of the last decade: the gruesome murder of a handsome virile young man by those who envy him his virility.

The plot of *Dutchman* is similar, except that here there is an added fillip of anxiety. In place of the veiled homoerotic hang-ups of *Blues for Mister Charlie*, there is class anxiety. As his contribution to the mystique of Negro sexuality, Jones brings up the question—which is never raised in *Blues for Mister Charlie*—of being authentically Negro. (Baldwin's play takes place in the South; perhaps one can only have such a problem up North.) Clay, the hero of *Dutchman*, is a middle-class Negro from New Jersey, who has gone to college and wanted to write poetry like Baudelaire, and has Negro friends who speak with English accents. In the early part of the play, he is in limbo. But in the end, poked and prodded by Lula, Clay strips down to his true self; he stops being nice, well-spoken, reasonable, and assumes his full Negro identity: that is, he announces the homicidal rage toward whites that Negroes bear in their hearts, whether they act on it or not. He will not kill, he says. Whereupon, he is killed.

Dutchman is, of course, a smaller work than *Blues for Mister*

Charlie. In only one act and with only two speaking characters, it is a descendant of the sexual duels to the death dramatized by Strindberg. At its best, in some of the early exchanges between Lula and Clay, it is neat and powerful. But as a whole—and one does look back on the play in the light of the astonishing fantasy revealed at the end—it is altogether too frantic, too overstated. Robert Hooks played Clay with some subtlety, but I found the spasmic sexual contortions and raucousness in Jennifer West's performance as Lula almost unbearable. There is a smell of a new, rather verbose style of emotional savagery in *Dutchman* that, for want of a better name, I should have to call Albee-esque. Undoubtedly, we shall see more of it. . . . In contrast, *Blues for Mister Charlie* is a long, overlong, rambling work which is virtually an anthology, a summa of the trends of serious big American plays of the last thirty years. It has lots of moral uplift. It carries on the good fight to talk dirty on the legitimate stage to new, splendid victories. And it adopts a complex, pretentious form of narration —the story is told in clumsy flashbacks, with the ornament of a non-functioning chorus, some kind of world-historical disc jockey ensconced stage-right, wearing earphones and fiddling with his apparatus all evening. The production itself, directed by Burgess Meredith, wobbles through several different styles. The realistic parts come off best. In roughly the last third of the play, which takes place in the courtroom, the play founders completely; all pretense at verisimilitude is dropped, there being no fidelity to courtroom rituals observed even in darkest Mississippi, and the play crumbles into bits of internal monologue, whose subjects have little bearing on the present action, which is Lyle's trial. In the last part of *Blues for Mister Charlie*, Baldwin seems bent on dissipating the play's dramatic power; the director needed only to follow. Despite the flabbiness of the direction, though, there are a number of affecting performances. Rip Torn, a sexy aggressive Lyle, rather upstaged the other actors; he was fun to watch. Al Freeman, Jr., was appealing as Richard, though he was saddled with some remarkably maudlin lines, especially in the Moment of Truth With Father scene, which has been obligatory in the serious Broadway theater for the last decade. Diana Sands, one of the loveliest actresses around, did well with the underrealized role of Juanita, except in what has been the most praised part of her performance, her downstage-center-and-face-the-audience aria of lament for Richard, which I thought terribly forced. As Parnell, Pat Hingle, an actor spectacularly embalmed in his own mannerisms, is still the very same indecisive lumbering old dear that he was last year as Nina Leeds' husband in the Actors Studio production of *Strange Interlude*.

The best occasions in the theater in the last months were freewheeling efforts, which made wholly comic use of the mask, the cliché of character.

At a small theater on East Fourth Street on two Monday evenings in late March, two short plays, *The General Returns From One Place to Another* by Frank O'Hara and *The Baptism* by LeRoi Jones, were performed. The O'Hara is a set of skits involving a kind of General MacArthur type and his entourage in perpetual orbit around the Pacific; the Jones play (like his *Dutchman*) starts more or less realistically, and ends in fantasy; it is about sex and religion and takes place in an evangelical church. Neither the O'Hara nor the Jones seemed very interesting as plays, but then, there is more to theater than plays, that is, than literature. Their main interest for me was as vehicles for the incredible Taylor Mead, poet and "Underground" movie actor. (He has been in Ron Rice's *Flower Thief*.) Mead is a skinny, balding, pot-bellied, round-shouldered, droopy, very pale young man—a sort of consumptive, faggot Harry Langdon. How it is possible for such a physically self-effacing, underprivileged-looking fellow to be so immensely attractive on the stage is hard to explain. But one simply cannot take one's eyes off him. In *The Baptism*, Mead is delightfully inventive and funny as a homosexual in long red underwear camping-in in the church, prancing, wisecracking, kibbitzing, flirting, while all the spiritual doings are taking place. In *The General Returns From One Place to Another*, he was more varied, and even more captivating. Rather than a role, this part is more like a set of charades: the General saluting while his pants are falling down, the General courting an inane widow who keeps popping up along his route, the General making a political speech, the General mowing down a field of flowers with his swagger stick, the General trying to crawl into a sleeping bag, the General dressing down his two adjutants, and so on. It was not, of course, what Mead did, but the somnambulistic concentration with which he did it. The source of his art is the deepest and purest of all: he just gives himself, wholly and without reserve, to some bizarre autistic fantasy. Nothing is more attractive in a person, but it is extremely rare after the age of four. This is the quality Harpo Marx has; Langdon and Keaton among the great silent comics have it; so do those four wonderful floppy Raggedy Andy dolls, the Beatles. Tammy Grimes projects something of it in her very stylized and exciting performance in an otherwise unremarkable Broadway musical now running, *High Spirits*, which is based on Noel Coward's *Blithe Spirit*. (The marvellous Bea Lillie is in it, too; but either she doesn't have enough scope for her gifts in this play or she just isn't up to form.)

What all these performers, from Buster Keaton to Taylor Mead, have in common is their total lack of self-consciousness, in the pursuit of some absolutely invented idea of action. With even a touch of self-consciousness, the effect is spoiled. It becomes insincere, distasteful, even grotesque. I am speaking of course of something rarer than acting ability. And since the ordinary conditions of work in the theater promote a great deal of self-consciousness, one is at least as likely to find this kind of thing in informal circumstances, such as those in which *The General* and *The Baptism* were put on. I am not sure whether Taylor Mead's performances would have prospered in another setting.

My favorite theatrical event of recent months, though, did survive the jump from semi-amateur production to off-Broadway; at least it was still surviving the last time I saw it. *Home Movies* opened in March in the choir loft of the Judson Memorial Church off Washington Square and eventually moved to the Provincetown Playhouse. The scene is A Home. The characters are: a Margaret Dumont mother; a super-athletic mustachioed father; a shrivelled whiny virgin daughter; a girlish youth; a red-cheeked stuttering poet sporting a muffler; a pair of bouncy clericals named Father Shenanigan and Sister Thalia; and an affable Negro delivery man with a thick foot-long pencil. Certain gestures are made in the direction of a plot. The father is believed dead, mother and daughter are lamenting his absence, friends of the family and clergy are paying condolence calls, and in the middle of it all father is delivered, alive and kicking, in a wardrobe. But it doesn't matter. In *Home Movies*, only the present exists—charming people coming and going, reclining in various tableaux, and singing at each other. There is a fast and witty script by Rosalyn Drexler, in which the oldest cliché and the fanciest fancy are meant to be uttered with the same solemnity. "It's the truth," says one character. "Yes," answers another, "a terrible truth like a rash." The gentleness and warmth of *Home Movies* delighted me even more than its wit; and this seemed the work of the adorable music composed by Al Carmines (who is assistant minister at the Judson Memorial Church) and played by him on the piano. The best numbers are a tango sung and danced by Sister Thalia (Sheindi Tokayer) and Father Shenanigan (Al Carmines), the winsome strip tease done by Peter (Freddy Herko) and the duets between him and Mrs. Verdun (Gretel Cummings); and the song "Peanut Brittle" belted out by the maid Violet (Barbara Ann Teer). *Home Movies* is great fun. The people on the stage look happy to be doing what they are doing, too. One could hardly ask for more in the theater—except for great plays, great actors, and great spectacles. Lacking these, one hopes for vitality and joy; and these seem more likely to turn up on out-of-the-way stages, like the Judson Memorial Church or the Sierra Leone pavilion at the World's Fair, than in midtown or even off-Broadway theaters. It helps that neither *Home Movies*, nor *The General* or *The Baptism*, is, strictly, a play. They are theatrical events of a use-and-throw-away kind—spoofs, joyous and insouciant, full of irreverence for "the theater" and "the play." Something similar is taking place with the movies: there is more vitality and art in the Maysles brothers' film on the Beatles in America, *What's Happening*, than in all American story films made this year.

Last, and I suppose least, a few words about two Shakespeare productions.

From John Gielgud's excellent essay, "The Hamlet Tradition—

Some Notes on Costume, Scenery and Stage," published in 1937, one could educe most of the particular mistakes in Gielgud's present production of *Hamlet* in New York. For instance, Gielgud cautions against playing Act I, Scene 2—the scene in which Hamlet, Claudius, and Gertrude all appear for the first time—as a family quarrel, rather than a formal privy council meeting, the first (according to tradition) held after the accession of Claudius to the throne. Yet this is just what Gielgud has allowed in the New York production, with Claudius and Gertrude looking like a weary suburban couple having it out with a spoiled only son. Another instance: in staging the Ghost, Gielgud in his essay argues convincingly against increasing ghostliness by using a miked voice coming from offstage, rather than the voice of the actor who is on stage and being seen by the audience. Everything must work toward making the Ghost as real as possible. But in the present production, Gielgud has forfeited the entire physical presence of the Ghost. This time the Ghost is really ghostly: a taped voice, Gielgud's own, resonating hollowly through the theater, and a giant silhouette thrown on the rear wall of the stage. . . . But it is a waste of time to look for reasons for this or that feature of the current production. The overall impression is of complete indifference, as if the play hadn't really been directed at all—except that one gathers that some of the dullness, at least the visual dullness, is actually deliberate. There is the matter of the clothes: most of the actors, whether courtiers or soldiers, wear old slacks and sweaters and windbreakers, though Hamlet's pants and shirt match (they're black), and Claudius and Polonius wear natty business suits, and Gertrude and Ophelia have long skirts (Gertrude has a mink, too), and the Player King and Queen have gorgeous costumes and gold masks. This silly conceit appears to be the one idea in the present production, and is called "playing *Hamlet* in rehearsal clothes."

The production affords exactly two pleasures. Hearing John Gielgud's voice on tape, even thus Cineramarized, reminded one of how beautiful Shakespeare's verse sounds when it is spoken with grace and intelligence. And the excellent George Rose, in the brief role of the gravedigger, rendered all the delights of Shakespeare's prose. The rest of the performances gave only various degrees of pain. Everyone spoke too fast; that fault apart, some performances rose to the height of mediocrity, while others, for example the performances of Laertes and Ophelia, deserve to be singled out as particularly immature, unfelt. It might be mentioned, though, that Eileen Herlie, who does a perfunctory Gertrude, gave a striking performance in the same role in Olivier's movie some fifteen years ago. And that Richard Burton, who does as little as possible with the part of Hamlet, is indeed a very handsome man. Correction: he does play the whole of Hamlet's death scene standing, when he could have sat down.

But no sooner had one recovered from Gielgud's effrontery in presenting a Shakespeare play absolutely nude, without any interpretation at all, than a Shakespeare production arrived which, putting the best face on it, was marred by overinterpretation and too much thought. This was Peter Brook's celebrated King Lear which was staged at Stratford-on-Avon two years ago, was received with great acclaim in Paris, throughout Eastern Europe, and in Russia, and played—more or less inaudibly—in the New York State Theater (which, it is now discovered, was designed for music and ballet) at Lincoln Center. If Gielgud's Hamlet was without thought or style, Brook's King Lear came laden with ideas. One read that, inspired by a recent essay by Jan Kott, the Polish Shakespearean scholar, comparing Shakespeare and Beckett, Brook had decided to play King Lear as Endgame, so to speak. Gielgud has mentioned, in an interview this April in England, that Brook told him it was his controversial "Japanese" King Lear (sets and costumes by Noguchi) in 1955 which gave him the basic idea for the current production. And by consulting the "Lear Log" of Charles Marowitz, Brook's assistant at Stratford in 1962, one can find other influences, too. But in the end none of the ideas that fed into the production matter. What matters is what one saw and, hopefully, heard. What I saw was rather dull—if you liked it, it was austere—and arbitrary, too. I can't see what is gained by going against the emotional climaxes of the play—leveling off Lear's tirades, bringing the Gloucester plot almost to equal scale with the Lear plot, cutting out "humanist" passages such as where Regan's servants move to aid the newly blinded Gloucester and where Edmund attempts to revoke the execution of Cordelia and Lear ("Some good I mean to do, Despite of mine own nature"). There were a number of graceful and intelligent performances—Edmund, Gloucester, the Fool. But all the actors seemed to work under an almost palpable constraint, the desire simultaneously to make explicit and to underplay, which must have been what led Brook, in one of the most curious choices of the production, to keep the stage fully lit and bare during the storm scenes. Paul Scofield's Lear is an admirably studied performance. On Lear's great age—with its egotism, its awkward movements and appetites—he is especially good. But I cannot see the point of his throwing so much of the role away, Lear's madness for instance, by arbitrary vocal mannerisms that deadened the full emotional power of his lines. The only performance which seemed to me to survive this strange, crippling interpretation which Brook has imposed on his actors—even, to thrive on it—was Irene Worth's complex and partly sympathetic Goneril. Miss Worth appeared to have searched every corner of her role and, unlike Scofield, to have found more, rather than less, than others had before.

[Summer 1964]

> "The Primary and most beautiful of Nature's qualities is motion, which agitates her at all times. But this motion is simply the perpetual consequence of crimes; and it is conserved by means of crimes alone."
>
> SADE

> "Everything that acts is a cruelty. It is upon this idea of extreme action, pushed beyond all limits, that theatre must be rebuilt."
>
> ARTAUD

Marat/Sade/Artaud

THEATRICALITY and insanity—the two most potent subjects of the contemporary theater —are brilliantly fused in Peter Weiss' play, *The Persecution and Assassination of Marat as Performed by the Inmates of the Asylum at Charenton under the Direction of the Marquis de Sade*. The subject is a dramatic performance staged before the audience's eyes; the scene is a madhouse. The historical facts behind the play are that in the insane asylum just outside Paris where Sade was confined by order of Napoleon for the last eleven years of his life (1803–14), it was the enlightened policy of the director, M. Coulmier, to allow Charenton's inmates to stage theatrical productions of their own devising which were open to the Parisian public. In these circumstances Sade is known to have written and put on several plays (all lost), and Weiss' play ostensibly re-creates such a

performance. The year is 1808 and the stage is the stark tiled bath-
house of the asylum.

Theatricality permeates Weiss' cunning play in a peculiarly
modern sense: most of Marat/Sade consists of a play-within-a-play.
In Peter Brook's production, which opened in London last August,
the aged, disheveled, flabby Sade (acted by Patrick Magee) sits
quietly on the left side of the stage—prompting (with the aid of a
fellow-patient who acts as stage manager and narrator), supervis-
ing, commenting. M. Coulmier, dressed formally and wearing
some sort of honorific red sash, attended by his elegantly dressed
wife and daughter, sits throughout the performance on the right
side of the stage. There is also an abundance of theatricality in a
more traditional sense: the emphatic appeal to the senses with
spectacle and sound. A quartet of inmates with string hair and
painted faces, wearing colored sacks and floppy hats, sing sardonic
loony songs while the action described by the songs is mimed; their
motley getup contrasts with the shapeless white tunics and strait-
jackets, the whey-colored faces of most of the rest of the inmates
who act in Sade's passion play on the French Revolution. The
verbal action, conducted by Sade, is repeatedly interrupted by brilliant bits of acting-out performed by the lunatics, the most forceful
of which is a mass guillotining sequence, in which some inmates
make metallic rasping noises, bang together parts of the ingenious
set, and pour buckets of paint (blood) down drains, while other
madmen gleefully jump into a pit in the center of the stage, leaving
their heads piled above stage level, next to the guillotine.

In Brook's production, insanity proves the most authoritative
and sensuous kind of theatricality. Insanity establishes the inflec-
tion, the intensity of Marat/Sade, from the opening image of the
ghostly inmates who are to act in Sade's play, crouching in foetal
postures or in a catatonic stupor or trembling or performing some
obsessive ritual, then stumbling forward to greet the affable M. Coulmier and his family as they enter the stage and mount the plat-
form where they will sit. Insanity is the register of the intensity
of the individual performances as well: of Sade, who recites his
long speeches with a painful clenched singsong deliberateness; of
Marat (acted by Clive Revill), swathed in wet cloths (a treat-

ment for his skin disease) and encased throughout the action in a portable metal bathtub, even in the midst of the most passionate declamation staring straight ahead as though he were already dead; of Charlotte Corday, Marat's assassin, who is played by a beautiful somnambule who periodically goes blank, forgets her lines, even lies down on the stage and has to be awakened by Sade; of Duperret, the Girondist deputy and lover of Corday, played by a lanky stiff-haired patient, an erotomaniac, who is constantly breaking down in his role of gentleman and lover and lunging lustfully toward the patient playing Corday (in the course of the play, he has to be put in a strait-jacket); of Simone Everard, Marat's mistress and nurse, played by an almost wholly disabled patient who can barely speak and is limited to jerky idiot movements as she changes Marat's dressings. Insanity becomes the privileged, most authentic metaphor for passion; or, what's the same thing in this case, the logical terminus of any strong emotion. Both dream (as in the "Marat's Nightmare" sequence) and dream-like states must end in violence. Being "calm" amounts to a failure to understand one's real situation. Thus, the slow-motion staging of Corday's murder of Marat (history, i.e. theater) is followed by the inmates shouting and singing of the fifteen bloody years since then, and ends with the "cast" assaulting the Coulmiers as they attempt to leave the stage.

It is through its depiction of theatricality and insanity that Weiss' play is also a play of ideas. The heart of the play is a running debate between Sade, in his chair, and Marat, in his bath, on the meaning of the French Revolution, that is, on the psychological and political premises of modern history, but seen through a very modern sensibility, one equipped with the hindsight afforded by the Nazi concentration camps. But Marat/Sade does not lend itself to being formulated as a particular theory about modern experience. Weiss' play seems to be more about the range of sensibility that concerns itself with, or is at stake in, the modern experience, than it is about an argument or an interpretation of that experience. Weiss does not present ideas as much as he immerses his audience in them. Intellectual debate is the material of the play, but it is not its subject or its end. The Charenton setting insures that this debate takes place in a constant atmosphere of barely suppressed violence: all ideas are volatile at this temperature. Again, insanity proves to be the most austere (even abstract) and drastic mode of expressing in theatrical terms the reenacting of ideas, as members of the cast reliving the Revolution run amuck and have to be restrained and the cries of the Parisian mob for liberty are suddenly metamorphosed into the cries of the patients howling to be let out of the asylum.

Such theater, whose fundamental action is the irrevocable careening toward extreme states of feeling, can end in only two ways. It can turn in on itself and become formal, and end in strict da capo fashion, with its own opening lines. Or it can turn outward, breaking the "frame," and assault the audience. Ionesco has admitted that he originally envisaged his first play, The Bald Soprano, ending with a massacre of the audience; in another version of the same play (which now ends da capo), the author was to leap on the stage, and shout imprecations at the audience till they fled the theater. Brook, or Weiss, or both, have devised for the end of Marat/Sade an equivalent of the same hostile gesture toward the audience. The inmates, that is, the "cast" of Sade's play, have gone berserk and assaulted the Coulmiers; but this riot—that is, the play —is broken off by the entry of the stage manager of the Aldwych Theater, in modern skirt, sweater, and gym shoes. She blows a whistle; the actors abruptly stop, turn, and face the audience; but when the audience applauds, the company responds with a slow ominous handclap, drowning out the "free" applause and leaving everyone pretty uncomfortable.

My own admiration for, and pleasure in, Marat/Sade is virtually unqualified. The play that opened in London last August, and will, it's rumored, soon be seen in New York, is one of the great experiences of anyone's theater-going lifetime. Yet almost everyone, from the daily reviewers to the most serious critics, have voiced serious reservations about, if not outright dislike for, Brook's production of Weiss' play. Why?

Three ready-made ideas seem to me to underlie most caviling at Weiss' play in Brook's production of it.

The connection between theater and literature. One ready-made idea: a work of theater is a branch of literature. The truth is, some works of theater may be judged primarily as works of literature, others not.

It is because this is not admitted, or generally understood, that one reads all too frequently the statement that while *Marat/Sade* is, theatrically, one of the most stunning things anyone has seen on the stage, it's a "director's play," meaning a first-rate production of a second-rate play. A well-known English poet told me he detested the play for this reason: because although he thought it marvelous when he saw it, he knew that if it hadn't had the benefit of Peter Brook's production, he wouldn't have liked it. It's also reported that the play in Konrad Swinarski's production last year in West Berlin made nowhere near the striking impression it does in the current production in London.

Granted, *Marat/Sade* is not the supreme masterpiece of contemporary dramatic literature, but it is scarcely a second-rate play. Considered as a text alone, *Marat/Sade* is both sound and exciting. It is not the play which is at fault, but a narrow vision of theater which insists on one image of the director—as servant to the writer, bringing out meanings already resident in the text.

After all, to the extent that it is true that Weiss' text, in Adrian Mitchell's graceful translation, is enhanced greatly by being joined with Peter Brook's staging, what of it? Apart from a theater of dialogue (of language) in which the text is primary, there is also a theater of the senses. The first might be called "play," the second "theater work." In the case of a pure theater work, the writer who sets down words which are to be spoken by actors and staged by a director loses his primacy. In this case, the "author" or "creator" is, to quote Artaud, none other than "the person who controls the direct handling of the stage." The director's art is a material art—an art in which he deals with the bodies of actors, the props, the lights, the music. And what Brook has put together is particularly brilliant and inventive—the rhythm of the staging, the costumes, the ensemble mime scenes. In every detail of the production—one of the most remarkable elements of which is the clangorous tuneful music (by Richard Peaslee) featuring bells, cymbals, and the organ—there is an inexhaustible material inventiveness, a relentless address to the senses. Yet, something about Brook's sheer virtuosity in stage effects offends. It seems, to most people, to overwhelm the text. But perhaps that's just the point.

I'm not suggesting that Marat/Sade is simply theater of the senses. Weiss has supplied a complex and highly literate text which demands to be responded to. But Marat/Sade also demands to be taken on the sensory level as well, and only the sheerest prejudice about what theater must be (the prejudice, namely, that a work of theater is to be judged, in the last analysis, as a branch of literature) lies behind the demand that the written, and subsequently spoken, text of a theater work carry the whole play.

The connection between theater and psychology. Another ready-made idea: drama consists of the revelation of character, built on the conflict of realistically credible motives. But the most interesting modern theater is a theater which goes beyond psychology.

Again, to cite Artaud: "We need true action, but without practical consequences. It is not on the social level that the action of theater unfolds. Still less on the ethical and psychological levels. . . . This obstinacy in making characters talk about feelings, passions, desires, and impulses of a strictly psychological order, in which a single word is to compensate for innumerable gestures, is the reason . . . the theater has lost its true *raison d'être.*"

It's from this point of view, tendentiously formulated by Artaud, that one may properly approach the fact that Weiss has situated his argument in an insane asylum. The fact is that with the exception of the audience-figures on stage—M. Coulmier, who frequently interrupts the performance to remonstrate with Sade, and his wife and daughter, who have no lines—all the characters in the play are mad. But the setting of Marat/Sade does not amount to a statement that the world is insane. Nor is it an instance of a fashionable interest in the psychology of psychopathic behavior. On the contrary, the concern with insanity in art today usually reflects the desire to go beyond psychology. By representing characters with deranged behavior or deranged styles of speech, such dramatists as Pirandello, Genet, Beckett, and Ionesco make it unnecessary for their characters to embody in their acts or voice in their speech sequential and credible accounts of their motives. Freed from the limitations of what Artaud calls "psychological and dialogue painting of the individual," the dramatic representation is open to levels of experience which are more heroic, more rich in fantasy, more philosophical. The point applies, of course, not only to the drama. The choice of "insane" behavior as the subject-matter of art is, by now, the virtually classic strategy of modern artists who wish to transcend traditional "realism," that is, psychology.

Take the scene to which many people particularly objected, in which Sade persuades Charlotte Corday to whip him (Peter Brook has her do it with her hair)—while he, meanwhile, continues to recite, in agonized tones, some point about the Revolution, and the nature of human nature. The purpose of this scene is surely not to inform the audience that, as one critic put it, Sade is "sick, sick, sick"; nor is it fair to reproach Weiss' Sade, as the same critic does, with "using the theater less to advance an argument than to excite himself." (Anyway, why not both?) By combining rational or near-rational argument with irrational behavior, Weiss is not inviting the audience to make a judgment on Sade's character, mental competence, or state of mind. Rather, he is shifting to a kind of theater focused not on characters, but on intense trans-personal emotions borne by characters. He is providing a kind of vicarious emotional experience (in this case, frankly erotic) from which the theater has shied away too long.

Language is used in Marat/Sade primarily as a form of incantation, instead of being limited to the revelation of character and the exchange of ideas. This use of language as incantation is the point of another scene which many who saw the play have found objectionable, upsetting, and gratuitous—the bravura soliloquy of Sade, in which he illustrates the cruelty in the heart of man by relating in excruciating detail the public execution by slow dismemberment of Damiens, the would-be assassin of Louis XV.

The connection between theater and ideas. Another ready-made idea: a work of art is to be understood as being "about" or representing or arguing for an "idea." That being so, an implicit standard for a work of art is the value of the ideas it contains, and whether these are clearly and consistently expressed.

It is only to be expected that Marat/Sade would be subjected to these standards. Weiss' play, theatrical to its core, is also full of intelligence. It contains discussions of the deepest issues of contemporary morality and history and feeling that put to shame the banalities peddled by such would-be diagnosticians of these issues as Arthur Miller (see his current *After the Fall* and *Incident at Vichy*), Friedrich Duerrenmatt (*The Visit, The Physicists*), and Max Frisch (*The Firebugs, Andorra*). Yet, there is no doubt that Marat/Sade is intellectually puzzling. Argument is offered, only (seemingly) to be undermined by the context of the play—the insane asylum, and the avowed theatricality of the proceedings. People do seem to represent positions in Weiss' play. Roughly, Sade represents the claim of the permanence of human nature, in all its vileness, against Marat's revolutionary fervor and his belief that man can be changed by history. Sade thinks that "the world is made of bodies," Marat that it is made of forces. Secondary characters, too, have their moments of passionate advocacy: Duperret hails the eventual dawn of freedom, the priest Jacques Roux denounces Napoleon. But Sade and "Marat" are both madmen, each in a different style; "Charlotte Corday" is a sleepwalker, "Duperret" has satyriasis; "Roux" is hysterically violent. Doesn't this undercut their arguments? And, apart from the question of the context of insanity in which the ideas are presented, there is the device of the play-within-a-play. At one level, the running debate between Sade and Marat, in which the moral and social idealism attributed to Marat is countered by Sade's trans-moral advocacy of the claims of individual passion, seems a debate between equals. But, on another level, since the fiction of Weiss' play is that it is Sade's script which Marat is reciting, presumably Sade carries the argument. One critic goes so far as to say that because Marat has to double as a puppet in Sade's psychodrama, and as Sade's opponent in an evenly matched ideological contest, the debate between them is stillborn. And, lastly, some critics have attacked the play on the grounds of its lack of historical fidelity to the actual views of Marat, Sade, Duperret, and Roux.

These are some of the difficulties which have led people to charge Marat/Sade with being obscure or intellectually shallow.

But most of these difficulties, and the objections made to them, are misunderstandings—misunderstandings of the connection between the drama and didacticism. Weiss' play cannot be treated like an argument of Arthur Miller, or even of Brecht. We have to do here with a kind of theater as different from these as Antonioni and Godard are from Eisenstein. Weiss' play contains an argument, or rather it employs the material of intellectual debate and historical reevaluation (the nature of human nature, the betrayal of the Revolution, etc.). But Weiss' play is only secondarily an argument. There is another use of ideas to be reckoned with in art: ideas as sensory stimulants. Antonioni has said of his films that he wants them to dispense with "the superannuated casuistry of positives and negatives." The same impulse discloses itself in a complex way in Marat/Sade. Such a position does not mean that these artists wish to dispense with ideas. What it does mean is that ideas, including moral ideas, are proffered in a new style. Ideas may function as décor, props, sensuous material.

One might perhaps compare the Weiss play with the long prose narratives of Genet. Genet is not really arguing that "cruelty is good" or "cruelty is holy" (a moral statement, albeit the opposite of traditional morality), but rather shifting the argument to another plane, from the moral to the aesthetic. But this is not quite the case with Marat/Sade. While the "cruelty" in Marat/Sade is not, ultimately, a moral issue, it is not an aesthetic one either. It is an ontological issue. While those who propose the aesthetic version of "cruelty" interest themselves in the richness of the surface of life, the proponents of the ontological version of "cruelty" want their art to act out the widest possible context for human action, at least a wider context than that provided by realistic art. That wider context is what Sade calls "nature" and what Artaud means when he says that "everything that acts is a cruelty." There is a moral vision in art like Marat/Sade, though clearly it cannot (and this has made its audience uncomfortable) be summed up with the slogans of "humanism." But "humanism" is not identical with morality. Precisely, art like Marat/Sade entails a rejection of "humanism," of the task of moralizing the world and thereby refusing to acknowledge the "crimes" of which Sade speaks.

•

I have repeatedly cited the writings of Artaud on the theater in discussing Marat/Sade. But Artaud—unlike Brecht, the other great theoretician of 20th century theater—did not create a body of work to illustrate his theory and sensibility.

Often, the sensibility (the theory, at a certain level of discourse) which governs certain works of art is formulated before there exist substantial works to embody that sensibility. Or, the theory may apply to works other than those for which they are developed. Thus, right now in France writers and critics such as Alain Robbe-Grillet (Pour un Nouveau Roman), Roland Barthes (Essais Critiques), and Michel Foucault (essays in Tel Quel and elsewhere) have worked out an elegant and persuasive anti-rhetorical aesthetic for the novel. But the novels produced by the nouveau roman writers and analyzed by them are in fact not as important or satisfying an illustration of this sensibility as certain films, and, moreover, films by directors, Italian as well as French, who have no connection with this school of new French writers, such as Bresson, Melville, Antonioni, Godard, and Bertolucci (Before the Revolution).

Similarly, it seems doubtful that the only stage production which Artaud personally supervised, of Shelley's The Cenci, or the 1948 radio broadcast Pour en Finir avec le Jugement de Dieu, came close to following the brilliant recipes for the theater in his writings, any more than did his public readings of Seneca's tragedies. We have up to now lacked a full-fledged example of Artaud's category, "the theater of cruelty." The closest thing to it are the theatrical events done in New York and elsewhere in the last five years, largely by painters (such as Alan Kaprow, Claes Oldenberg, Jim Dine, Bob Whitman, Red Grooms, Robert Watts) and without text or at least intelligible speech, called Happenings. Another example of work in a quasi-Artaudian spirit: the brilliant staging by Lawrence Kornfield and Al Carmines of Gertrude Stein's prose poem "What Happened," at the Judson Memorial Church last year. Another example: the final production of The Living Theater in New York, Kenneth H. Brown's The Brig, directed by Judith Malina.

All the works I have mentioned so far suffer, though, apart from all questions of individual execution, from smallness of scope and conception—as well as a narrowness of sensory means. Hence, the great interest of *Marat/Sade*, for it, more than any modern theater work I know of, comes near the scope, as well as the intent, of Artaud's theater. (I must reluctantly except, because I have never seen it, what sounds like the most interesting and ambitious theater group in the world today—the Theater Laboratory of Jerzy Grotowski in Opole, Poland. For an account of this work, which is an ambitious extension of Artaudian principles, see the *Tulane Drama Review*, Spring 1965.)

Yet Artaud's is not the only major influence reflected in the Weiss-Brook production. Weiss is reported to have said that in this play he wished—staggering ambition!—to combine Brecht and Artaud. And, to be sure, one can see what he means. Certain features of *Marat/Sade* are reminiscent of Brecht's theater—constructing the action around a debate on principles and reasons; the songs; the appeals to the audience through an M.C. And these blend well with the Artaudian texture of the situation and the staging. Yet the matter is not that simple. Indeed, the final question that Weiss' play raises is precisely the one of the ultimate compatibility of these two sensibilities and ideals. How could one reconcile Brecht's conception of a didactic theater, a theater of intelligence, with Artaud's theater of magic, of gesture, of "cruelty," of feeling?

The answer seems to be that, if one could effect such a reconciliation or synthesis, Weiss' play has taken a big step toward doing so. Hence the obtuseness of the critic who complained: "Useless ironies, insoluble conundrums, double meanings which could be multipled indefinitely: Brecht's machinery without Brecht's incisiveness or firm commitment," forgetting about Artaud altogether. If one does put the two together, one sees that new perceptions must be allowed, new standards devised. For isn't an Artaudian theater of commitment, much less "firm commitment," a contradiction in terms? Or is it? The problem is not solved by ignoring the fact that Weiss in *Marat/Sade* means to employ ideas in a fugue form (rather than as literal assertions), and thereby necessarily refers beyond the arena of social material and didactic statement. A misunderstanding of the artistic aims implicit in

Marat/Sade due to a narrow vision of the theater accounts for most of the critics' dissatisfaction with Weiss' play—an ungrateful dissatisfaction, considering the extraordinary richness of the text and of the Brook production. That the ideas taken up in Marat/Sade are not resolved, in an intellectual sense, is far less important than the extent to which they do work together in the sensory arena.

[1965]

IV

Spiritual style
in the films of
Robert Bresson

SOME art aims directly at arousing the feelings; some art appeals to the feelings through the route of the intelligence. There is art that involves, that creates empathy. There is art that detaches, that provokes reflection.

Great reflective art is not frigid. It can exalt the spectator, it can present images that appall, it can make him weep. But its emotional power is mediated. The pull toward emotional involvement is counterbalanced by elements in the work that promote distance, disinterestedness, impartiality. Emotional involvement is always, to a greater or lesser degree, postponed.

The contrast can be accounted for in terms of techniques or means—even of ideas. No doubt, though, the sensibility of the artist is, in the end, decisive. It is a reflective art, a detached art that Brecht is advocating when he talks about the "Alienation Effect."

The didactic aims which Brecht claimed for his theater are really a vehicle for the cool temperament that conceived those plays.

2

In the film, the master of the reflective mode is Robert Bresson.

Though Bresson was born in 1911, his extant work in the cinema has all been done in the last twenty years, and consists of six feature films. (He made a short film in 1934 called *Les Affaires Publiques*, reportedly a comedy in the manner of René Clair, all copies of which have been lost; did some work on the scripts of two obscure commercial films in the mid-thirties; and in 1940 was assistant director to Clair on a film that was never finished.) Bresson's first full-length film was begun when he returned to Paris in 1941 after spending eighteen months in a German prison camp. He met a Dominican priest and writer, Father Bruckberger, who suggested that they collaborate on a film about Bethany, the French Dominican order devoted to the care and rehabilitation of women ex-convicts. A scenario was written, Jean Giraudoux was enlisted to write the dialogue, and the film—at first called *Béthanie*, and finally, at the producers' insistence, *Les Anges du Peché* (The Angels of Sin) —was released in 1943. It was enthusiastically acclaimed by the critics and had a success with the public as well.

The plot of his second film, begun in 1944 and released in 1945, was a modern version of one of the interpolated stories in Diderot's great anti-novel *Jacques le Fataliste*; Bresson wrote the scenario and Jean Cocteau the dialogue. Bresson's first success was not repeated, however. *Les Dames du Bois de Boulogne* (sometimes called, here, *The Ladies of the Park*) was panned by the critics and failed at the box-office, too.

Bresson's third film, *Le Journal d'un Curé de Campagne* (The Diary of a Country Priest), did not appear until 1951; his fourth film, *Un Condamné à Mort s'est Échappé* (called, here, A Man Escaped), in 1956; his fifth film, *Pickpocket*, in 1959; and his sixth film, *Procès de Jeanne d'Arc* (The Trial of Joan of Arc), in 1962. All have had a certain success with critics but scarcely any with the public—with the exception of the last film, which most critics disliked, too. Once hailed as the new hope of the French cinema,

Bresson is now firmly labeled as an esoteric director. He has never had the attention of the art-house audience that flocks to Buñuel, Bergman, Fellini—though he is a far greater director than these; even Antonioni has almost a mass audience compared with Bresson's. And, except among a small coterie, he has had only the scantest critical attention.

The reason that Bresson is not generally ranked according to his merits is that the tradition to which his art belongs, the reflective or contemplative, is not well understood. Particularly in England and America, Bresson's films are often described as cold, remote, overintellectualized, geometrical. But to call a work of art "cold" means nothing more or less than to compare it (often unconsciously) to a work that is "hot." And not all art is—or could be—hot, any more than all persons have the same temperament. The generally accepted notions of the range of temperament in art are provincial. Certainly, Bresson is cold next to Pabst or Fellini. (So is Vivaldi cold next to Brahms, and Keaton cold next to Chaplin.) One has to understand the aesthetics—that is, find the beauty —of such coldness. And Bresson offers a particularly good case for sketching such an aesthetic, because of his range. Exploring the possibilities of a reflective, as opposed to an emotionally immediate, art, Bresson moves from the diagrammatic perfection of *Les Dames du Bois de Boulogne* to the almost lyrical, almost "humanistic" warmth of *Un Condamné à Mort s'est Échappé*. He also shows—and this is instructive, too—how such art can become too rarefied, in his last film, *Procès de Jeanne d'Arc*.

3

In reflective art, the form of the work of art is present in an emphatic way.

The effect of the spectator's being aware of the form is to elongate or to retard the emotions. For, to the extent that we are conscious of form in a work of art, we become somewhat detached; our emotions do not respond in the same way as they do in real life. Awareness of form does two things simultaneously: it gives a sensuous pleasure independent of the "content," and it invites the use of intelligence. It may be a very low order of reflection which is invited, as, for instance, by the narrative form (the interweaving of the four separate stories) of Griffith's *Intolerance*. But it is reflection, nonetheless.

The typical way in which "form" shapes "content" in art is by doubling, duplicating. Symmetry and the repetition of motifs in painting, the double plot in Elizabethan drama, and rhyme schemes in poetry are a few obvious examples.

The evolution of forms in art is partly independent of the evolution of subject-matters. (The history of forms is dialectical. As types of sensibility become banal, boring, and are overthrown by their opposites, so forms in art are, periodically, exhausted. They become banal, unstimulating, and are replaced by new forms which are at the same time anti-forms.) Sometimes the most beautiful effects are gained when the material and the form are at cross purposes. Brecht does this often: placing a hot subject in a cold frame. Other times, what satisfies is that the form is perfectly appropriate to the theme. This is the case with Bresson.

Why Bresson is not only a much greater, but also a more interesting director than, say, Buñuel is that he has worked out a form that perfectly expresses and accompanies what he wants to say. In fact, it *is* what he wants to say.

Here, one must carefully distinguish between form and manner. Welles, the early René Clair, Sternberg, Ophuls are examples of directors with unmistakable stylistic inventions. But they never created a rigorous narrative form. Bresson, like Ozu, has. And the form of Bresson's films is designed (like Ozu's) to discipline the emotions at the same time that it arouses them: to induce a certain tranquillity in the spectator, a state of spiritual balance that is itself the subject of the film.

Reflective art is art which, in effect, imposes a certain discipline on the audience—postponing easy gratification. Even boredom can be a permissible means of such discipline. Giving prominence to what is artifice in the work of art is another means. One thinks here of Brecht's idea of theater. Brecht advocated strategies of staging—like having a narrator, putting musicians on stage, interposing filmed scenes—and a technique of acting so that the audience could distance itself, and not become uncritically "involved" in the plot and the fate of the characters. Bresson wishes distance, too. But his aim, I would imagine, is not to keep hot emotions cool so that intelligence can prevail. The emotional distance typical of Bresson's films seems to exist for a different reason altogether: because all identification with characters, deeply conceived, is an impertinence—an affront to the mystery that is human action and the human heart.

But—all claims for intellectual coolness or respect for the mystery of action laid aside—surely Brecht knew, as must Bresson, that such distancing is a source of great emotional power. It is precisely the defect of the naturalistic theater and cinema that, giving itself too readily, it easily consumes and exhausts its effects. Ultimately, the greatest source of emotional power in art lies not in any particular subject-matter, however passionate, however universal. It lies in form. The detachment and retarding of the emotions, through the consciousness of form, makes them far stronger and more intense in the end.

4

Despite the venerable critical slogan that film is primarily a visual medium, and despite the fact that Bresson was a painter before he turned to making films, form for Bresson is not mainly visual. It is, above all, a distinctive form of narration. For Bresson film is not a plastic but a narrative experience.

Bresson's form fulfills beautifully the prescription of Alexandre Astruc, in his famous essay "Le Camera-Stylo," written in the late forties. According to Astruc, the cinema will, ideally, become a language.

By a language I mean the form in which and through which an artist can express his thoughts, however abstract they may be, or translate his obsessions, just as in an essay or a novel . . . The film will gradually free itself from the tyranny of the visual, of the image for its own sake, of the immediate and concrete anecdote, to become a means of writing as supple and subtle as the written word . . . What interests us in the cinema today is the creation of this language.

Cinema-as-language means a break with the traditional dramatic and visual way of telling a story in film. In Bresson's work, this creation of a language for films entails a heavy emphasis on the word. In the first two films, where the action is still relatively dramatic, and the plot employs a group of characters,* language (in the literal sense) appears in the form of dialogue. This dialogue definitely calls attention to itself. It is very theatrical dialogue, concise, aphoristic, deliberate, literary. It is the opposite of the improvised-sounding dialogue favored by the new French directors—including Godard in *Vivre Sa Vie* and *Une Femme Mariée*, the most Bressonian of the New Wave films.

But in the last four films, in which the action has contracted from that which befalls a group to the fortunes of the lonely self, dialogue is often displaced by first-person narration. Sometimes the narration can be justified as providing links between scenes. But, more interestingly, it often doesn't tell us anything we don't know or are about to learn. It "doubles" the action. In this case, we usually get the word first, then the scene. For example, in *Pickpocket*: we see the hero writing (and hear his voice reading) his memoirs. Then we see the event which he has already curtly described.

But sometimes we get the scene first, then the explanation, the description of what has just happened. For example, in *Le Journal d'un Curé de Campagne*, there is a scene in which the priest calls anxiously on the Vicar of Torcy. We see the priest wheeling his bicycle up to the Vicar's door, then the housekeeper answering (the Vicar is obviously not at home, but we don't hear the housekeeper's voice), then the door shutting, and the priest leaning against it. Then, we hear: "I was so disappointed, I had to lean against the door." Another example: in *Un Condamné à Mort s'est Échappé*,

---

* Even here, though, there is a development. In *Les Anges du Péché*, there are five main characters—the young novice Anne-Marie, another novice Madeleine, the Prioress, the Prioress' assistant Mother Saint-Jean, and the murderess Thérèse—as well as a great deal of background: the daily life of the convent, and so forth. In *Les Dames du Bois de Boulogne*, there is already a simplification, less background. Four characters are clearly outlined—Hélène, her former lover Jean, Agnès, and Agnès' mother. Everyone else is virtually invisible. We never see the servants' faces, for instance.

we see Fontaine tearing up the cloth of his pillow, then twisting the cloth around wire which he has stripped off the bed frame. Then, the voice: "I twisted it strongly."

The effect of this "superfluous" narration is to punctuate the scene with intervals. It puts a brake on the spectator's direct imaginative participation in the action. Whether the order is from comment to scene or from scene to comment, the effect is the same: such doublings of the action both arrest and intensify the ordinary emotional sequence.

Notice, too, that in the first type of doubling—where we hear what's going to happen before we see it—there is a deliberate flouting of one of the traditional modes of narrative involvement: suspense. Again, one thinks of Brecht. To eliminate suspense, at the beginning of a scene Brecht announces, by means of placards or a narrator, what is to happen. (Godard adopts this technique in Vivre Sa Vie.) Bresson does the same thing, by jumping the gun with narration. In many ways, the perfect story for Bresson is that of his last film, Procès de Jeanne d'Arc—in that the plot is wholly known, foreordained; the words of the actors are not invented but those of the actual trial record. Ideally, there is no suspense in a Bresson film. Thus, in the one film where suspense should normally play a large role, Un Condamné à Mort s'est Échappé, the title deliberately—even awkwardly—gives the outcome away: we know Fontaine is going to make it.* In this respect, of course, Bresson's escape film differs from Jacques Becker's last work, Le Trou (called, here, Nightwatch), though in other ways Becker's excellent film owes a great deal to Un Condamné à Mort s'est Échappé. (It is to Becker's credit that he was the only prominent person in the French film world who defended Les Dames du Bois de Boulogne when it came out.)

Thus, form in Bresson's films is anti-dramatic, though strongly linear. Scenes are cut short, and set end to end without obvious emphasis. In Le Journal d'un Curé de Campagne, there must be thirty such short scenes. This method of constructing the story is most rigorously observed in Procès de Jeanne d'Arc. The film is

* The film has a co-title, which expresses the theme of inexorability: Le Vent Souffle où il Veut.

composed of static, medium shots of people talking; the scenes are the inexorable sequence of Jeanne's interrogations. The principle of eliding anecdotal material—in *Un Condamné à Mort s'est Échappé*, for instance, one knows little about why Fontaine is in prison in the first place—is here carried to its extreme. There are no interludes of any sort. An interrogation ends; the door slams behind Jeanne; the scene fades out. The key clatters in the lock; another interrogation; again the door clangs shut; fadeout. It is a very dead-pan construction, which puts a sharp brake on emotional involvement.

Bresson also came to reject the species of involvement created in films by the expressiveness of the acting. Again, one is reminded of Brecht by Bresson's particular way of handling actors, in the exercise of which he has found it preferable to use non-professionals in major roles. Brecht wanted the actor to "report" a role rather than "be" it. He sought to divorce the actor from identifying with the role, as he wanted to divorce the spectator from identifying with the events that he saw being "reported" on the stage. "The actor," Brecht insists, "must remain a demonstrator; he must present the person demonstrated as a stranger, he must not suppress the 'he did that, he said that' element in his performance." Bresson, working with non-professional actors in his last four films (he used professionals in *Les Anges du Peché* and *Les Dames du Bois de Boulogne*), also seems to be striving for the same effect of strangeness. His idea is for the actors not to act out their lines, but simply to say them with as little expression as possible. (To get this effect, Bresson rehearses his actors for several months before shooting begins.) Emotional climaxes are rendered very elliptically.

But the reason is really quite different in the two cases. The reason that Brecht rejected acting reflects his idea of the relation of dramatic art to critical intelligence. He thought that the emotional force of the acting would get in the way of the ideas represented in plays. (From what I saw of the work of the Berliner Ensemble six years ago, though, it didn't seem to me that the somewhat low-keyed acting really diminished emotional involvement; it was the highly stylized staging which did that.) The reason that Bresson rejects acting reflects his notion of the purity of the art itself.

"Acting is for the theater, which is a bastard art," he has said. "The film can be a true art because in it the author takes fragments of reality and arranges them in such a way that their juxtaposition transforms them." Cinema, for Bresson, is a total art, in which acting corrodes. In a film,

each shot is like a word, which means nothing by itself, or rather means so many things that in effect it is meaningless. But a word in a poem is transformed, its meaning made precise and unique, by its placing in relation to the words around it: in the same way a shot in a film is given its meaning by its context, and each shot modifies the meaning of the previous one until with the last shot a total, unparaphrasable meaning has been arrived at. Acting has nothing to do with that, it can only get in the way. Films can only be made by bypassing the will of those who appear in them; using not what they do, but what they are.

In sum: there are spiritual resources beyond effort, which appear only when effort is stilled. One imagines that Bresson never treats his actors to an "interpretation" of their roles: Claude Laydu, who plays the priest in Le Journal d'un Curé de Campagne, has said that while he was making the film he was never told to try to represent sanctity, though that is what it appears, when viewing the film, that he does. In the end, everything depends on the actor, who either has this luminous presence or doesn't. Laydu has it. So does François Leterrier, who is Fontaine in Un Condamné à Mort s'est Échappé. But Martin Lassalle as Michel in Pickpocket conveys something wooden, at times evasive. With Florence Carrez in Procès de Jeanne d'Arc, Bresson has experimented with the limit of the unexpressive. There is no acting at all; she simply reads the lines. It could have worked. But it doesn't—because she is the least luminous of all the presences Bresson has "used" in his later films. The thinness of Bresson's last film is, partly, a failure of communicated intensity on the part of the actress who plays Jeanne, upon whom the film depends.

5

All of Bresson's films have a common theme: the meaning of confinement and liberty. The imagery of the religious vocation and of crime are used jointly. Both lead to "the cell."

The plots all have to do with incarceration and its sequel. *Les Anges du Peché* takes place mostly inside a convent. Thérèse, an ex-convict who (unknown to the police) has just murdered the lover who betrayed her, is delivered into the hands of the Bethany nuns. One young novice, who tries to create a special relationship with Thérèse and, learning her secret, to get her to surrender herself voluntarily to the police, is expelled from the convent for insubordination. One morning, she is found dying in the convent garden. Thérèse is finally moved, and the last shot is of her extending her hands to the policeman's manacles. . . . In *Les Dames du Bois de Boulogne*, the metaphor of confinement is repeated several times. Hélène and Jean have been confined in their love; he urges her to return to the world now that she is "free." But she doesn't, and instead devotes herself to setting a trap for him—a trap which requires that she find two pawns (Agnès and. her mother), whom she virtually confines in an apartment while they await her orders. Like *Les Anges du Peché,* this is the story of the redemption of a lost girl. In *Les Anges du Peché*, Thérèse is liberated by accepting imprisonment; in *Les Dames du Bois de Boulogne*, Agnès is imprisoned, and then, arbitrarily, as by a miracle, is forgiven, set free. . . . In *Le Journal d'un Curé de Campagne*, the emphasis has shifted. The bad girl, Chantal, is kept in the background. The drama of confinement is in the priest's confinement in himself, his despair, his weakness, his mortal body. ("I was a prisoner of the Holy Agony.") He is liberated by accepting his senseless and agonizing death from stomach cancer. . . . In *Un Condamné à Mort s'est Échappé,* which is set in a German-run prison in occupied France, confinement is most literally represented. So is liberation: the hero triumphs over himself (his despair, the temptation of inertia) and escapes. The obstacles are embodied both in material things and in the incalculability of the human beings in the vicinity of the solitary hero. But Fontaine risks trusting the two strangers in the courtyard at the beginning of his imprisonment, and his trust is not betrayed. And because he risks trusting the youthful collaborationist who is thrown into his cell with him on the eve of his escape (the alternative is to kill the boy), he is able to get out. . . . In *Pickpocket*, the hero is a young recluse who lives in a closet of a room, a petty criminal who, in Dostoevskian fashion, appears to crave punishment. Only at the end, when he has been caught and is in jail, talking through the bars with the girl who has loved him, is he depicted as being, possibly, able to love. . . . In *Procès de Jeanne d'Arc*, again the entire film is set in prison. As in *Le Journal d'un Curé de Campagne*, Jeanne's liberation comes through a hideous death; but Jeanne's martyrdom is much less affecting than the priest's, because she is so depersonalized (unlike Falconetti's Jeanne in Dreyer's great film) that she does not seem to mind dying.

The nature of drama being conflict, the real drama of Bresson's stories is interior conflict: the fight against oneself. And all the static and formal qualities of his films work to that end. Bresson has said, of his choice of the highly stylized and artificial plot of *Les Dames du Bois de Boulogne*, that it allowed him to "eliminate anything which might distract from the interior drama." Still, in that film and the one before it, interior drama is represented in an exterior form, however fastidious and stripped down. *Les Anges du Peché* and *Les Dames du Bois de Boulogne* depict conflicts of wills among the various characters as much or more than they concern a conflict within the self.

It is only in the films following *Les Dames du Bois de Boulogne* that Bresson's drama has been really interiorized. The theme of *Le Journal d'un Curé de Campagne* is the young priest's conflict with himself: only secondarily is this acted out in his relation with the Vicar of Torcy, with Chantal, and with the Countess, Chantal's mother. This is even clearer in *Un Condamné à Mort s'est Échappé* —where the principal character is literally isolated in a cell, struggling against despair. Solitude and interior conflict pair off in another way in *Pickpocket*, where the solitary hero refuses despair only at the price of refusing love, and gives himself over to masturbatory acts of theft. But in the last film, where we know the drama should be taking place, there is scarcely any evidence of it. Conflict has been virtually suppressed; it must be inferred. Bresson's Jeanne is an automaton of grace. But, however interior the drama, there must be drama. This is what *Procès de Jeanne d'Arc* withholds.

Notice, though, that the "interior drama" which Bresson seeks to depict does not mean psychology. In realistic terms, the motives of Bresson's characters are often hidden, sometimes downright incredible. In *Pickpocket*, for instance, when Michel sums up his two years in London with "I lost all my money on gambling and women," one simply does not believe it. Nor is it any more convincing that during this time the good Jacques, Michel's friend, has made Jeanne pregnant and then deserted her and their child.

Psychological implausibility is scarcely a virtue; and the narrative passages I have just cited are flaws in *Pickpocket*. But what is central to Bresson and, I think, not to be caviled at, is his evident belief that psychological analysis is superficial. (Reason: it assigns to action a paraphrasable meaning that true art transcends.) He does not intend his characters to be implausible, I'm sure; but he does, I think, intend them to be opaque. Bresson is interested in the forms of spiritual action—in the physics, as it were, rather than in the psychology of souls. Why persons behave as they do is, ultimately, not to be understood. (Psychology, precisely, does claim to understand.) Above all, persuasion is inexplicable, unpredictable. That the priest *does* reach the proud and unyielding Countess (in *Le Journal d'un Curé de Campagne*), that Jeanne doesn't persuade Michel (in *Pickpocket*) are just facts—or mysteries, if you like.

Such a physics of the soul was the subject of Simone Weil's most remarkable book, *Gravity and Grace*. And the following sentences of Simone Weil's—

All the natural movements of the soul are controlled by laws analogous to those of physical gravity. Grace is the only exception.

Grace fills empty spaces, but it can only enter where there is a void to receive it, and it is grace itself which makes this void.

The imagination is continually at work filling up all the fissures through which grace might pass.

supply the three basic theorems of Bresson's "anthropology." Some souls are heavy, others light; some are liberated or capable of being liberated, others not. All one can do is be patient, and as empty as possible. In such a regimen there is no place for the imagination, much less for ideas and opinions. The ideal is neutrality, transparence. This is what is meant when the Vicar of Torcy tells the young priest in Le Journal d'un Curé de Campagne, "A priest has no opinions."

Except in an ultimate unrepresentable sense, a priest has no attachments either. In the quest for spiritual lightness ("grace"), attachments are a spiritual encumbrance. Thus, the priest, in the climactic scene of Le Journal d'un Curé de Campagne, forces the Countess to relinquish her passionate mourning for her dead son. True contact between persons is possible, of course; but it comes not through will but unasked for, through grace. Hence in Bresson's films human solidarity is represented only at a distance—as it is between the priest and the Vicar of Torcy in Le Journal d'un Curé de Campagne, or between Fontaine and the other prisoners in Un Condamné à Mort s'est Échappé. The actual coming together of two people in a relation of love can be stated, ushered in, as it were, before our eyes: Jean crying out "Stay! I love you!" to the nearly dead Agnès in Les Dames du Bois de Boulogne; Fontaine putting his arm around Jost in Un Condamné à Mort s'est Échappé; Michel in Pickpocket saying to Jeanne through prison bars, "How long it has taken me to come to you." But we do not see love lived. The moment in which it is declared terminates the film.

In Un Condamné à Mort s'est Échappé, the elderly man in the adjoining cell asks the hero, querulously, "Why do you fight?" Fontaine answers, "To fight. To fight against myself." The true fight against oneself is against one's heaviness, one's gravity. And the instrument of this fight is the idea of work, a project, a task. In Les Anges du Peché, it is Anne-Marie's project of "saving" Thérèse. In Les Dames du Bois de Boulogne, it is the revenge plot of Hélène. These tasks are cast in traditional form—constantly referring back to the intention of the character who performs them, rather than decomposed into separately engrossing acts of behavior. In Le Journal d'un Curé de Campagne (which is transitional in this respect) the most affecting images are not those of the priest in his role, struggling for the souls of his parishioners, but of the priest in his homely moments: riding his bicycle, removing his vestments, eating bread, walking. In Bresson's next two films, work has dissolved into the idea of the-infinite-taking-of-pains. The project has become totally concrete, incarnate, and at the same time more impersonal. In *Un Condamné à Mort s'est Échappé*, the most powerful scenes are those which show the hero absorbed in his labors: Fontaine scraping at his door with the spoon, Fontaine sweeping the wood shavings which have fallen on the floor into a tiny pile with a single straw pulled from his broom. ("One month of patient work—my door opened.") In *Pickpocket*, the emotional center of the film is where Michel is wordlessly, disinterestedly, taken in hand by a professional pickpocket and initiated into the real art of what he has only practiced desultorily: difficult gestures are demonstrated, the necessity of repetition and routine is made clear. Large sections of *Un Condamné à Mort s'est Échappé* and *Pickpocket* are wordless; they are about the beauties of personality effaced by a project. The face is very quiet, while other parts of the body, represented as humble servants of projects, become expressive, transfigured. One remembers Thérèse kissing the white feet of the dead Anne-Marie at the end of *Les Anges du Peché*, the bare feet of the monks filing down the stone corridor in the opening sequence of *Procès de Jeanne d'Arc*. One remembers Fontaine's large graceful hands at their endless labors in *Un Condamné à Mort s'est Échappé*, the ballet of agile thieving hands in *Pickpocket*.

Through the "project"—exactly contrary to "imagination"—one overcomes the gravity that weighs down the spirit. Even *Les Dames du Bois de Boulogne*, whose story seems most un-Bressonian, rests on this contrast between a project and gravity (or, immobility). Hélène has a project—revenging herself on Jean. But she is immobile, too—from suffering and vengefulness. Only in *Procès de Jeanne d'Arc*, the most Bressonian of stories, is this contrast (to the detriment of the film) not exploited. Jeanne has no project. Or if she may be said to have a project, her martyrdom, we only know about it; we are not privy to its development and consummation. She appears to be passive. If only because Jeanne is not portrayed for us in her solitude, alone in her cell, Bresson's last film seems, next to the others, so undialectical.

6

Jean Cocteau has said (*Cocteau on the Film*, A Conversation Recorded by André Fraigneau, 1951) that minds and souls today "live without a syntax, that is to say, without a moral system. This moral system has nothing to do with morality proper, and should be built up by each one of us as an inner style, without which no outer style is possible." Cocteau's films may be understood as portraying this inwardness which is the true morality; so may Bresson's. Both are concerned, in their films, with depicting spiritual style. This similarity is less than obvious because Cocteau conceives of spiritual style aesthetically, while in at least three of his films (*Les Anges du Peché, Le Journal d'un Curé de Campagne*, and *Procès de Jeanne d'Arc*) Bresson seems committed to an explicit religious point of view. But the difference is not as great as it appears. Bresson's Catholicism is a language for rendering a certain vision of human action, rather than a "position" that is stated. (For contrast, compare the direct piety of Rossellini's *The Flowers of Saint Francis* and the complex debate on faith expounded in Melville's *Leon Morin, Prêtre*.) The proof of this is that Bresson is able to say the same thing without Catholicism—in his three other films. In fact, the most entirely successful of all Bresson's films—*Un Condamné à Mort s'est Échappé*—is one which, while it has a sensitive and intelligent priest in the background (one of the prisoners), bypasses the religious way of posing the problem. The religious vocation supplies one setting for ideas about gravity, lucidity, and martyrdom. But the drastically secular subjects of crime, the revenge of betrayed love, and solitary imprisonment also yield the same themes.

Bresson is really more like Cocteau than appears—an ascetic Cocteau, Cocteau divesting himself of sensuousness, Cocteau without poetry. The aim is the same: to build up an image of spiritual style. But the sensibility, needless to say, is altogether different. Cocteau's is a clear example of the homosexual sensibility that is one of the principal traditions of modern art: both romantic and witty, langorously drawn to physical beauty and yet always decorating itself with stylishness and artifice. Bresson's sensibility is antiromantic and solemn, pledged to ward off the easy pleasures of physical beauty and artifice for a pleasure which is more permanent, more edifying, more sincere.

In the evolution of this sensibility, Bresson's cinematic means become more and more chaste. His first two films, which were photographed by Philippe Agostini, stress visual effects in a way that the other four do not. Bresson's very first film, *Les Anges du Peché*, is more conventionally beautiful than any which have followed. And in *Les Dames du Bois de Boulogne*, whose beauty is more muted, there are lyrical camera movements, like the shot which follows Hélène running down the stairs to arrive at the same time as Jean, who is descending in an elevator, and stunning cuts, like the one which moves from Hélène alone in her bedroom, stretched out on the bed, saying, "I will be revenged," to the first shot of Agnès, in a crowded nightclub, wearing tights and net stockings and top hat, in the throes of a sexy dance. Extremes of black and white succeed one another with great deliberateness. In *Les Anges du Peché*, the darkness of the prison scene is set off by the whiteness of the convent wall and of the nuns' robes. In *Les Dames du Bois de Boulogne*, the contrasts are set by clothes even more than by interiors. Hélène always wears long black velvet dresses, whatever the occasion. Agnès has three costumes: the scant black dancing outfit in which she appears the first time, the light-colored trench-coat she wears during most of the film, and the white wedding dress at the end. . . . The last four films, which were photographed by L. H. Burel, are much less striking visually, less chic. The photography is almost self-effacing. Sharp contrasts, as between black and white, are avoided. (It is almost impossible to imagine a Bresson film in color.) In *Le Journal d'un Curé de Campagne*, for instance, one is not particularly aware of the blackness of the priest's habit. One barely notices the bloodstained shirt and dirty pants which Fontaine has on throughout *Un Condamné à Mort s'est Échappé*, or the drab suits which Michel wears in *Pickpocket*. Clothes and interiors are as neutral, inconspicuous, functional as possible.

Besides refusing the visual, Bresson's later films also renounce "the beautiful." None of his non-professional actors are handsome in an outward sense. One's first feeling, when seeing Claude Laydu (the priest in *Le Journal d'un Curé de Campagne*), François Leterrier (Fontaine in *Un Condamné à Mort s'est Échappé*),

Martin Lassalle (Michel in *Pickpocket*), and Florence Carrez (Jeanne in *Procès de Jeanne d'Arc*), is how plain they are. Then, at some point or other, one begins to see the face as strikingly beautiful. The transformation is most profound, and satisfying, with François Leterrier as Fontaine. Here lies an important difference between the films of Cocteau and Bresson, a difference which indicates the special place of *Les Dames du Bois de Boulogne* in Bresson's work; for this film (for which Cocteau wrote the dialogue) is in this respect very Cocteauish. Maria Casarès' black-garbed demonic Hélène is, visually and emotionally, of a piece with her brilliant performance in Cocteau's *Orphée* (1950). Such a hard-edge character, a character with a "motive" that remains constant throughout the story, is very different from the treatment of character, typical of Bresson, in *Le Journal d'un Curé de Campagne*, *Un Condamné à Mort s'est Échappé*, and *Pickpocket*. In the course of each of these three films, there is a subliminal revelation: a face which at first seems plain reveals itself to be beautiful; a character which at first seems opaque becomes oddly and inexplicably transparent. But in Cocteau's films—and in *Les Dames du Bois de Boulogne*—neither character nor beauty is revealed. They are there to be assumed, to be transposed into drama.

While the spiritual style of Cocteau's heroes (who are played, usually, by Jean Marais) tends toward narcissism, the spiritual style of Bresson's heroes is one variety or other of unself-consciousness. (Hence the role of the project in Bresson's films: it absorbs the energies that would otherwise be spent on the self. It effaces personality, in the sense of personality as what is idiosyncratic in each human being, the limit inside which we are locked.) Consciousness of self is the "gravity" that burdens the spirit; the surpassing of the consciousness of self is "grace," or spiritual lightness. The climax of Cocteau's films is a voluptuous movement: a falling down, either in love (*Orphée*) or death (*L'Aigle à Deux Têtes*, *L'Éternel Retour*); or a soaring up (*La Belle et la Bête*). With the exception of *Les Dames du Bois de Boulogne* (with its final glamorous image, shot from above, of Jean bending over Agnès, who lies on the floor like a great white bird), the end of Bresson's films is counter-voluptuous, reserved.

While Cocteau's art is irresistibly drawn to the logic of dreams, and to the truth of invention over the truth of "real life," Bresson's art moves increasingly away from the story and toward documentary. *Le Journal d'un Curé de Campagne* is a fiction, drawn from the superb novel of the same name by Georges Bernanos. But the journal device allows Bresson to relate the fiction in a quasi-documentary fashion. The film opens with a shot of a notebook and a hand writing in it, followed by a voice on the sound track reading what has been written. Many scenes start with the priest writing in his journal. The film ends with a letter from a friend to the Vicar of Torcy relating the priest's death—we hear the words while the whole screen is occupied with the silhouette of a cross. Before *Un Condamné à Mort s'est Échappé* begins we read the words on the screen: "This story actually happened. I have set it down without embellishment," and then: "Lyons, 1943." (Bresson had the original of Fontaine constantly present while the film was being made, to check on its accuracy.) *Pickpocket*, again a fiction, is told—partly—through journal form. Bresson returned to documentary in *Procès de Jeanne d'Arc*, this time with the greatest severity. Even music, which aided in setting tone in the earlier films, has been discarded. The use of the Mozart Mass in C minor in *Un Condamné à Mort s'est Échappé*, of Lully in *Pickpocket*, is particularly brilliant; but all that survives of music in *Procès de Jeanne d'Arc* is the drum beat at the opening of the film.

Bresson's attempt is to insist on the irrefutability of what he is presenting. Nothing happens by chance; there are no alternatives, no fantasy; everything is inexorable. Whatever is not necessary, whatever is merely anecdotal or decorative, must be left out. Unlike Cocteau, Bresson wishes to pare down—rather than to enlarge—the dramatic and visual resources of the cinema. (In this, Bresson again reminds one of Ozu, who in the course of his thirty years of film-making renounced the moving camera, the dissolve, the fade.) True, in the last, most ascetic of all his films, Bresson seems to have left out too much, to have overrefined his conception. But a conception as ambitious as this cannot help but have its extremism, and Bresson's "failures" are worth more than most directors' successes. For Bresson, art is the discovery of what is necessary—of that, and nothing more. The power of Bresson's six films lies in the fact that his purity and fastidiousness are not just an assertion about the resources of the cinema, as much of modern painting is mainly a comment in paint about painting. They are at the same time an idea about life, about what Cocteau called "inner style," about the most serious way of being human.

[1964]

Godard's
Vivre Sa Vie

PREFACE : Vivre Sa Vie invites a rather theoretical treatment, because it is—intellectually, aesthetically—extremely complex. Godard's films are about ideas, in the best, purest, most sophisticated sense in which a work of art can be "about" ideas. I have discovered, while writing these notes, that in an interview in the Paris weekly, L'Express, July 27, 1961, he said: "My three films all have, at bottom, the same subject. I take an individual who has an idea, and who tries to go to the end of his idea." Godard said this after he had made, besides a number of short films, A Bout de Souffle (1959) with Jean Seberg and Jean-Paul Belmondo, Le Petit Soldat (1960) with Michel Subor and Anna Karina, and Une Femme est Une Femme (1961) with Karina, Belmondo, and Jean-Claude Brialy. How this is true of Vivre Sa Vie, his fourth film, which he made in 1962, is what I have attempted to show.

NOTE: Godard, who was born in Paris in 1930, has now completed ten feature films. After the four mentioned above, he made Les Carabiniers (1962-63) with Marino Mase and Albert Juross, Le Mépris (1963) with Brigitte Bardot, Jack Palance, and Fritz Lang, Bande à Part (1964) with Karina, Sami Frey, and Claude Brasseur, Une Femme Mariée (1964) with Macha Méril and Bernard Noël, Alphaville (1965) with Karina, Eddie Constantine, and Akim Tamiroff, and Pierrot le Fou (1965) with Karina and Belmondo. Six of the films have been shown in America. The first called Breathless here, is by now established as an art-house classic; the eighth, The Married Woman, has had a mixed reception; but the others, under the titles A Woman Is a Woman, My Life to Live, Contempt, and Band of Outsiders, have been both critical and box-office flops. The brilliance of A Bout de Souffle is now obvious to everybody and I shall explain my esteem for Vivre Sa Vie. While I am not claiming that all his other work is on the same level of excellence, there is no film of Godard's which does not have many remarkable passages of the highest quality. The obtuseness of serious critics here to the merits of Le Mépris, a deeply flawed but nonetheless extraordinarily ambitious and original film, seems to me particularly lamentable.

1

"The cinema is still a form of graphic art," Cocteau wrote in his Journals. "Through its mediation, I write in pictures, and secure for my own ideology a power in actual fact. I show what others tell. In Orphée, for example, I do not narrate the passing through mirrors; I show it, and in some manner, I prove it. The means I use are not important, if my characters perform publicly what I want them to perform. The greatest power of a film is to be indisputable with respect to the actions it determines and which are carried out before our eyes. It is normal for the witness of an action to transform it for his own use, to distort it, and to testify to it inaccurately. But the action was carried out, and is carried out as often as the machine resurrects it. It combats inexact testimonies and false police reports."

2

All art may be treated as a mode of proof, an assertion of accuracy in the spirit of maximum vehemence. Any work of art may be seen as an attempt to be indisputable with respect to the actions it represents.

3

Proof differs from analysis. Proof establishes that something happened. Analysis shows why it happened. Proof is a mode of argument that is, by definition, complete; but the price of its completeness is that proof is always formal. Only what is already contained in the beginning is proven at the end. In analysis, however, there are always further angles of understanding, new realms of causality. Analysis is substantive. Analysis is a mode of argument that is, by definition, always incomplete; it is, properly speaking, interminable.

The extent to which a given work of art is designed as a mode of proof is, of course, a matter of proportion. Surely, some works of art are more directed toward proof, more based on considerations of form, than others. But still, I should argue, all art tends toward the formal, toward a completeness that must be formal rather than substantive—endings that exhibit grace and design, and only secondarily convince in terms of psychological motives or social forces. (Think of the barely credible but immensely satisfying endings of most of Shakespeare's plays, particularly the comedies.) In great art, it is form—or, as I call it here, the desire to prove rather than the desire to analyze—that is ultimately sovereign. It is form that allows one to terminate.

4

An art concerned with proof is formal in two senses. Its subject is the form (above and beyond the matter) of events, and the forms (above and beyond the matter) of consciousness. Its means are formal; that is, they include a conspicuous element of design (symmetry, repetition, inversion, doubling, etc.). This can be true even when the work is so laden with "content" that it virtually proclaims itself as didactic—like Dante's *Divine Comedy*.

5

Godard's films are particularly directed toward proof, rather than analysis. *Vivre Sa Vie* is an exhibit, a demonstration. It shows *that* something happened, not *why* it happened. It exposes the inexorability of an event.

For this reason, despite appearances, Godard's films are drastically untopical. An art concerned with social, topical issues can never simply show that something is. It must indicate *how*. It must show *why*. But the whole point of *Vivre Sa Vie* is that it does not explain anything. It rejects causality. (Thus, the ordinary causal sequence of narrative is broken in Godard's film by the extremely arbitrary decomposition of the story into twelve episodes—episodes which are serially, rather than causally, related.) *Vivre Sa Vie* is certainly not "about" prostitution, any more than *Le Petit Soldat* is "about" the Algerian War. Neither does Godard in *Vivre Sa Vie* give us any explanation, of an ordinary recognizable sort, as to what led the principal character, Nana, ever to become a prostitute. Is it because she couldn't borrow 2,000 francs toward her back rent from her former husband or from one of her fellow clerks at the record store in which she works and was locked out of her apartment? Hardly that. At least, not that alone. But we scarcely know any more than this. All Godard shows us is that she did become a prostitute. Again, Godard does not show us why, at the end of the film, Nana's pimp Raoul "sells" her, or what has happened between them, or what lies behind the final gun battle in the street in which Nana is killed. He only shows us that she is sold, that she does die. He does not analyze. He proves.

6

Godard uses two means of proof in *Vivre Sa Vie*. He gives us a collection of images illustrating what he wants to prove, and a series of "texts" explaining it. In keeping the two elements separate, Godard's film employs a genuinely novel means of exposition.

7

Godard's intention is Cocteau's. But Godard discerns difficulties, where Cocteau saw none. What Cocteau wanted to show, to be indisputable with reference to, was magic—things like the reality of fascination, the eternal possibility of metamorphosis. (Passing through mirrors, etc.) What Godard wishes to show is the opposite: the anti-magical, the structure of lucidity. This is why Cocteau used techniques that, by means of the alikeness of images, bind together events—to form a total sensuous whole. Godard makes no effort to exploit the beautiful in this sense. He uses techniques that would fragment, dissociate, alienate, break up. Example: the famous staccato editing (jump cuts et al.) in *A Bout de Souffle*. Another example: the division of *Vivre Sa Vie* into twelve episodes, with long titles like chapter headings at the beginning of each episode, telling us more or less what is going to happen.

The rhythm of *Vivre Sa Vie* is stopping-and-starting. (In another style, this is also the rhythm of *Le Mépris*.) Hence, *Vivre Sa Vie* is divided into separate episodes. Hence, too, the repeated halting and resuming of the music in the credit sequence; and the abrupt presentation of Nana's face—first in left profile, then (without transition) full face, then (again without transition) in right profile. But, above all, there is the dissociation of word and image which runs through the entire film, permitting quite separate accumulations of intensity for both idea and feeling.

8

Throughout the history of film, image and word have worked in tandem. In the silent film, the word—set down in the form of titles—alternated with, literally linked together, the sequences of images. With the advent of sound films, image and word became simultaneous rather than successive. While in silent films the word could be either comment on the action or dialogue by the participants in the action, in sound films the word became (except for documentaries) almost exclusively, certainly preponderantly dialogue.

Godard restores the dissociation of word and image characteristic of silent film, but on a new level. *Vivre Sa Vie* is clearly composed of two discrete types of material, the seen and the heard. But in the distinguishing of these materials, Godard is very ingenious, even playful. One variant is the television documentary or *cinéma-vérité* style of Episode VIII—while one is taken, first, on a car ride through Paris, then sees, in rapid montage, shots of a dozen clients, one hears a dry flat voice rapidly detailing the routine, hazards, and appalling arduousness of the prostitute's vocation. Another variant is in Episode XII, where the happy banalities exchanged by Nana and her young lover are projected on the screen in the form of subtitles. The speech of love is not heard at all.

9

Thus, *Vivre Sa Vie* must be seen as an extension of a particular cinematic genre: the narrated film. There are two standard forms of this genre, which give us images plus a text. In one, an impersonal voice, the author, as it were, narrates the film. In the other, we hear the interior monologue of the main character, narrating the events as we see them happening to him.

Two examples of the first type, featuring an anonymous commenting voice which oversees the action, are Resnais' *L'Année Dernière à Marienbad* and Melville's *Les Enfants Terribles*. An example of the second type, featuring an interior monologue of the main character, is Franju's *Thérèse Desqueyroux*. Probably the greatest examples of the second type, in which the entire action is recited by the hero, are Bresson's *Le Journal d'un Curé de Campagne* and *Un Condamné à Mort s'est Échappé*.

Godard used the technique brought to perfection by Bresson in his second film, *Le Petit Soldat*, made in 1960 in Geneva though not released (because for three years it was banned by the French censors) until January 1963. The film is the sequence of the reflections of the hero, Bruno Forestier, a man embroiled in a right-wing terrorist organization who is assigned the job of killing a Swiss agent for the FLN. As the film opens, one hears Forestier's voice saying: "The time for action is passed. I have grown older. The time for reflection has come." Bruno is a photographer. He says, "To photograph a face is to photograph the soul behind it. Photography is truth. And the cinema is the truth twenty-four times a second." This central passage in *Le Petit Soldat*, in which Bruno meditates on the relation between the image and truth, anticipates the complex meditation on the relation between language and truth in *Vivre Sa Vie*.

Since the story itself in *Le Petit Soldat*, the factual connections between the characters, are mostly conveyed through Forestier's monologue, Godard's camera is freed to become an instrument of contemplation—of certain aspects of events, and of characters. Quiet "events"—Karina's face, the façade of buildings, passing through the city by car—are studied by the camera, in a way that somewhat isolates the violent action. The images seem arbitrary sometimes, expressing a kind of emotional neutrality; at other times, they indicate an intense involvement. It is as though Godard hears, then looks at what he hears.

In Vivre Sa Vie, Godard takes this technique of hearing first, then seeing, to new levels of complexity. There is no longer a single unified point of view, either the protagonist's voice (as in Le Petit Soldat) or a godlike narrator, but a series of documents (texts, narrations, quotations, excerpts, set pieces) of various description. These are primarily words; but they may also be worldless sounds, or even wordless images.

10

All the essentials of Godard's technique are present in the opening credit sequence and in the first episode. The credits occur over a left profile view of Nana, so dark that it is almost a silhouette. (The title of the film is Vivre Sa Vie. A Film in Twelve Episodes.) As the credits continue, she is shown full face, and then from the right side, still in deep shadow. Occasionally she blinks or shifts her head slightly (as if it were uncomfortable to hold still so long), or wets her lips. Nana is posing. She is being seen.

Next we are given the first titles. "Episode I: Nana and Paul. Nana Feels Like Giving Up." Then the images begin, but the emphasis is on what is heard. The film proper opens in the midst of a conversation between Nana and a man; they are seated at the counter of a café; their backs are to the camera; besides their conversation, we hear the noises of the barman, and snatches of the voices of other customers. As they talk, always facing away from the camera, we learn that the man (Paul) is Nana's husband, that they have a child, and that she has recently left both husband and child to try to become an actress. In this brief public reunion (it is never clear on whose initiative it came about) Paul is stiff and hostile, but wants her to come back; Nana is oppressed, desperate, and revolted by him. After weary, bitter words, Nana says to Paul, "The more you talk, the less it means." Throughout this opening sequence, Godard systematically deprives the viewer. There is no cross-cutting. The viewer is not allowed to see, to become involved. He is only allowed to hear.

Only after Nana and Paul break off their fruitless conversation to leave the counter and play a game at the pinball machine, do we see them. Even here, the emphasis remains on hearing. As they go on talking, we continue to see Nana and Paul mainly from behind. Paul has stopped pleading and being rancorous. He tells Nana of the droll theme his father, a schoolteacher, received from one of his pupils on an assigned topic, The Chicken. "The chicken has an inside and an outside," wrote the little girl. "Remove the outside and you find the inside. Remove the inside, and you find the soul." On these words, the image dissolves and the episode ends.

11

The story of the chicken is the first of many "texts" in the film which establish what Godard wants to say. For the story of the chicken, of course, is the story of Nana. (There is a pun in French —the French *poule* being something like, but a good deal rougher than, the American "chick.") In *Vivre Sa Vie*, we witness the stripping down of Nana. The film opens with Nana having divested herself of her outside: her old identity. Her new identity, within a few episodes, is to be that of a prostitute. But Godard's interest is in neither the psychology nor the sociology of prostitution. He takes up prostitution as the most radical metaphor for the separating out of the elements of a life—as a testing ground, a crucible for the study of what is essential and what is superfluous in a life.

12

The whole of *Vivre Sa Vie* may be seen as a text. It is a text in, a study of, lucidity; it is about seriousness.

And it "uses" texts (in the more literal sense), in all but two of its twelve episodes. The little girl's essay on the chicken told by Paul in Episode I. The passage from the pulp magazine story recited by the salesgirl in Episode II. ("You exaggerate the importance of logic.") The excerpt from Dreyer's *Jeanne d'Arc* which Nana watches in Episode III. The story of the theft of 1,000 francs which Nana relates to the police inspector in Episode IV. (We learn that her full name is Nana Klein and that she was born in 1940.) Yvette's story—how she was abandoned by Raymond two years ago—and Nana's speech in reply ("I am responsible") in Episode VI. The letter of application Nana composes to the madam of a brothel in Episode VII. The documentary narration of the life and routine of the prostitute in Episode VIII. The record of dance music in Episode IX. The conversation with the philosopher in Episode XI. The excerpt from the story by Edgar Allan Poe ("The Oval Portrait") read aloud by Luigi in Episode XII.

13

The most elaborate, intellectually, of all the texts in the film is the conversation in Episode XI between Nana and a philosopher (played by the philosopher, Brice Parain) in a café. They discuss the nature of language. Nana asks why one can't live without words; Parain explains that it is because talking equals thinking, and thinking talking, and there is no life without thought. It is not a question of speaking or not speaking, but of speaking well. Speaking well demands an ascetic discipline (*une ascèse*), detachment. One has to understand, for one thing, that there is no going straight at the truth. One needs error.

Early in their conversation, Parain relates the story of Dumas' Porthos, the man of action, whose first thought killed him. (Running away from a dynamite charge he had planted, Porthos suddenly wondered how one could walk, how anyone ever placed one foot in front of the other. He stopped. The dynamite exploded. He was killed.) There is a sense in which this story, too, like the story of the chicken, is about Nana. And through both the story and the Poe tale told in the next (and last) episode, we are being prepared—formally, not substantively—for Nana's death.

14

Godard takes his motto for this film-essay on freedom and responsibility from Montaigne: "Lend yourself to others; give yourself to yourself." The life of the prostitute is, of course, the most radical metaphor for the act of lending oneself to others. But if we ask, how has Godard shown us Nana keeping herself for herself, the answer is: he has *not* shown it. He has, rather, expounded on it. We don't know Nana's motives except at a distance, by inference. The film eschews all psychology; there is no probing of states of feeling, of inner anguish.

Nana knows herself to be free, Godard tells us. But that freedom has no psychological interior. Freedom is not an inner, psychological something—but more like physical grace. It is being *what, who* one is. In Episode I, Nana says to Paul, "I want to die." In Episode II, we see her desperately trying to borrow money, trying unsuccessfully to force her way past the concierge and get into her own apartment. In Episode III, we see her weeping in the cinema over Jeanne d'Arc. In Episode IV, at the police station, she weeps again as she relates the humiliating incident of the theft of 1,000 francs. "I wish I were someone else," she says. But in Episode V ("On the Street. The First Client") Nana has become what she is. She has entered the road that leads to her affirmation and to her death. Only as prostitute do we see a Nana who can affirm herself. This is the meaning of Nana's speech to her fellow prostitute Yvette in Episode VI, in which she declares serenely, "I am responsible. I turn my head, I am responsible. I lift my hand, I am responsible."

Being free means being responsible. One is free, and therefore responsible, when one realizes that things are as they are. Thus, the speech to Yvette ends with the words: "A plate is a plate. A man is a man. Life is . . . life."

15

That freedom has no psychological interior—that the soul is something to be found not upon but after stripping away the "inside" of a person—is the radical spiritual doctrine which *Vivre Sa Vie* illustrates.

One would guess that Godard is quite aware of the difference between his sense of the "soul" and the traditional Christian one. The difference is precisely underscored by the quotation from

Dreyer's *Jeanne d'Arc*; for the scene which we see is the one in which the young priest (played by Antonin Artaud) comes to tell Jeanne (Mlle Falconetti) that she is to be burned at the stake. Her martyrdom, Jeanne assures the distraught priest, is really her deliverance. While the choice of a quotation from a film does distance our emotional involvement with these ideas and feelings, the reference to martyrdom is not ironic in this context. Prostitution, as *Vivre Sa Vie* allows us to see it, has entirely the character of an ordeal. "Pleasure isn't all fun," as the title to Episode X announces laconically. And Nana does die.

The twelve episodes of *Vivre Sa Vie* are Nana's twelve stations of the cross. But in Godard's film the values of sanctity and martyrdom are transposed to a totally secular plane. Godard offers us Montaigne instead of Pascal, something akin to the mood and intensity of Bressonian spirituality but without Catholicism.

16

The one false step in *Vivre Sa Vie* comes at the end, when Godard breaks the unity of his film by referring to it from the outside, as maker. Episode XII begins with Nana and Luigi in a room together; he is a young man with whom she has apparently fallen in love (we have seen him once before, in Episode IX, when Nana meets him in a billiard parlor and flirts with him). At first the scene is silent, and the dialogue—"Shall we go out?" "Why don't you move in with me?" etc.—rendered in subtitles. Then Luigi, lying on the bed, begins to read aloud from Poe's "The Oval Portrait," a story about an artist engaged in painting a portrait of his wife; he strives for the perfect likeness, but at the moment he finally achieves it his wife dies. The scene fades out on these words, and opens to show Raoul, Nana's pimp, roughly forcing her through the courtyard of her apartment house, pushing her into a car. After a car ride (one or two brief images), Raoul hands Nana over to another pimp; but it is discovered that the money exchanged is not enough, guns are drawn, Nana is shot, and the last image shows the cars speeding away and Nana lying dead in the street.

What is objectionable here is not the abruptness of the ending.

It is the fact that Godard is clearly making a reference outside the film, to the fact that the young actress who plays Nana, Anna Karina, is his wife. He is mocking his own tale, which is unforgivable. It amounts to a peculiar failure of nerve, as if Godard did not dare to let us have Nana's death—in all its horrifying arbitrariness—but had to provide, at the last moment, a kind of subliminal causality. (The woman is my wife.—The artist who portrays his wife kills her.—Nana must die.)

17

This one lapse aside, *Vivre Sa Vie* seems to me a perfect film. That is, it sets out to do something that is both noble and intricate, and wholly succeeds in doing it. Godard is perhaps the only director today who is interested in "philosophical films" and possessses an intelligence and discretion equal to the task. Other directors have had their "views" on contemporary society and the nature of our humanity; and sometimes their films survive the ideas they propose. Godard is the first director fully to grasp the fact that, in order to deal seriously with ideas, one must create a new film language for expressing them—if the ideas are to have any suppleness and complexity. This he has been trying to do in different ways: in *Le Petit Soldat*, *Vivre Sa Vie*, *Les Carabiniers*, *Le Mépris*, *Une Femme Mariée*, and *Alphaville*—*Vivre Sa Vie* being, I think, his most successful film. For this conception, and the formidable body of work in which he has pursued it, Godard is in my opinion the most important director to have emerged in the last ten years.

APPENDIX: The advertisement drawn up by Godard when the film was first released in Paris:

VIVRE SA VIE

Un	Une
Film	Série
Sur	D'Aventures
La	Qui
Prostitution	Lui
Qui	Font
Raconte	Connaître
Comment	Tous
Une	Les
Jeune	Sentiments
Et	Humains
Jolie	Profonds
Vendeuse	Possibles
Parisienne	Et
Donne	Qui
Son	Ont
Corps	Eté
Mais	Filmés
Garde	Par
Son	Jean-Luc
Ame	Godard
Alors	Et
Qu'elle	Joués
Traverse	Par
Comme	Anna Karina
Des	Vivre
Apparences	Sa Vie

[1964]

The imagination
of disaster

THE typical science fiction film has a form as predictable as a Western, and is made up of elements which, to a practiced eye, are as classic as the saloon brawl, the blonde schoolteacher from the East, and the gun duel on the deserted main street.

One model scenario proceeds through five phases.

(1) The arrival of the thing. (Emergence of the monsters, landing of the alien spaceship, etc.) This is usually witnessed or suspected by just one person, a young scientist on a field trip. Nobody, neither his neighbors nor his colleagues, will believe him for some time. The hero is not married, but has a sympathetic though also incredulous girl friend.

(2) Confirmation of the hero's report by a host of witnesses to a great act of destruction. (If the invaders are beings from another planet, a fruitless attempt to parley with them and get them to

leave peacefully.) The local police are summoned to deal with the situation and massacred.

(3) In the capital of the country, conferences between scientists and the military take place, with the hero lecturing before a chart, map, or blackboard. A national emergency is declared. Reports of further destruction. Authorities from other countries arrive in black limousines. All international tensions are suspended in view of the planetary emergency. This stage often includes a rapid montage of news broadcasts in various languages, a meeting at the UN, and more conferences between the military and the scientists. Plans are made for destroying the enemy.

(4) Further atrocities. At some point the hero's girl friend is in grave danger. Massive counter-attacks by international forces, with brilliant displays of rocketry, rays, and other advanced weapons, are all unsuccessful. Enormous military casualties, usually by incineration. Cities are destroyed and/or evacuated. There is an obligatory scene here of panicked crowds stampeding along a highway or a big bridge, being waved on by numerous policemen who, if the film is Japanese, are immaculately white-gloved, preternaturally calm, and call out in dubbed English, "Keep moving. There is no need to be alarmed."

(5) More conferences, whose motif is: "They must be vulnerable to something." Throughout the hero has been working in his lab to this end. The final strategy, upon which all hopes depend, is drawn up; the ultimate weapon—often a super-powerful, as yet untested, nuclear device—is mounted. Countdown. Final repulse of the monster or invaders. Mutual congratulations, while the hero and girl friend embrace cheek to cheek and scan the skies sturdily. "But have we seen the last of them?"

The film I have just described should be in color and on a wide screen. Another typical scenario, which follows, is simpler and suited to black-and-white films with a lower budget. It has four phases.

(1) The hero (usually, but not always, a scientist) and his girl friend, or his wife and two children, are disporting themselves in some innocent ultra-normal middle-class surroundings—their house

in a small town, or on vacation (camping, boating). Suddenly, someone starts behaving strangely; or some innocent form of vegetation becomes monstrously enlarged and ambulatory. If a character is pictured driving an automobile, something gruesome looms up in the middle of the road. If it is night, strange lights hurtle across the sky.

(2) After following the thing's tracks, or determining that It is radioactive, or poking around a huge crater—in short, conducting some sort of crude investigation—the hero tries to warn the local authorities, without effect; nobody believes anything is amiss. The hero knows better. If the thing is tangible, the house is elaborately barricaded. If the invading alien is an invisible parasite, a doctor or friend is called in, who is himself rather quickly killed or "taken possession of" by the thing.

(3) The advice of whoever further is consulted proves useless. Meanwhile, It continues to claim other victims in the town, which remains implausibly isolated from the rest of the world. General helplessness.

(4) One of two possibilities. Either the hero prepares to do battle alone, accidentally discovers the thing's one vulnerable point, and destroys it. Or, he somehow manages to get out of town and succeeds in laying his case before competent authorities. They, along the lines of the first script but abridged, deploy a complex technology which (after initial setbacks) finally prevails against the invaders.

Another version of the second script opens with the scientist-hero in his laboratory, which is located in the basement or on the grounds of his tasteful, prosperous house. Through his experiments, he unwittingly causes a frightful metamorphosis in some class of plants or animals which turn carnivorous and go on a rampage. Or else, his experiments have caused him to be injured (sometimes irrevocably) or "invaded" himself. Perhaps he has been experimenting with radiation, or has built a machine to communicate with beings from other planets or transport him to other places or times.

Another version of the first script involves the discovery of some fundamental alteration in the conditions of existence of our planet, brought about by nuclear testing, which will lead to the extinction in a few months of all human life. For example: the temperature of the earth is becoming too high or too low to support life, or the earth is cracking in two, or it is gradually being blanketed by lethal fallout.

A third script, somewhat but not altogether different from the first two, concerns a journey through space—to the moon, or some other planet. What the space-voyagers discover commonly is that the alien terrain is in a state of dire emergency, itself threatened by extra-planetary invaders or nearing extinction through the practice of nuclear warfare. The terminal dramas of the first and second scripts are played out there, to which is added the problem of getting away from the doomed and/or hostile planet and back to Earth.

I am aware, of course, that there are thousands of science fiction novels (their heyday was the late 1940s), not to mention the transcriptions of science fiction themes which, more and more, provide the principal subject-matter of comic books. But I propose to discuss science fiction films (the present period began in 1950 and continues, considerably abated, to this day) as an independent sub-genre, without reference to other media—and, most particularly, without reference to the novels from which, in many cases, they were adapted. For, while novel and film may share the same plot, the fundamental difference between the resources of the novel and the film makes them quite dissimilar.

Certainly, compared with the science fiction novels, their film counterparts have unique strengths, one of which is the immediate representation of the extraordinary: physical deformity and mutation, missile and rocket combat, toppling skyscrapers. The movies are, naturally, weak just where the science fiction novels (some of them) are strong—on science. But in place of an intellectual work-out, they can supply something the novels can never provide—sensuous elaboration. In the films it is by means of images and sounds, not words that have to be translated by the imagination, that one can participate in the fantasy of living through one's own death and more, the death of cities, the destruction of humanity itself.

Science fiction films are not about science. They are about disaster, which is one of the oldest subjects of art. In science fiction films disaster is rarely viewed intensively; it is always extensive. It is a matter of quantity and ingenuity. If you will, it is a question of scale. But the scale, particularly in the wide-screen color films (of which the ones by the Japanese director Inoshiro Honda and the American director George Pal are technically the most convincing and visually the most exciting), does raise the matter to another level.

Thus, the science fiction film (like that of a very different contemporary genre, the Happening) is concerned with the aesthetics of destruction, with the peculiar beauties to be found in wreaking havoc, making a mess. And it is in the imagery of destruction that the core of a good science fiction film lies. Hence, the disadvantage of the cheap film—in which the monster appears or the rocket lands in a small dull-looking town. (Hollywood budget needs usually dictate that the town be in the Arizona or California desert. In *The Thing From Another World* [1951] the rather sleazy and confined set is supposed to be an encampment near the North Pole.) Still, good black-and-white science fiction films have been made. But a bigger budget, which usually means color, allows a much greater play back and forth among several model environments. There is the populous city. There is the lavish but ascetic interior of the spaceship—either the invaders' or ours—replete with streamlined chromium fixtures and dials and machines whose complexity is indicated by the number of colored lights they flash and strange noises they emit. There is the laboratory crowded with formidable boxes and scientific apparatus. There is a comparatively old-fashioned-looking conference room, where the scientists unfurl charts to explain the desperate state of things to the military. And each of these standard locales or backgrounds is subject to two modalities—intact and destroyed. We may, if we are lucky, be treated to a panorama of melting tanks, flying bodies, crashing walls, awesome craters and fissures in the earth, plummeting spacecraft, colorful deadly rays; and to a symphony of screams, weird electronic signals, the noisiest military hardware going, and the leaden tones of the laconic denizens of alien planets and their subjugated earthlings.

Certain of the primitive gratifications of science fiction films—
for instance, the depiction of urban disaster on a colossally magni-
fied scale—are shared with other types of films. Visually there
is little difference between mass havoc as represented in the old
horror and monster films and what we find in science fiction films,
except (again) scale. In the old monster films, the monster always
headed for the great city, where he had to do a fair bit of rampag-
ing, hurling busses off bridges, crumpling trains in his bare hands,
toppling buildings, and so forth. The archetype is King Kong, in
Schoedsack and Cooper's great film of 1933, running amok, first in
the native village (trampling babies, a bit of footage excised from
most prints), then in New York. This is really no different in spirit
from the scene in Inoshiro Honda's *Rodan* (1957) in which two
giant reptiles—with a wingspan of 500 feet and supersonic speeds—
by flapping their wings whip up a cyclone that blows most of Tokyo
to smithereens. Or the destruction of half of Japan by the gigantic
robot with the great incinerating ray that shoots forth from his eyes,
at the beginning of Honda's *The Mysterians* (1959). Or, the dev-
astation by the rays from a fleet of flying saucers of New York,
Paris, and Tokyo, in *Battle in Outer Space* (1960). Or, the inunda-
tion of New York in *When Worlds Collide* (1951). Or, the end
of London in 1966 depicted in George Pal's *The Time Machine*
(1960). Neither do these sequences differ in aesthetic intention
from the destruction scenes in the big sword, sandal, and orgy
color spectaculars set in Biblical and Roman times—the end of
Sodom in Aldrich's *Sodom and Gomorrah*, of Gaza in De Mille's
Samson and Delilah, of Rhodes in *The Colossus of Rhodes*, and of
Rome in a dozen Nero movies. Griffith began it with the Babylon
sequence in *Intolerance*, and to this day there is nothing like the
thrill of watching all those expensive sets come tumbling down.

In other respects as well, the science fiction films of the 1950s
take up familiar themes. The famous 1930s movie serials and comics
of the adventures of Flash Gordon and Buck Rogers, as well as
the more recent spate of comic book super-heroes with extrater-
restrial origins (the most famous is Superman, a foundling from
the planet Krypton, currently described as having been exploded by
a nuclear blast), share motifs with more recent science fiction

movies. But there is an important difference. The old science fiction films, and most of the comics, still have an essentially innocent relation to disaster. Mainly they offer new versions of the oldest romance of all—of the strong invulnerable hero with a mysterious lineage come to do battle on behalf of good and against evil. Recent science fiction films have a decided grimness, bolstered by their much greater degree of visual credibility, which contrasts strongly with the older films. Modern historical reality has greatly enlarged the imagination of disaster, and the protagonists—perhaps by the very nature of what is visited upon them—no longer seem wholly innocent.

The lure of such generalized disaster as a fantasy is that it releases one from normal obligations. The trump card of the end-of-the-world movies—like *The Day the Earth Caught Fire* (1962)—is that great scene with New York or London or Tokyo discovered empty, its entire population annihilated. Or, as in *The World, The Flesh, and The Devil* (1957), the whole movie can be devoted to the fantasy of occupying the deserted metropolis and starting all over again, a world Robinson Crusoe.

Another kind of satisfaction these films supply is extreme moral simplification—that is to say, a morally acceptable fantasy where one can give outlet to cruel or at least amoral feelings. In this respect, science fiction films partly overlap with horror films. This is the undeniable pleasure we derive from looking at freaks, beings excluded from the category of the human. The sense of superiority over the freak conjoined in varying proportions with the titillation of fear and aversion makes it possible for moral scruples to be lifted, for cruelty to be enjoyed. The same thing happens in science fiction films. In the figure of the monster from outer space, the freakish, the ugly, and the predatory all converge—and provide a fantasy target for righteous bellicosity to discharge itself, and for the aesthetic enjoyment of suffering and disaster. Science fiction films are one of the purest forms of spectacle; that is, we are rarely inside anyone's feelings. (An exception is Jack Arnold's *The Incredible Shrinking Man* [1957].) We are merely spectators; we watch.

But in science fiction films, unlike horror films, there is not much horror. Suspense, shocks, surprises are mostly abjured in favor of a steady, inexorable plot. Science fiction films invite a dispassionate, aesthetic view of destruction and violence—a technological view. Things, objects, machinery play a major role in these films. A greater range of ethical values is embodied in the décor of these films than in the people. Things, rather than the helpless humans, are the locus of values because we experience them, rather than people, as the sources of power. According to science fiction films, man is naked without his artifacts. They stand for different values, they are potent, they are what get destroyed, and they are the indispensable tools for the repulse of the alien invaders or the repair of the damaged environment.

The science fiction films are strongly moralistic. The standard message is the one about the proper, or humane, use of science, versus the mad, obsessional use of science. This message the science fiction films share in common with the classic horror films of the 1930s, like *Frankenstein, The Mummy, Island of Lost Souls, Dr. Jekyll and Mr. Hyde.* (Georges Franju's brilliant *Les Yeux Sans Visage* [1959], called here *The Horror Chamber of Doctor Faustus,* is a more recent example.) In the horror films, we have the mad or obsessed or misguided scientist who pursues his experiments against good advice to the contrary, creates a monster or monsters, and is himself destroyed—often recognizing his folly himself, and dying in the successful effort to destroy his own creation. One science fiction equivalent of this is the scientist, usually a member of a team, who defects to the planetary invaders because "their" science is more advanced than "ours."

This is the case in *The Mysterians,* and, true to form, the renegade sees his error in the end, and from within the Mysterian space ship destroys it and himself. In *This Island Earth* (1955), the inhabitants of the beleaguered planet Metaluna propose to conquer earth, but their project is foiled by a Metalunan scientist named Exeter who, having lived on earth a while and learned to love Mozart, cannot abide such viciousness. Exeter plunges his spaceship into the ocean after returning a glamorous pair (male and female) of American physicists to earth. Metaluna dies. In *The Fly*

(1958), the hero, engrossed in his basement-laboratory experiments on a matter-transmitting machine, uses himself as a subject, exchanges head and one arm with a housefly which had accidentally gotten into the machine, becomes a monster, and with his last shred of human will destroys his laboratory and orders his wife to kill him. His discovery, for the good of mankind, is lost.

Being a clearly labeled species of intellectual, scientists in science fiction films are always liable to crack up or go off the deep end. In *Conquest of Space* (1955), the scientist-commander of an international expedition to Mars suddenly acquires scruples about the blasphemy involved in the undertaking, and begins reading the Bible mid-journey instead of attending to his duties. The commander's son, who is his junior officer and always addresses his father as "General," is forced to kill the old man when he tries to prevent the ship from landing on Mars. In this film, both sides of the ambivalence toward scientists are given voice. Generally, for a scientific enterprise to be treated entirely sympathetically in these films, it needs the certificate of utility. Science, viewed without ambivalence, means an efficacious response to danger. Disinterested intellectual curiosity rarely appears in any form other than caricature, as a maniacal dementia that cuts one off from normal human relations. But this suspicion is usually directed at the scientist rather than his work. The creative scientist may become a martyr to his own discovery, through an accident or by pushing things too far. But the implication remains that other men, less imaginative—in short, technicians—could have administered the same discovery better and more safely. The most ingrained contemporary mistrust of the intellect is visited, in these movies, upon the scientist-as-intellectual.

The message that the scientist is one who releases forces which, if not controlled for good, could destroy man himself seems innocuous enough. One of the oldest images of the scientist is Shakespeare's Prospero, the overdetached scholar forcibly retired from society to a desert island, only partly in control of the magic forces in which he dabbles. Equally classic is the figure of the scientist as satanist (*Doctor Faustus*, and stories of Poe and Hawthorne). Science is magic, and man has always known that there is black magic as well as white. But it is not enough to remark that contemporary attitudes—as reflected in science fiction films—remain ambivalent, that the scientist is treated as both satanist and savior. The proportions have changed, because of the new context in which the old admiration and fear of the scientist are located. For his sphere of influence is no longer local, himself or his immediate community. It is planetary, cosmic.

One gets the feeling, particularly in the Japanese films but not only there, that a mass trauma exists over the use of nuclear weapons and the possibility of future nuclear wars. Most of the science fiction films bear witness to this trauma, and, in a way, attempt to exorcise it.

The accidental awakening of the super-destructive monster who has slept in the earth since prehistory is, often, an obvious metaphor for the Bomb. But there are many explicit references as well. In The Mysterians, a probe ship from the planet Mysteroid has landed on earth, near Tokyo. Nuclear warfare having been practiced on Mysteroid for centuries (their civilization is "more advanced than ours"), ninety percent of those now born on the planet have to be destroyed at birth, because of defects caused by the huge amounts of Strontium 90 in their diet. The Mysterians have come to earth to marry earth women, and possibly to take over our relatively un-contaminated planet . . . In The Incredible Shrinking Man, the John Doe hero is the victim of a gust of radiation which blows over the water, while he is out boating with his wife; the radiation causes him to grow smaller and smaller, until at the end of the movie he steps through the fine mesh of a window screen to become "the infinitely small." . . . In Rodan, a horde of monstrous carnivorous prehistoric insects, and finally a pair of giant flying reptiles (the prehistoric Archeopteryx), are hatched from dormant eggs in the depths of a mine shaft by the impact of nuclear test explosions, and go on to destroy a good part of the world before they are felled by the molten lava of a volcanic eruption. . . . In the English film, The Day the Earth Caught Fire, two simultaneous hydrogen bomb tests by the United States and Russia change by 11 degrees the tilt of the earth on its axis and alter the earth's orbit so that it begins to approach the sun.

Radiation casualties—ultimately, the conception of the whole world as a casualty of nuclear testing and nuclear warfare—is the most ominous of all the notions with which science fiction films deal. Universes become expendable. Worlds become contaminated, burnt out, exhausted, obsolete. In *Rocketship X-M* (1950) explorers from the earth land on Mars, where they learn that atomic warfare has destroyed Martian civilization. In George Pal's *The War of the Worlds* (1953), reddish spindly alligator-skinned creatures from Mars invade the earth because their planet is becoming too cold to be inhabitable. In *This Island Earth*, also American, the planet Metaluna, whose population has long ago been driven underground by warfare, is dying under the missile attacks of an enemy planet. Stocks of uranium, which power the force field shielding Metaluna, have been used up; and an unsuccessful expedition is sent to earth to enlist earth scientists to devise new sources for nuclear power. In Joseph Losey's *The Damned* (1961), nine icy-cold radioactive children are being reared by a fanatical scientist in a dark cave on the English coast to be the only survivors of the inevitable nuclear Armageddon.

There is a vast amount of wishful thinking in science fiction films, some of it touching, some of it depressing. Again and again, one detects the hunger for a "good war," which poses no moral problems, admits of no moral qualifications. The imagery of science fiction films will satisfy the most bellicose addict of war films, for a lot of the satisfactions of war films pass, untransformed, into science fiction films. Examples: the dogfights between earth "fighter rockets" and alien spacecraft in the *Battle in Outer Space* (1960); the escalating firepower in the successive assaults upon the invaders in *The Mysterians*, which Dan Talbot correctly described as a non-stop holocaust; the spectacular bombardment of the underground fortress of Metaluna in *This Island Earth*.

Yet at the same time the bellicosity of science fiction films is neatly channeled into the yearning for peace, or for at least peaceful coexistence. Some scientist generally takes sententious note of the fact that it took the planetary invasion to make the warring nations of the earth come to their senses and suspend their own conflicts. One of the main themes of many science fiction films—the color ones usually, because they have the budget and resources to develop the military spectacle—is this UN fantasy, a fantasy of united warfare. (The same wishful UN theme cropped up in a recent spectacular which is not science fiction, *Fifty-Five Days in Peking* [1963]. There, topically enough, the Chinese, the Boxers, play the role of Martian invaders who unite the earthmen, in this case the United States, England, Russia, France, Germany, Italy, and Japan.) A great enough disaster cancels all enmities and calls upon the utmost concentration of earth resources.

Science—technology—is conceived of as the great unifier. Thus the science fiction films also project a Utopian fantasy. In the classic models of Utopian thinking—Plato's Republic, Campanella's City of the Sun, More's Utopia, Swift's land of the Houyhnhnms, Voltaire's Eldorado—society had worked out a perfect consensus. In these societies reasonableness had achieved an unbreakable supremacy over the emotions. Since no disagreement or social conflict was intellectually plausible, none was possible. As in Melville's *Typee*, "they all think the same." The universal rule of reason meant universal agreement. It is interesting, too, that societies in which reason was pictured as totally ascendant were also traditionally pictured as having an ascetic or materially frugal and economically simple mode of life. But in the Utopian world community projected by science fiction films, totally pacified and ruled by scientific consensus, the demand for simplicity of material existence would be absurd.

Yet alongside the hopeful fantasy of moral simplification and international unity embodied in the science fiction films lurk the deepest anxieties about contemporary existence. I don't mean only the very real trauma of the Bomb—that it has been used, that there are enough now to kill everyone on earth many times over, that those new bombs may very well be used. Besides these new anxieties about physical disaster, the prospect of universal mutilation and even annihilation, the science fiction films reflect powerful anxieties about the condition of the individual psyche.

For science fiction films may also be described as a popular mythology for the contemporary negative imagination about the impersonal. The other-world creatures that seek to take "us" over are an "it," not a "they." The planetary invaders are usually zombie-like. Their movements are either cool, mechanical, or lumbering, blobby. But it amounts to the same thing. If they are non-human in form, they proceed with an absolutely regular, unalterable movement (unalterable save by destruction). If they are human in form —dressed in space suits, etc.—then they obey the most rigid military discipline, and display no personal characteristics whatsoever. And it is this regime of emotionlessness, of impersonality, of regimentation, which they will impose on the earth if they are successful. "No more love, no more beauty, no more pain," boasts a converted earthling in The Invasion of the Body Snatchers (1956). The half-earthling, half-alien children in The Children of the Damned (1960) are absolutely emotionless, move as a group and understand each others' thoughts, and are all prodigious intellects. They are the wave of the future, man in his next stage of development.

These alien invaders practice a crime which is worse than murder. They do not simply kill the person. They obliterate him. In The War of the Worlds, the ray which issues from the rocket ship disintegrates all persons and objects in its path, leaving no trace of them but a light ash. In Honda's The H-Man (1959), the creeping blob melts all flesh with which it comes in contact. If the blob, which looks like a huge hunk of red Jello and can crawl across floors and up and down walls, so much as touches your bare foot, all that is left of you is a heap of clothes on the floor. (A more articulated, size-multiplying blob is the villain in the English film The Creeping Unknown [1956].) In another version of this fantasy, the body is preserved but the person is entirely reconstituted as the automatized servant or agent of the alien powers. This is, of course, the vampire fantasy in new dress. The person is really dead, but he doesn't know it. He is "undead," he has become an "unperson." It happens to a whole California town in The Invasion of the Body Snatchers, to several earth scientists in This Island Earth, and to assorted innocents in It Came From Outer Space, Attack of the Puppet People (1958), and The Brain Eaters (1958). As the victim always backs away from the vampire's horrifying embrace, so in science fiction films the person always fights being "taken over"; he wants to retain his humanity. But once the deed has been done, the victim is eminently satisfied with his condition. He has not been converted from human amiability to monstrous "animal" bloodlust (a metaphoric exaggeration of sexual desire), as in the old vampire fantasy. No, he has simply become far more efficient—the very model of technocratic man, purged of emotions, volitionless, tranquil, obedient to all orders. (The dark secret behind human nature used to be the upsurge of the animal—as in *King Kong*. The threat to man, his availability to dehumanization, lay in his own animality. Now the danger is understood as residing in man's ability to be turned into a machine.)

The rule, of course, is that this horrible and irremediable form of murder can strike anyone in the film except the hero. The hero and his family, while greatly threatened, always escape this fate and by the end of the film the invaders have been repulsed or destroyed. I know of only one exception, *The Day That Mars Invaded Earth* (1963), in which after all the standard struggles the scientist-hero, his wife, and their two children are "taken over" by the alien invaders—and that's that. (The last minutes of the film show them being incinerated by the Martians' rays and their ash silhouettes flushed down their empty swimming pool, while their simulacra drive off in the family car.) Another variant but upbeat switch on the rule occurs in *The Creation of the Humanoids* (1964), where the hero discovers at the end of the film that he, too, has been turned into a metal robot, complete with highly efficient and virtually indestructible mechanical insides, although he didn't know it and detected no difference in himself. He learns, however, that he will shortly be upgraded into a "humanoid" having all the properties of a real man.

Of all the standard motifs of science fiction films, this theme of dehumanization is perhaps the most fascinating. For, as I have indicated, it is scarcely a black-and-white situation, as in the old vampire films. The attitude of the science fiction films toward depersonalization is mixed. On the one hand, they deplore it as the ultimate horror. On the other hand, certain characteristics of the dehumanized invaders, modulated and disguised—such as the ascendancy of reason over feelings, the idealization of teamwork and the consensus-creating activities of science, a marked degree of moral simplification—are precisely traits of the savior-scientist. It is interesting that when the scientist in these films is treated negatively, it is usually done through the portrayal of an individual scientist who holes up in his laboratory and neglects his fiancée or his loving wife and children, obsessed by his daring and dangerous experiments. The scientist as a loyal member of a team, and therefore considerably less individualized, is treated quite respectfully.

There is absolutely no social criticism, of even the most implicit kind, in science fiction films. No criticism, for example, of the conditions of our society which create the impersonality and dehumanization which science fiction fantasies displace onto the influence of an alien It. Also, the notion of science as a social activity, interlocking with social and political interests, is unacknowledged. Science is simply either adventure (for good or evil) or a technical response to danger. And, typically, when the fear of science is paramount—when science is conceived of as black magic rather than white—the evil has no attribution beyond that of the perverse will of an individual scientist. In science fiction films the antithesis of black magic and white is drawn as a split between technology, which is beneficent, and the errant individual will of a lone intellectual.

Thus, science fiction films can be looked at as thematically central allegory, replete with standard modern attitudes. The theme of depersonalization (being "taken over") which I have been talking about is a new allegory reflecting the age-old awareness of man that, sane, he is always perilously close to insanity and unreason. But there is something more here than just a recent, popular image which expresses man's perennial, but largely unconscious, anxiety about his sanity. The image derives most of its power from a supplementary and historical anxiety, also not experienced consciously by most people, about the depersonalizing conditions of modern urban life. Similarly, it is not enough to note that science fiction allegories are one of the new myths about—that is, one of the ways of accommodating to and negating—the perennial human anxiety about death. (Myths of heaven and hell, and of ghosts, had the same function.) For, again, there is a historically specifiable twist which intensifies the anxiety. I mean, the trauma suffered by every-one in the middle of the 20th century when it became clear that, from now on to the end of human history, every person would spend his individual life under the threat not only of individual death, which is certain, but of something almost insupportable psychologically—collective incineration and extinction which could come at any time, virtually without warning.

From a psychological point of view, the imagination of disaster does not greatly differ from one period in history to another. But from a political and moral point of view, it does. The expectation of the apocalypse may be the occasion for a radical disaffiliation from society, as when thousands of Eastern European Jews in the 17th century, hearing that Sabbatai Zevi had been proclaimed the Messiah and that the end of the world was imminent, gave up their homes and businesses and began the trek to Palestine. But people take the news of their doom in diverse ways. It is reported that in 1945 the populace of Berlin received without great agitation the news that Hitler had decided to kill them all, before the Allies arrived, because they had not been worthy enough to win the war. We are, alas, more in the position of the Berliners of 1945 than of the Jews of 17th century Eastern Europe; and our response is closer to theirs, too. What I am suggesting is that the imagery of disaster in science fiction is above all the emblem of an inadequate response. I don't mean to bear down on the films for this. They themselves are only a sampling, stripped of sophistication, of the inadequacy of most people's response to the unassimilable terrors that infect their consciousness. The interest of the films, aside from their considerable amount of cinematic charm, consists in this intersection between a naïve and largely debased commercial art product and the most profound dilemmas of the contemporary situation.

Ours is indeed an age of extremity. For we live under continual threat of two equally fearful, but seemingly opposed, destinies: unremitting banality and inconceivable terror. It is fantasy, served out in large rations by the popular arts, which allows most people to cope with these twin specters. For one job that fantasy can do is to lift us out of the unbearably humdrum and to distract us from terrors—real or anticipated—by an escape into exotic, dangerous situations which have last-minute happy endings. But another of the things that fantasy can do is to normalize what is psychologically unbearable, thereby inuring us to it. In one case, fantasy beautifies the world. In the other, it neutralizes it.

The fantasy in science fiction films does both jobs. The films reflect world-wide anxieties, and they serve to allay them. They inculcate a strange apathy concerning the processes of radiation, contamination, and destruction which I for one find haunting and depressing. The naïve level of the films neatly tempers the sense of otherness, of alien-ness, with the grossly familiar. In particular, the dialogue of most science fiction films, which is of a monumental but often touching banality, makes them wonderfully, unintentionally funny. Lines like "Come quickly, there's a monster in my bathtub," "We must do something about this," "Wait, Professor. There's someone on the telephone," "But that's incredible," and the old American stand-by, "I hope it works!" are hilarious in the context of picturesque and deafening holocaust. Yet the films also contain something that is painful and in deadly earnest.

There is a sense in which all these movies are in complicity with the abhorrent. They neutralize it, as I have said. It is no more, perhaps, than the way all art draws its audience into a circle of complicity with the thing represented. But in these films we have to do with things which are (quite literally) unthinkable. Here, "thinking about the unthinkable"—not in the way of Herman Kahn, as a subject for calculation, but as a subject for fantasy—becomes, however inadvertently, itself a somewhat questionable act from a moral point of view. The films perpetuate clichés about identity, volition, power, knowledge, happiness, social consensus, guilt, responsibility which are, to say the least, not serviceable in our present extremity. But collective nightmares cannot be banished by demonstrating that they are, intellectually and morally, fallacious. This nightmare—the one reflected, in various registers, in the science fiction films—is too close to our reality.

[1965]

Jack Smith's
Flaming Creatures

T H E only thing to be regretted
about the close-ups of limp penises and bouncing breasts, the shots
of masturbation and oral sexuality, in Jack Smith's *Flaming Creatures* is that they make it hard simply to talk about this remarkable
film; one has to *defend* it. But in defending as well as talking about
the film, I don't want to make it seem less outrageous, less shocking
than it is. For the record: in *Flaming Creatures*, a couple of women
and a much larger number of men, most of them clad in flamboyant
thrift-shop women's clothes, frolic about, pose and posture, dance
with one another, enact various scenes of voluptuousness, sexual
frenzy, romance, and vampirism—to the accompaniment of a sound
track which includes some Latin pop favorites (*Siboney, Amapola*),
rock-'n'-roll, scratchy violin playing, bullfight music, a Chinese song,
the text of a wacky ad for a new brand of "heart-shaped lipstick"
being demonstrated on the screen by a host of men, some in drag

and some not, and the chorale of flutey shrieks and screams which accompany the group rape of a bosomy young woman, rape happily converting itself into an orgy. Of course, *Flaming Creatures* is outrageous, and intends to be. The very title tells us that.

As it happens, *Flaming Creatures* is not pornographic, if pornography be defined as the manifest intention and capacity to excite sexually. The depiction of nakedness and various sexual embraces (with the notable omission of straight screwing) is both too full of pathos and too ingenuous to be prurient. Rather than being sentimental or lustful, Smith's images of sex are alternately childlike and witty.

The police hostility to *Flaming Creatures* is not hard to understand. It is, alas, inevitable that Smith's film will have to fight for its life in the courts. What is disappointing is the indifference, the squeamishness, the downright hostility to the film evinced by almost everyone in the mature intellectual and artistic community. Almost its only supporters are a loyal coterie of film-makers, poets, and young "Villagers." *Flaming Creatures* has not yet graduated from being a cult object, the prize exhibit of the New American Cinema group whose house organ is the magazine *Film Culture*. Everyone should be grateful to Jonas Mekas, who almost single-handedly, with tenacity and even heroism, has made it possible to see Smith's film and many other new works. Yet it must be admitted that the pronouncements of Mekas and his entourage are shrill and often positively alienating. It is absurd of Mekas to argue that this new group of films, which includes *Flaming Creatures*, is a totally unprecedented departure in the history of cinema. Such truculence does Smith a disservice, making it unnecessarily hard to grasp what is of merit in *Flaming Creatures*. For *Flaming Creatures* is a small but valuable work in a particular tradition, the poetic cinema of shock. In this tradition are to be found Buñuel's *Le Chien Andalou* and *L'Âge d'Or*, parts of Eisenstein's first film, *Strike*, Tod Browning's *Freaks*, Jean Rouch's *Les Maîtres-Fous*, Franju's *Le Sang des Bêtes*, Lenica's *Labyrinth*, the films of Kenneth Anger (*Fireworks, Scorpio Rising*), and Noël Burch's *Noviciat*.

The older avant-garde film-makers in America (Maya Deren, James Broughton, Kenneth Anger) turned out short films which

were technically quite studied. Given their very low budgets, the
color, camera work, acting, and synchronization of image and
sound were as professional as possible. The hallmark of one of the
two new avant-garde styles in American cinema (Jack Smith, Ron
Rice, et al., but not Gregory Markopolous or Stan Brakhage) is its
willful technical crudity. The newer films—both the good ones and
the poor, uninspired work—show a maddening indifference to
every element of technique, a studied primitiveness. This is a very
contemporary style, and very American. Nowhere in the world has
the old cliché of European romanticism—the assassin mind versus
the spontaneous heart—had such a long career as in America.
Here, more than anywhere else, the belief lives on that neatness
and carefulness of technique interfere with spontaneity, with truth,
with immediacy. Most of the prevailing techniques (for even to be
against technique demands a technique) of avant-garde art express
this conviction. In music, there is aleatory performance now as
well as composition, and new sources of sound and new ways of
mutilating the old instruments; in painting and sculpture, there is
the favoring of impermanent or found materials, and the transformation of objects into perishable (use-once-and-throw-away) environments or "happenings." In its own way Flaming Creatures
illustrates this snobbery about the coherence and technical finish of
the work of art. There is, of course, no story in Flaming Creatures,
no development, no necessary order of the seven (as I count them)
clearly separable sequences of the film. One can easily doubt that a
certain piece of footage was indeed intended to be overexposed. Of
no sequence is one convinced that it had to last this long, and not
longer or shorter. Shots aren't framed in the traditional way; heads
are cut off; extraneous figures sometimes appear on the margin of
the scene. The camera is hand-held most of the time, and the image often quivers (where this is wholly effective, and no doubt deliberate, is in the orgy sequence).

But in Flaming Creatures, amateurishness of technique is not
frustrating, as it is in so many other recent "underground" films.
For Smith is visually very generous; at practically every moment
there is simply a tremendous amount to see on the screen. And
then, there is an extraordinary charge and beauty to his images, even

when the effect of the strong ones is weakened by the ineffective ones, the ones that might have been better through planning. Today indifference to technique is often accompanied by bareness; the modern revolt against calculation in art often takes the form of aesthetic asceticism. (Much of Abstract Expressionist painting has this ascetic quality.) _Flaming Creatures_, though, issues from a different aesthetic: it is crowded with visual material. There are no ideas, no symbols, no commentary on or critique of anything in _Flaming Creatures_. Smith's film is strictly a treat for the senses. In this it is the very opposite of a "literary" film (which is what so many French avant-garde films were). It is not in the knowing about, or being able to interpret, what one sees, that the pleasure of _Flaming Creatures_ lies; but in the directness, the power, and the lavish quantity of the images themselves. Unlike most serious modern art, this work is not about the frustrations of consciousness, the dead ends of the self. Thus Smith's crude technique serves, beautifully, the sensibility embodied in _Flaming Creatures_—a sensibility which disclaims ideas, which situates itself beyond negation.

Flaming Creatures is that rare modern work of art: it is about joy and innocence. To be sure, this joyousness, this innocence is composed out of themes which are—by ordinary standards—perverse, decadent, at the least highly theatrical and artificial. But this, I think, is precisely how the film comes by its beauty and modernity. _Flaming Creatures_ is a lovely specimen of what currently, in one genre, goes by the flippant name of "pop art." Smith's film has the sloppiness, the arbitrariness, the looseness of pop art. It also has pop art's gaiety, its ingenuousness, its exhilarating freedom from moralism. One great virtue of the pop-art movement is the way it blasts through the old imperative about taking a _position_ toward one's subject matter. (Needless to say, I'm not denying that there are certain events about which it is necessary to take a position. An extreme instance of a work of art dealing with such events is _The Deputy_. All I'm saying is that there are some elements of life— above all, sexual pleasure—about which it isn't necessary to have a position.) The best works among those that are called pop art intend, precisely, that we abandon the old task of always either approving or disapproving of what is depicted in art—or, by extension, experienced in life. (This is why those who dismiss pop art as a symptom of a new conformism, a cult of acceptance of the artifacts of mass civilization, are being obtuse.) Pop art lets in wonderful and new mixtures of attitude, which would before have seemed contradictions. Thus *Flaming Creatures* is a brilliant spoof on sex and at the same time full of the lyricism of erotic impulse. Simply in a visual sense, too, it is full of contradictions. Very studied visual effects (lacy textures, falling flowers, tableaux) are introduced into disorganized, clearly improvised scenes in which bodies, some shapely and convincingly feminine and others scrawny and hairy, tumble, dance, make love.

One can regard Smith's film as having, for its subject, the poetry of transvestitism. *Film Culture*, in awarding *Flaming Creatures* its Fifth Independent Film Award, said of Smith: "He has struck us with not the mere pity or curiosity of the perverse, but the glory, the pageantry of Transylvestia and the magic of Fairyland. He has lit up a part of life, although it is a part which most men scorn." The truth is that *Flaming Creatures* is much more about intersexuality than about homosexuality. Smith's vision is akin to the vision in Bosch's paintings of a paradise and a hell of writhing, shameless, ingenious bodies. Unlike those serious and stirring films about the beauties and terrors of homoerotic love, Kenneth Anger's *Fireworks* and Genet's *Chant d'Amour*, the important fact about the figures in Smith's film is that one cannot easily tell which are men and which are women. These are "creatures," flaming out in intersexual, polymorphous joy. The film is built out of a complex web of ambiguities and ambivalences, whose primary image is the confusion of male and female flesh. The shaken breast and the shaken penis become interchangeable with each other.

Bosch constructed a strange, aborted, ideal nature against which he situated his nude figures, his androgynous visions of pain and pleasure. Smith has no literal background (it's hard to tell in the film whether one is indoors or outdoors), but instead the thoroughly artificial and invented landscape of costume, gesture, and music. The myth of intersexuality is played out against a background of banal songs, ads, clothes, dances, and above all, the repertory of fantasy drawn from corny movies. The texture of *Flaming Creatures* is made up of a rich collage of "camp" lore: a woman in white (a transvestite) with drooping head holding a stalk of lilies; a gaunt woman seen emerging from a coffin, who turns out to be a vampire and, eventually, male; a marvelous Spanish dancer (also a transvestite) with huge dark eyes, black lace mantilla and fan; a tableau from the *Sheik of Araby*, with reclining men in burnooses and an Arab temptress stolidly exposing one breast; a scene between two women, reclining on flowers and rags, which recalls the dense, crowded texture of the movies in which Sternberg directed Dietrich in the early thirties. The vocabulary of images and textures on which Smith draws includes pre-Raphaelite languidness; Art Nouveau; the great exotica styles of the twenties, the Spanish and the Arab; and the modern "camp" way of relishing mass culture.

Flaming Creatures is a triumphant example of an aesthetic vision of the world—and such a vision is perhaps always, at its core, epicene. But this type of art has yet to be understood in this country. The space in which *Flaming Creatures* moves is not the space of moral ideas, which is where American critics have traditionally located art. What I am urging is that there is not only moral space, by whose laws *Flaming Creatures* would indeed come off badly; there is also aesthetic space, the space of pleasure. Here Smith's film moves and has its being.

[1964]

Resnais' *Muriel*

Muriel is the most difficult,
by far, of Resnais' three feature films, but it is clearly drawn from
the same repertoire of themes as the first two. Despite the special
mannerisms of the very independent scriptwriters he has employed
—Marguerite Duras in *Hiroshima, Mon Amour*, Alain Robbe-
Grillet in *L'Année Dernière à Marienbad*, and Jean Cayrol in
Muriel—all three films share a common subject: the search for the
inexpressible past. Resnais' new film even has a co-title to this
effect, like an old-fashioned novel. It is called *Muriel, ou Le Temps
d'un Retour*.

In *Hiroshima, Mon Amour*, the subject is the collation of two
disjunct and clashing pasts. The story of the film is the unsuccessful
attempt of the two principals, a Japanese architect and a French
actress, to extract from their pasts the substance of feeling (and
concordance of memory) that could sustain a love in the present.

At the beginning of the film, they are in bed. They spend the rest of the film literally reciting themselves to each other. But they fail to transcend their "statements," their guilt and separateness.

L'Année Dernière à Marienbad is another version of the same theme. But here the theme is put in a deliberately theatrical, static setting, at a tangent to both the brash modern ugliness of the new Hiroshima and the solid provincial authenticity of Nevers. This story entombs itself in an outlandish, beautiful, barren place and plays out the theme of *le temps retrouvé* with abstract personages, who are denied a solid consciousness or memory or past. *Marienbad* is a formal inversion of the idea of *Hiroshima*, with more than one note of melancholic parody of its own theme. As the idea of *Hiroshima* is the weight of the inescapably remembered past, so the idea of *Marienbad* is the openness, the abstractness of memory. The claim of the past upon the present is reduced to a cipher, a ballet, or—in the controlling image of the film—a game, whose results are entirely determined by the first move (if he who makes the first move knows what he is doing). The past is a fantasy of the present, according to both *Hiroshima* and *Marienbad*. *Marienbad* develops the meditation on the form of memory implicit in *Hiroshima*, cutting away the ideological clothing of the first film.

The reason *Muriel* is difficult is that it attempts to do both what *Hiroshima* and what *Marienbad* did. It attempts to deal with substantive issues—the Algerian War, the OAS, the racism of the colons—even as *Hiroshima* dealt with the bomb, pacifism, and collaboration. But it also, like *Marienbad*, attempts to project a purely abstract drama. The burden of this double intention—to be both concrete and abstract—doubles the technical virtuosity and complexity of the film.

Again, the story concerns a group of people haunted by their memories. Hélène Aughain, a fortyish widow living in the provincial city of Boulogne, impulsively summons a former lover whom she has not seen for twenty years to visit her. Her motive is never named; in the film, it has the character of a gratuitous act. Hélène runs a touch-and-go antique furniture business from her apartment, gambles compulsively, and is badly in debt. Living with her in a painful loving stalemate is her uncommunicative stepson,

Bernard Aughain, another memory addict, who has recently returned from serving in the army in Algeria. Bernard is unable to
forget his share in a crime: the torturing of an Algerian political
prisoner, a girl named Muriel. He is not merely too distraught to
work; he is in an agony of restlessness. On the pretext of visiting a
nonexistent fiancée in the town (whom he has named Muriel), he
often flees his stepmother's modern apartment, where every item
of furniture is beautiful and for sale, to a room he maintains in the
ruins of the old family apartment, which was bombed during
World War II. . . . The film opens with the arrival from Paris of
Hélène's old lover, Alphonse. He is accompanied by his mistress,
Françoise, whom he passes off as his niece. It ends, several months
later, the unsuccessful reunion of Hélène and Alphonse having run
its course. Alphonse and Françoise, their relationship permanently
embittered, leave for Paris. Bernard—after shooting the boyhood
friend who, as a soldier, led the torture of Muriel and who is now a
civilian member of the OAS underground in France—says good-
bye to his stepmother. In a coda, we are shown the arrival in
Hélène's empty apartment of the wife of Alphonse, Simone, who
has come to reclaim her husband.

Unlike *Hiroshima* and *Marienbad*, *Muriel* directly suggests an
elaborate plot and complex interrelationships. (In the sketch above
I have omitted important minor characters, including friends of
Hélène, who figure in the film.) Yet, for all this complexity, Resnais conscientiously avoids direct narration. He gives us a chain of
short scenes, horizontal in emotional tone, which focus on selected
undramatic moments in the lives of the four main characters:
Hélène and her stepson and Alphonse and Françoise eating together; Hélène going up, or coming down, the steps of the gambling casino; Bernard riding his bicycle in the town; Bernard going
horseback riding on the cliffs outside the town; Bernard and
Françoise walking and talking; and so forth. The film is not really
hard to follow. I have seen it twice, and expected after I saw it once
that I would see more in it the second time. I didn't. *Muriel*, like
Marienbad, should not puzzle, because there is nothing "behind"
the lean, staccato statements that one sees. They can't be deci-
phered, because they don't say more than they say. It is rather as if

Resnais had taken a story, which could be told quite straightforwardly, and cut it against the grain. This "against the grain" feeling —the sense of being shown the action at an angle—is the peculiar mark of *Muriel*. It is Resnais' way of making a realistic story over into an examination of the *form* of emotions.

Thus, although the story is not difficult to follow, Resnais' techniques for telling it deliberately estrange the viewer from the story. Most conspicuous of these techniques is his elliptical, off-center conception of a scene. The film opens with the strained good-byes of Hélène and a demanding client at the threshold of Hélène's apartment; then there is a brief exchange between the harried Hélène and the disgruntled Bernard. Throughout both sequences, Resnais denies the viewer a chance to orient himself visually in traditional story terms. We are shown a hand on the doorknob, the vacant insincere smile of the client, a coffee pot boiling. The way the scenes are photographed and edited decomposes, rather than explains, the story. Then Hélène hurries off to the station to meet Alphonse, whom she finds accompanied by Françoise, and leads them from the station back to her apartment on foot. On this walk from the station—it is night—Hélène is nervously chattering about Boulogne, which was mostly destroyed during the war and has been rebuilt in a bright functional modern style; and shots of the city in the daytime are interspersed with shots of the three walking through the city at night. Hélène's voice bridges this high-speed visual alternation. In Resnais' films, all speech, including dialogue, tends to become narration—to hover over the visible action, rather than to issue directly from it.

The extremely rapid cutting of *Muriel* is unlike the jumpy, jazzy cutting of Godard in *Breathless* and *Vivre Sa Vie*. Godard's abrupt cutting pulls the viewer into the story, makes him restless and heightens his appetite for action, creating a kind of visual suspense. When Resnais cuts abruptly, he pulls the viewer away from the story. His cutting acts as a brake on the narrative, a kind of aesthetic undertow, a sort of filmic alienation effect.

Resnais' use of speech has a similar "alienating" effect on the viewer's feelings. Because his main characters have something not only benumbed but positively hopeless about them, their words are

never emotionally moving. Speaking in a Resnais film is typically
an occasion of frustration—whether it is the trance-like recitation
of the uncommunicable distress of an event in the past; or the trun-
cated, distracted words his characters address to each other in the
present. (Because of the frustrations of speech, eyes have great authority in Resnais' films. A standard dramatic moment, insofar as he
allows such a thing, is a few banal words followed by silence and a
look.) Happily, there is nothing in *Muriel* of the insufferable incantatory style of the dialogue of *Hiroshima* and the narration of
Marienbad. Apart from a few stark, unanswered questions, the
characters in *Muriel* mostly speak in dull, evasive phrases, especially
when they are very unhappy. But the firm prosiness of the dialogue in *Muriel* is not intended to mean anything different from
the awful poetizing of the earlier two long films. Resnais proposes
the same subject in all his films. All his films are about the *inexpressible*. (The main topics which are inexpressible are two: guilt
and erotic longing.) And the twin notion to inexpressibility is banality. In high art, banality is the modesty of the inexpressible.
"Ours is really *une histoire banale*," the anguished Hélène says
ruefully at one moment to the suave, furtive Alphonse. "The story
of Muriel can't be told," says Bernard to a stranger in whom he
has confided his excruciating memory. The two declarations really
amount to the same thing.

Resnais' techniques, despite the visual brilliance of his films, seem
to me to owe more to literature than to the tradition of the cinema
as such. (Bernard, in *Muriel*, is a film-maker—he is collecting "evidence," as he calls it, about the case of Muriel—for the same reason
that the central consciousness in so many modern novels is that of a
character who is a writer.) Most literary of all is Resnais' formalism.
Formalism itself is not literary. But to appropriate a complex and
specific narrative in order deliberately to obscure it—to write an abstract text on top of it, as it were—is a very literary procedure.
There *is* a story in *Muriel*, the story of a troubled middle-aged
woman attempting to reinstate the love of twenty years ago and a
young ex-soldier wracked by guilt over his complicity in a barbarous
war. But *Muriel* is designed so that, at any given moment of it, it's

not about anything at all. At any given moment it is a formal composition; and it is to this end that individual scenes are shaped so obliquely, the time sequence scrambled, and dialogue kept to a minimum of informativeness.

This is exactly the point of many new novels coming out of France today—to suppress the story, in its traditional psychological or social meaning, in favor of a formal exploration of the structure of an emotion or event. Thus, the real concern of Michel Butor in his novel *La Modification* is not to show whether the hero will or will not leave his wife to live with his mistress, and even less to base some theory of love on his decision. What interests Butor is the "modification" itself, the formal structure of the man's behavior. It's exactly in this spirit that Resnais handles the story of *Muriel*.

The typical formula of the new formalists of the novel and film is a mixture of coldness and pathos: coldness enclosing and subduing an immense pathos. Resnais' great discovery is the application of this formula to "documentary" material, to true events locked in the historical past. Here—in Resnais' short films, particularly *Guernica*, *Van Gogh*, and above all, *Night and Fog*—the formula works brilliantly, educating and liberating the viewer's feelings. *Night and Fog* shows us Dachau, ten years later. The camera moves about (the film is in color), nosing out the grass growing up between the cracks in the masonry of the crematoria. The ghastly serenity of Dachau—now a hollow, silent, evacuated shell—is posed against the unimaginable reality of what went on there in the past; this past is represented by a quiet voice describing life in the camps and reciting the statistics of extermination (text by Jean Cayrol), and some interpolated black-and-white newsreel footage of the camp when it was liberated. (This is the parent of the scene in *Muriel* when Bernard recites the story of the torture and murder of Muriel, while running off a home-movie type film of his smiling uniformed comrades in Algeria. Muriel herself is never shown.) The triumph of *Night and Fog* is its absolute control, its supreme refinement in dealing with a subject that incarnates the purest, most agonizing pathos. For the danger of such a subject is that it can numb, instead of stir, our feelings. Resnais has overcome this danger by adopting a distance from his subject which is not sentimental, and which yet does not cheat the horror of its horrifyingness. *Night and Fog* is overwhelming in its directness, yet full of tact about the unimaginable.

But in Resnais' three feature films, the same strategy is not so apt or satisfying. It would be too simple to say that it is because the lucid and brilliantly compassionate documentarist has been superseded by the aesthete, the formalist. (After all, films are an art.) But there is an undeniable loss of power, since Resnais wants very much to have it both ways—as "*homme de gauche*" and as formalist. The aim of formalism is to break up content, to question content. The questionable reality of the past is the subject of all Resnais' films. More exactly, for Resnais, the past is that reality which is both unassimilable and dubious. (The new formalism of the French novels and films is thus a dedicated agnosticism about reality itself.) But at the same time, Resnais does believe in, and want us to share in a certain attitude toward, the past insofar as it has the signature of history. This does not create a problem in *Night and Fog*, where the memory of the past is situated objectively, outside the film, so to speak, in an impersonal narrator. But when Resnais decided to take as his subject, not "a memory," but "remembering," and to situate memories in characters within the film, a muted collision between the aims of formalism and the ethic of engagement occurred. The result of using admirable sentiments— like guilt for the bomb (in *Hiroshima*) and for the French atrocities in Algeria (*Muriel*)—as subjects for aesthetic demonstration is a palpable strain and diffuseness in the structure, as if Resnais did not know where the center of his film really was. Thus, the disturbing anomaly of *Hiroshima* is the implicit equating of the grandiose horror of the Japanese hero's memory, the bombing and its mutilated victims, with the comparatively insignificant horror from the past that plagues the French heroine, an affair with a German soldier during the war for which, after the liberation, she was humiliated by having her head shaved.

I have said that not a memory but remembering is Resnais' subject: nostalgia itself becomes an object of nostalgia, the memory of an unrecapturable feeling becomes the subject of feeling. The only one of Resnais' feature films which does not reveal this confusion about its center is *Marienbad*. Here, a strong emotion—the pathos of erotic frustration and longing—is raised to the level of a meta-emotion by being set in a place that has the character of an abstraction, a vast palace peopled with *haute couture* mannequins. This method is plausible because it is a totally ahistorical, apolitical memory which Resnais has located in what is a kind of generalized Past. But abstraction through generality, at least in this film, seems to produce a certain deflection of energy. The mood is stylized reticence, but one does not feel, sufficiently, the pressure of what the characters are being reticent about. *Marienbad* has its center, but the center seems frozen. It has an insistent, sometimes sluggish stateliness in which visual beauty and exquisiteness of composition are continually undermined by a lack of emotional tension.

There is greater energy in *Muriel*, which is a far more ambitious film. For Resnais has come back to the problem which, given his sensibility and the themes he wishes to pursue, he cannot evade: the reconciliation of formalism and the ethic of engagement. He cannot be said to have solved the problem, and in an ultimate sense *Muriel* must be judged a noble failure, but he has shown a good deal more about the problem and the complexities of any solution to it. He does not make the mistake of implicitly coordinating historical atrocity with a private grief (as in *Hiroshima*). Both simply exist, in an extended network of relationships whose psychological "insides" we never know. For Resnais has sought to represent his materials, the burden of an anguishing memory of participation in a real historical event (Bernard in Algeria) and the inexplicit anguish of a purely private past (Hélène and her affair with Alphonse) in a manner which is both abstract and concrete. It is neither the understated documentary realism of his rendering of the city of Hiroshima, nor the sensuous realism of the photography of Nevers; nor is it the abstract museum stillness, embodied in the exotic locale of *Marienbad*. Abstraction in *Muriel* is subtler and more complex, because it is discovered in the real everyday world rather than by departing from it in time (the flashbacks in *Hiroshima*) or in space (the château of *Marienbad*). It is conveyed in the rigor of its compositional sense, first of all, but this is to be found in all Resnais' films. And it is in the rapid cutting-away-from-scenes which I have already mentioned, a rhythm new in Resnais' films; and in the use of color. About the last, much could be said. Sacha Vierny's color photography in *Muriel* stuns and delights, giving one that sense of having never before appreciated the resources of color in the cinema that such films as *Gate of Hell* and Visconti's *Senso* once also did. But the impact of the colors in Resnais' film is not just that they are beautiful. It is the aggressive inhuman intensity they possess, which gives to quotidian objects, up-to-date kitchenware, modern apartment buildings and stores, a peculiar abstractness and distance.

Another resource for intensification through abstractness is the music of Hans Werner Henze for voice and orchestra, one of those rare film scores that stands as a musical composition by itself. Sometimes the music is used for conventional dramatic purposes: to confirm or comment on what is happening. Thus, in the scene when Bernard shows the crude film he made of his ex-comrades in Algeria, cavorting and smiling, the music becomes harsh and jolting—contradicting the innocence of the image. (We know these are the soldiers who share with Bernard the guilt of Muriel's death.) But the more interesting use which Resnais makes of the music is as a structural element in the narration. The atonal vocal line sung by Rita Streich is sometimes used, like the dialogue, to soar over the action. It is through the music that we know when Hélène is most tormented by her barely named emotions. And, in its most powerful use, the music constitutes a kind of purified dialogue, displacing speech altogether. In the brief wordless final scene, when Simone comes looking for her husband in Hélène's apartment and finds no one, the music becomes her speech; voice and orchestra rise to a crescendo of lament.

But, for all the beauty and effectiveness of the resources I have mentioned (and those I have not mentioned, which include acting performances of great clarity, restraint, and intelligence*), the prob-

---

* Most of the principals of *Muriel* are remarkable as actors and in the clarity of their physical presences. But it must be noted that, unlike the other two feature films of Resnais, *Muriel* is dominated by a single performance, that of Delphine Seyrig as Hélène. In this film (but not in *Marienbad*) Seyrig has the nourishing irrelevant panoply of mannerisms of a star, in the peculiarly cinematic sense of that word. That is to say, she doesn't simply play (or even perfectly fill) a role. She becomes an independent aesthetic object in herself. Each

lem of *Muriel*—and of Resnais' work—remains. A cleavage of intention, which Resnais has thus far failed to transcend, has given rise to a multiplicity of devices, each one justifiable and largely successful, but the whole giving an unpleasant feeling of clutteredness. Perhaps this is why *Muriel*, however admirable, is not a very likable film. The trouble, let me repeat, is not formalism. Bresson's *Les Dames du Bois de Boulogne* and Godard's *Vivre Sa Vie*—to mention only two great films in the formalist tradition—are emotionally exalting, even when they are being most dead-pan and cerebral. But *Muriel* is somehow depressing, weighty. Its virtues, such as its intelligence and its extraordinary rewards on a purely visual level, still retain something (though a good deal less) of that preciousness, that studied air, that artiness that infests *Hiroshima* and *Marienbad*. Resnais knows all about beauty. But his films lack tonicity and vigor, directness of address. They are cautious, somehow, overburdened and synthetic. They do not go to the end, either of the idea or of the emotion which inspires them, which all great art must do.

[1963]

___

detail of her appearance—her graying hair, her tilted loping walk, her wide-brimmed hats and smartly dowdy suits, her gauche manner in enthusiasm and regret—is unnecessary and indelible.

A note on
novels and films

THE fifty years of the cinema
present us with a scrambled recapitulation of the more than two
hundred year history of the novel. In D. W. Griffith, the cinema
had its Samuel Richardson; the director of *Birth of a Nation*
(1915), *Intolerance* (1916), *Broken Blossoms* (1919), *Way Down
East* (1920), *One Exciting Night* (1922), and hundreds of other
films voiced many of the same moral conceptions and occupied an
approximately similar position with respect to the development of
the film art as the author of *Pamela* and *Clarissa* did with respect
to the development of the novel. Both Griffith and Richardson
were innovators of genius; both had intellects of supreme vulgarity
and even inanity; and the work of both men reeks of a fervid moralizing about sexuality and violence whose energy comes from suppressed voluptuousness. The central figure in Richardson's two
novels, the pure young virgin assailed by the brute-seducer, finds its

exact counterpart—stylistically and conceptually—in the Pure Young Girl, the Perfect Victim, of Griffith's many films, played often either by Lillian Gish (who is famous for these roles) or by the now-forgotten but much better actress, Mae Marsh. Like Richardson, Griffith's moral drivel (expressed in his inimitable and lengthy titles written in a brand of English all his own, replete with capital letters for the names of all the virtues and sins) concealed an essential lasciviousness; and, like Richardson, what is best in Griffith is his extraordinary capacity for representing the most tremulous feminine sentiments in all their *longueurs*, which the banality of his "ideas" does not obscure. Like Richardson, too, the world of Griffith seems cloying and slightly mad to modern taste. Yet it was these two who discovered "psychology" for the respective genres in which they are the pioneers.

Of course, not every great film director can be matched with a great novelist. The comparisons cannot be pressed too literally. Nevertheless, the cinema has had not only its Richardson, but its Dickens, its Tolstoy, its Balzac, its Proust, its Nathanael West. And then there are the curious marriages of style and conception in the cinema. The masterpieces that Erich Von Stroheim directed in Hollywood in the 1920s (*Blind Husbands, Foolish Wives, Greed, The Merry Widow, Wedding March, Queen Kelly*) might be described as an improbable and brilliant synthesis of Anthony Hope and Balzac.

This is not to assimilate the cinema to the novel, or even to claim that the cinema can be analyzed in the same terms as a novel. The cinema has its own methods and logic of representation, which one does not exhaust by saying that they are primarily visual. The cinema presents us with a new language, a way of talking about emotion through the direct experience of the language of faces and gestures. Nevertheless, there are useful analogies which may be drawn between the cinema and the novel—far more, it seems to me, than between the cinema and the theater. Like the novel, the cinema presents us with a view of an action which is absolutely under the control of the director (writer) at every moment. Our eye cannot wander about the screen, as it does about the stage. The camera is an absolute dictator. It shows us a face when we are to see a face, and nothing else; a pair of clenched hands, a landscape, a speeding train, the façade of a building in the middle of a tête-à-tête, when and only when it wants us to see these things. When the camera moves we move, when it remains still we are still. In a similar way the novel presents a selection of the thoughts and descriptions which are relevant to the writer's conception, and we must follow these serially, as the author leads us; they are not spread out, as a background, for us to contemplate in the order we choose, as in painting or the theater.

A further caveat. Traditions exist within the cinema—less frequently exploited than that tradition which plausibly can be compared with the novel—which are analogous to literary forms other than the novel. Eisenstein's *Strike, Potemkin, Ten Days That Shook the World, The Old and the New;* Pudovkin's *The Mother, The End of St. Petersburg, Storm Over Asia;* Kurosawa's *The Seven Samurai, The Throne of Blood, The Hidden Fortress;* Inagaki's *Chushingura;* Okamoto's *Samurai Assassin;* most films of John Ford (*The Searchers,* etc.) belong rather to a conception of the cinema as epic. There is also a tradition of the cinema as poetry; many of the "avant-garde" short films which were made in France in the 1920s (Buñuel's *Le Chien Andalou* and *L'Age d'Or;* Cocteau's *Le Sang d'un Poète;* Jean Renoir's *La Petite Marchande d'Allumettes;* Antonin Artaud's *La Coquille et le Clergyman*) are best compared with the work of Baudelaire, Rimbaud, Mallarmé, and Lautréamont. Nevertheless, the dominant tradition in the film has centered upon the more or less novelistic unfolding of plot and idea, employing highly individuated characters located in a precise social setting.

Of course, the cinema does not obey the same schedule of contemporaneity as the novel; thus, it would appear anachronistic to us if someone wrote a novel like Jane Austen, but it would be very "advanced" if someone makes a film which is the cinematic equivalent of Jane Austen. This is no doubt because the history of films is so much shorter than the history of narrative fiction; and has emerged under the peculiarly accelerated tempo at which the arts move in our century. Thus its various possibilities overlap and double back on each other. Another reason is the fact that cinema, as a late-comer to the serious arts, is in a position to raid the other arts and can deploy even relatively stale elements in innumerable fresh combinations. Cinema is a kind of pan-art. It can use, incorporate, engulf virtually any other art: the novel, poetry, theater, painting, sculpture, dance, music, architecture. Unlike opera, which is a (virtually) frozen art form, the cinema is and has been a fruitfully conservative medium of ideas and styles of emotion. All the trappings of melodrama and high emotion may be found in the most recent and sophisticated cinema (for example, Visconti's *Senso* and *Rocco and His Brothers*), while these have been banished from most recent sophisticated novels.

One link between novels and films that is frequently made, however, does not seem very useful. That is the old saw about dividing directors into those who are primarily "literary" and those who are primarily "visual." Actually, there are few directors whose work can be so simply characterized. A distinction at least as useful is that between films which are "analytic" and those which are "descriptive" and "expository." Examples of the first would be the films of Carné, Bergman (especially *Through a Glass Darkly*, *Winter Light*, and *The Silence*), Fellini, and Visconti; examples of the second would be the films of Antonioni, Godard, and Bresson. The first kind could be described as psychological films, those concerned with the revelation of the characters' motives. The second kind is antipsychological, and deals with the transaction between feeling and things; the persons are opaque, "in situation." The same contrast could be carried through in the novel. Dickens and Dostoevsky are examples of the first; Stendhal of the second.

[1961]

V

Piety
without content

As we may learn from such disparate sources as the *Oresteia* and *Psycho*, matricide is of all possible individual crimes the most insupportable psychologically. And, of all possible crimes which an entire culture can commit, the one most difficult to bear, psychologically, is deicide. We live in a society whose entire way of life testifies to the thoroughness with which the deity has been dispatched, but philosophers, writers, men of conscience everywhere squirm under the burden. For it is a far simpler matter to plot and commit a crime than it is to live with it afterwards.

While the act of killing the Judeo-Christian God was still under way, antagonists on both sides took up their positions with a great deal of sureness and self-righteousness. But once it was clear that the deed had been done, the battle lines began to blur. In the

19th century, melancholy attempts at promoting a revived pagan
religion to replace the vanquished Biblical tradition (Goethe,
Hölderlin) and tremulous hopes that something humane could be
saved (George Eliot, Matthew Arnold) are heard amidst the loud
and somewhat shrill voices of the victors proclaiming the triumph
of reason and maturity over faith and childishness, and the inevitable advance of humanity under the banner of science. In the
20th century, the sturdy Voltairean optimism of the rationalist attack on religion is even less convincing and less attractive,
though we still find it in conscientiously emancipated Jews like
Freud and, among American philosophers, in Morris Cohen and
Sidney Hook. It seems that such optimism is possible only to those
whom the "bad tidings," the dysangel of which Nietzsche speaks,
that God is dead, have not reached.

More common in our own generation, particularly in America
in the backwash of broken radical political enthusiasms, is a stance
that can only be called religious fellow-travelling. This is a piety
without content, a religiosity without either faith or observance. It
includes in differing measures both nostalgia and relief: nostalgia
over the loss of the sense of sacredness and relief that an intolerable burden has been lifted. (The conviction that what befell the
old faiths could not be avoided was held with a nagging sense of im-
poverishment.) Unlike political fellow-travelling, religious fellow-
travelling does not proceed from the attraction which a massive and
increasingly successful idealism exercises, an attraction which is
powerfully felt at the same time that one cannot completely identify with the movement. Rather, religious fellow-travelling proceeds
from a sense of the weakness of religion: knowing the good old
cause is down, it seems superfluous to kick it. Modern religious
fellow-travelling is nourished on the awareness that the contemporary religious communities are on the defensive; thus to be anti-
religious (like being a feminist) is old hat. Now one can afford to
look on sympathetically and derive nourishment from whatever
one can find to admire. Religions are converted into "religion," as
painting and sculpture of different periods and motives are converted into "art." For the modern post-religious man the religious
museum, like the world of the modern spectator of art, is without

walls; he can pick and choose as he likes, and be committed to
nothing except his own reverent spectatorship.

Religious fellow-travelling leads to several highly undesirable
consequences. One is that the sense of what religions are and have
been historically becomes coarse and intellectually dishonest. It is
understandable, if not sound, when Catholic intellectuals attempt
to reclaim Baudelaire, Rimbaud, and James Joyce—passionate
atheists all—as true, if highly tormented, sons of the Church. But
the same strategy is entirely indefensible on the part of the religious fellow-travellers operating within the Nietzschean "God is
dead," who apparently see no harm in making everybody religious.
They stand for no tradition to which they seek to reclaim errant
members. They merely collect exemplars of seriousness, or moral
earnestness, or intellectual passion, which is what they identify the
religious possibility with today.

The present book under review* is just such an example of religious fellow-travelling, worth examining because it clearly reflects
the lack of intellectual definition in this attitude which is so wide-
spread. It consists of an assemblage of writings by twenty-three authors "from Tolstoy to Camus," selected and edited by Walter
Kaufmann, an associate professor of philosophy at Princeton.

Of the order of the book one need not speak since it has no
order, except a vague chronological one. There are a few selections
with which one could hardly quarrel, such as the two chapters
"Rebellion" and "The Grand Inquisitor" from *The Brothers Kara-
mazov* (certainly Kaufmann is correct in saying that one cannot
understand the Grand Inquisitor story without the preceding dis-
quisition by Ivan on the sufferings of children), the excerpts from
Nietzsche's *The Antichrist* and Freud's *The Future of an Illusion*,
and William James' essay "The Will to Believe." There are also
a few imaginative choices of writings which deserve to be better
known: e.g. the Syllabus of Errors of Pope Pius IX, the exchange
of letters between Karl Barth and Emil Brunner on the Church's
stand against Communism, and the essay of W. K. Clifford which
prompted the famous reply of William James. But the majority of

* *Religion from Tolstoy to Camus.* Selected and introduced by Walter Kaufmann. New York, Harper.

the selections seem ill-chosen. Oscar Wilde cannot be regarded seriously as a religious writer. Neither is there any justification for Morton Scott Enslin's chapter on the New Testament, a conventionally sound account of the gospels and their historical setting, which is entirely out of place in an anthology of religious thought. The choices of Wilde and Enslin illustrate the two poles of irrelevance into which Kaufmann's book falls: frivolity and academicism.*

Kaufmann says in his introduction: "Almost all the men included were 'for' religion, though not the popular religion which scarcely any great religious figure has ever admired." But what does it mean to be "for" religion? Does the notion "religion" have any serious religious meaning at all? Put another way: can one teach or invite people to be sympathetic to religion-in-general? What does it mean to be "religious"? Obviously it is not the same thing as

* Kaufmann claims that he has presented "a heterogenous group, selected not to work toward some predetermined conclusion but to give a fair idea of the complexity of our story," but it's just this that he hasn't done. It is unfair to represent Catholicism by papal encyclicals plus two and one half pages by Maritain of neo-Scholastic argument on "the contingent and the necessary," which will be largely unintelligible to the audience to whom this anthology is directed. Selections from Gabriel Marcel, or Simone Weil, or some of the letters exchanged between Paul Claudel and André Gide on the latter's possible conversion, or Newman on "the grammar of assent," or Lord Acton, or Bernanos' Diary of a Country Priest—any of these would be more interesting and richer than what Kaufmann has given. Protestantism is more generously, but still inadequately, represented—by two sermons of Pastor Niemoller, a weak excerpt from Paul Tillich (one of the essays in The Protestant Era would have been far more appropriate here), the least interesting chapter from Albert Schweitzer's epochal book on eschatology in the New Testament, the Barth-Brunner correspondence, and the tame selection from Enslin mentioned above. Again, one may ask, why these? Why not something substantive from Barth or Bultmann? For Judaism, Kaufmann makes only the obvious choice, Martin Buber, represented by a chapter on the Hassidim. Why not more nourishing Buber, say, a chapter from I and Thou or Between Man and Man, or, better yet, a text by Franz Rosenzweig or Gershom Scholem? Of the fiction, why is there only Tolstoy and Dostoevsky? Why not Hesse (say, The Journey to the East) or some of Kafka's parables or D. H. Lawrence's Apocalypse? The emphasis on Camus, whose name appears in the title and whose great essay against capital punishment closes the book, seems particularly mysterious. Camus was not, nor ever claimed to be, religious. In fact, one of the points he makes in his essay is that capital punishment derives its only plausible rationale as a religious punishment and is therefore entirely inappropriate and ethically obscene in our present post-religious, secularized society.

being "devout" or "orthodox." My own view is that one cannot be religious in general any more than one can speak language in general; at any given moment one speaks French or English or Swahili or Japanese, but not "language." Similarly one is not "a religionist," but a believing Catholic, Jew, Presbyterian, Shintoist, or Tallensi. Religious beliefs may be options, as William James described them, but they are not generalized options. It is easy, of course, to misunderstand this point. I don't mean to say that one must be orthodox as a Jew, a Thomist as a Catholic, or a fundamentalist as a Protestant. The history of every important religious community is a complex one, and (as Kaufmann suggests) those figures who are afterwards acknowledged as great religious teachers have generally been in critical opposition to popular religious practices and to much within the past traditions of their own faiths. Nevertheless, for a believer the concept of "religion" (and of deciding to become religious) makes no sense as a category. (For the rationalist critic, from Lucretius to Voltaire to Freud, the term does have a certain polemical sense when, typically, he opposes "religion" on the one hand to "science" or "reason" on the other.) Neither does it make sense as a concept of objective sociological and historical inquiry. To be religious is always to be in some sense an adherent (even as a heretic) to a specific symbolism and a specific historic community, whatever the interpretation of these symbols and this historic community the believer may adopt. It is to be involved in specific beliefs and practices, not just to give assent to the philosophical assertions that a being whom we may call God exists, that life has meaning, etc. Religion is not equivalent to the theistic proposition.

The significance of Kaufmann's book is that it is one more example of a prevailing modern attitude which seems to me, at best, soft-headed and, more often, intellectually presumptuous. The attempts of modern secular intellectuals to help the faltering authority of "religion" ought to be rejected by every sensitive believer, and by every honest atheist. God-in-his-heaven, moral certitude, and cultural unity cannot be restored by nostalgia; the suspenseful piety of religious fellow-travelling demands a resolution, by acts of either commitment or disavowal. The presence of a religious faith may indeed be of unquestionable psychological benefit to the individual and of unquestionable social benefit to a society. But we shall never have the fruit of the tree without nourishing its roots as well; we shall never restore the prestige of the old faiths by demonstrating their psychological and sociological benefits.

Neither is it worth dallying with the lost religious consciousness because we unreflectively equate religion with seriousness, seriousness about the important human and moral issues. Most secular Western intellectuals have not really thought through or lived out the atheist option; they are only on the verge of it. Seeking to palliate a harsh choice, they often argue that all highmindedness and profundity has religious roots or can be viewed as a "religious" (or crypto-religious) position. The concern with the problems of despair and self-deception which Kaufmann singles out in *Anna Karenina* and *The Death of Ivan Ilyich* do not make Tolstoy in these writings a spokesman "for" religion, any more than they do Kafka, as Günther Anders has shown. If, finally, what we admire in religion is its "prophetic" or "critical" stance, as Kaufmann suggests, and we wish to salvage that (cf. also Erich Fromm's Terry lectures, *Psychoanalysis and Religion*, with its distinction between "humanistic" or good and "authoritarian" or bad religion), then we are deluding ourselves. The critical stance of the Old Testament prophets demands the priesthood, the cult, the specific history of Israel; it is rooted in that matrix. One cannot detach criticism from its roots and, ultimately, from that party to which it sets itself in antagonism. Thus Kierkegaard observed in his *Journals* that Protestantism makes no sense alone, without the dialectical opposition to Catholicism. (When there are no priests it makes no sense to protest that every layman is a priest; when there is no institutionalized other-worldliness, it makes no religious sense to denounce monasticism and asceticism and recall people to this world and to their mundane vocations.) The voice of the genuine critic always deserves the most specific hearing. It is simply misleading and vulgar to say of Marx, as Edmund Wilson in *To the Finland Station* and many others have done, that he was really a latter-day prophet; no more than it is true of Freud, though here people are following the cue of Freud's own rather ambivalent self-identification with Moses. The decisive element in Marx and Freud is the critical and entirely secular attitude which they took to all human problems. For their energies as persons and for their immense moral seriousness as thinkers, surely a better epithet of commendation can be found than these tired evocations of the prestige of the religious teacher. If Camus is a serious writer and worthy of respect, it is because he seeks to reason according to the post-religious premises. He does not belong in the "story" of modern religion.

If this is granted, we will become much clearer about the attempts which have been made to work out the serious consequences of atheism for reflective thought and personal morality. The heritage of Nietzsche constitutes one such tradition: the essays of E. M. Cioran, for example. The French moraliste and anti-moraliste tradition—Laclos, Sade, Breton, Sartre, Camus, Georges Bataille, Lévi-Strauss—constitutes another. The Hegelian-Marxist tradition is a third. And the Freudian tradition, which includes not only the work of Freud, but also that of dissidents such as Wilhelm Reich, Herbert Marcuse (*Eros and Civilization*) and Norman Brown (*Life Against Death*), is another. The creative phase of an idea coincides with the period during which it insists, cantankerously, on its boundaries, on what makes it different; but an idea becomes false and impotent when it seeks reconciliation, at cut-rate prices, with other ideas. Modern seriousness, in numerous traditions, exists. Only a bad intellectual end is served when we blur all boundaries and call it religious, too.

[1961]

Psychoanalysis
and Norman O. Brown's
Life Against Death

THE publication of Norman O. Brown's *Life Against Death* (1959) in a paperback edition is a noteworthy event. Together with Herbert Marcuse's *Eros and Civilization* (1955), it represents a new seriousness about Freudian ideas which reveals most previous writing on Freud published in America, be it the right-wing scholasticism of the psychoanalytic journals or the left-wing cultural studies of the Freudian "revisionists" (Fromm, Horney, etc.), as theoretically irrelevant or, at best, superficial. But, more important than its value as a reinterpretation of the most influential mind of our culture is its boldness as a discussion of the fundamental problems—about the hypocrisy of our culture, about art, money, religion, work, about sex and the motives of the body. Serious thinking about these problems—rightly, in my opinion, centered on the meaning of sexuality and of human freedom—has been continuous in France since Sade, Fourier,

Cabanis, and Enfantin; it is to be found today in such disparate works as the sections on the body and on concrete relations with others of Sartre's *Being and Nothingness*, in the essays of Maurice Blanchot, in *L'Histoire d'O*, in the plays and prose of Jean Genet.

But in America, the twin subjects of eroticism and liberty are just beginning to be treated in a serious way. Most of us still feel required to fight the stale battle against inhibitions and prudery, taking sexuality for granted as something which merely needs a freer expression. A country in which the vindication of so sexually reactionary a book as *Lady Chatterley's Lover* is a serious matter is plainly at a very elementary stage of sexual maturity. Lawrence's ideas on sex are seriously marred by his class-romanticism, by his mystique of male separateness, by his puritanical insistence on genital sexuality; and many of his recent literary defenders have admitted this. Yet Lawrence must still be defended, especially when many who reject him have retreated to an even more reactionary position than his: treating sex as a matter-of-fact adjunct to love. The truth is that love is more sexual, more bodily than even Lawrence imagined. And the revolutionary implications of sexuality in contemporary society are far from being fully understood.

Norman Brown's book is a step in this direction. *Life Against Death* cannot fail to shock, if it is taken personally; for it is a book which does not aim at eventual reconciliation with the views of common sense. Another distinction which it possesses: it shows, convincingly, that psychoanalysis is not to be written off—as many contemporary intellectuals have done—as one more vulgar and conformist "ism" (along with Marxism, original sin-ism, existentialism, Zen Buddhism, etc., etc.). The disenchantment with psychoanalysis which animates the most sophisticated voices of our culture is understandable; it is difficult not to reject a view which has become both so official and so bland. The vocabulary of psychoanalysis has become the routine weapon of personal aggression, and the routine way of formulating (and therefore defending oneself against) anxiety, in the American middle classes. Being psychoanalyzed has become as much a bourgeois institution as going to college; and psychoanalytic ideas, incarnated in Broadway plays, in television, in the movies, confront us everywhere. The trouble with psychoanalytic ideas, as it now appears to many, is that they constitute a form of retreat from, and, therefore, conformity to, the real world. Psychoanalytic treatment does not challenge society; it returns us to the world, only a little better able to bear it, and without hope. Psychoanalysis is understood as anti-Utopian and anti-political—a desperate, but fundamentally pessimistic, attempt to safeguard the individual against the oppressive but inevitable claims of society.

But the disenchantment of American intellectuals with psychoanalytic ideas, as with the earlier disenchantment with Marxist ideas (a parallel case), is premature. Marxism is not Stalinism or the suppression of the Hungarian revolution; psychoanalysis is not the Park Avenue analyst or the psychoanalytic journals or the suburban matron discussing her child's Oedipus complex. Disenchantment is the characteristic posture of contemporary American intellectuals, but disenchantment is often the product of laziness. We are not tenacious enough about ideas, as we have not been serious or honest enough about sexuality.

This is the importance of Brown's *Life Against Death*, as well as of Marcuse's *Eros and Civilization*. Brown, like Marcuse, pursues Freud's ideas as a general theory of human nature—not as a therapy which returns people to the society which enforces their conflicts. Psychoanalysis is conceived by Brown not as a mode of treatment to smooth away the neurotic edges of discontent, but as a project for the transformation of human culture, and as a new and higher level in human consciousness as a whole. Freud's psychological categories are thus correctly seen, in the terminology of Marcuse, as political categories.

The step which Brown takes, which moves beyond Freud's own conception of what he was doing, is to show that psychological categories are also bodily categories. For Brown, psychoanalysis (and he does not mean the institutions of current-day psychoanalysis) promises nothing less than the healing of the split between the mind and the body: the transformation of the human ego into a body ego, and the resurrection of the body that is promised in Christian mysticism (Boehme) and in Blake, Novalis, and Rilke. We are nothing but body; all values are bodily values, says Brown. He invites us to accept the androgynous mode of being and the narcissistic mode of self-expression that lie hidden in the body. According to Brown, mankind is unalterably, in the unconscious, in revolt against sexual differentiation and genital organization. The core of human neurosis is man's incapacity to live in the body—to live (that is, to be sexual) and to die.

In a time in which there is nothing more common or more acceptable than criticism of our society and revulsion against civilization, it is well to distinguish the arguments of Brown (and Marcuse) from the general run of criticism, which is either childishly nihilistic or ultimately conformist and irrelevant (or often both). And since both books are sharply critical of Freud at many points, it is also important to distinguish them from other attempts to modify Freudian theory and to extend it as a theory of human nature and a moral critique of society. Both Brown and Marcuse offer the sharpest opposition to the bland "revisionist" interpretation of Freud which rules American cultural and intellectual life—on Broadway, in the nursery, at the cocktail parties, and in the suburban marriage bed. This "revisionist" Freudianism (Fromm to Paddy Chayevsky) passes for a criticism of mechanized, anxious, television-brainwashed America. It seeks to reinstate the value of the individual against the mass society; it offers the worthy ideal of fulfillment through love. But the revisionist critique is superficial. To assert the claims of love, when love is understood as comfort, protection against loneliness, ego-security—while leaving all the claims of sublimation unchallenged—hardly does justice to Freud. It is no accident that Freud chose to use the word sex when, as he himself declared, he might as well have used "love." Freud insisted on sex; he insisted on the body. Few of his followers understood his meaning, or saw its applications in a theory of culture; two exceptions were Ferenczi and the ill-fated Wilhelm Reich. The fact that both Reich and Ferenczi, in Brown's account, misunderstood the implications of Freud's thought—mainly, in their acceptance of the primacy of the orgasm—is less important than the fact that they grasped the critical implications of the Freudian ideas. They are far truer to Freud than the orthodox psychoanalysts who, as a result of their inability to transform psychoanalysis into social criticism, send human desire back into repression again.

Of course, to some extent, the master does deserve the disciples he gets. The contemporary appearance of psychoanalysis as a form of expensive spiritual counselling on techniques of adjustment and reconciliation to culture proceeds from the limits in Freud's own thought, which Brown points out in careful detail. Revolutionary mind that he was, Freud nevertheless supported the perennial aspirations of repressive culture. He accepted the inevitability of culture as it is, with its two characteristics—"a strengthening of the intellect, which is beginning to govern instinctual life, and an internalization of the aggressive impulses, with all its consequent advantages and disadvantages." Those who think of Freud as the champion of libidinal expressiveness may be surprised at what he calls "the psychological ideal," for it is none other than "the primacy of the intellect."

More generally, Freud is heir to the Platonic tradition of Western thought in its two paramount, and related, assumptions: the dualism of mind and body, and the self-evident value (both theoretical and practical) of self-consciousness. The first assumption is reflected in Freud's own acceptance of the view that sexuality is "lower" and the sublimations in art, science, and culture "higher." Added to this is the pessimistic view of sexuality which regards the sexual as precisely the area of vulnerability in human personality. The libidinal impulses are in uncontrollable conflict in themselves, a prey to frustration, aggression, and internalization in guilt; and the repressive agency of culture is necessary to harness the self-repressive mechanisms installed in human nature itself. The second assumption is reflected in the way in which the Freudian therapy assumes the curative value of self-consciousness, of knowing in detail how and in what way we are ill. Bringing to light the hidden motives must, Freud thought, automatically dispel them. Neurotic illness, in his conception, is a form of amnesia, a forgetting (bungled repression) of the painful past. Not to know the past is to be in bondage to it, while to remember, to know, is to be set free.

Brown criticizes both of these assumptions of Freud. We are not body versus mind, he says; this is to deny death, and therefore to deny life. And self-consciousness, divorced from the experiences of the body, is also equated with the life-denying denial of death. Brown's argument, too involved to summarize here, does not entail a repudiation of the value of consciousness or reflectiveness. Rather, a necessary distinction is made. What is wanted, in his terminology, is not Apollonian (or sublimation) consciousness, but Dionysian (or body) consciousness.

The terms "Apollonian" and "Dionysian" will inevitably remind one of Nietzsche, and the association is appropriate. The key to this reinterpretation of Freud is Nietzsche. It is interesting, however, that Brown does not link his discussion to Nietzsche, but rather to the eschatological tradition within Christianity.

The specialty of Christian eschatology lies precisely in its rejection of the Platonic hostility to the human body and to 'matter,' its refusal to identify the Platonic path of sublimation with ultimate salvation, and its affirmation that eternal life can only be life in a body. Christian asceticism can carry punishment of the fallen body to heights inconceivable to Plato, but Christian hope is for the redemption of that fallen body. Hence the affirmation of Tertullian—'The body will rise again, all of the body, the identical body, the entire body.' The medieval Catholic synthesis between Christianity and Greek philosophy, with its notion of an immortal soul, compromised and confused the issue; only Protestantism carries the full burden of the peculiar Christian faith. Luther's break with the doctrine of sublimation (good works) is decisive, but the theologian of the resurrected body is the cobbler of Görlitz, Jacob Boehme.

The polemical drive, if not the exquisite detail, of Brown's book can be seen from this passage. It is at the same time an analysis of the whole range of Freudian theory, a theory of instinct and culture, and a set of historical case studies. Brown's commitment to Protestantism as the herald of a culture which has transcended sublimation is, however, historically dubious. To make only the most obvious criticism, Protestantism is also Calvinism, and the Calvinist ethic (as Max Weber has shown) provided the most powerful impetus for the ideals of sublimation and self-repression which are incarnated in modern urban culture.

Nevertheless, by putting his ideas in the framework of Christian eschatology (rather than in the terms of the passionate atheists like Sade, Nietzsche, and Sartre), Brown raises some additional is-

sues of great importance. The genius of Christianity has been its
development, from Judaism, of a historical view of the world and
the human condition. And Brown's analysis, by allying itself with
some of the submerged promises of Christian eschatology, opens
up the possibility of a psychoanalytic theory of history which does
not simply reduce cultural history to the psychology of individuals.
The originality of *Life Against Death* consists in its working out a
point of view which is simultaneously historical and psychological.
Brown demonstrates that the psychological point of view does not
necessarily imply a rejection of history, in terms of its eschatological
aspirations, and a resignation to the "limits of human nature" and
the necessity of repression through the agency of culture.

If this is so, however, we must reconsider the meaning of eschatology, or Utopianism, itself. Traditionally, eschatology has taken
the form of an expectation of the future transcendence of the human condition for all mankind in inexorably advancing history.
And it is against this expectation, whether in the form of Biblical
eschatology, enlightenment, progressivism, or the theories of Marx
and Hegel, that modern "psychological" critics have taken their
largely conservative stand. But not all eschatological theories are
theories of history. There is another kind of eschatology, which
might be called the eschatology of immanence (as opposed to the
more familiar eschatology of transcendence). It is this hope that
Nietzsche, the greatest critic of the Platonic devaluation of the
world (and of its heir, that "popular Platonism" known as Christianity), expressed in his theory of the "eternal return" and the "will
to power." However, for Nietzsche, the promise of fulfilled immanence was available only to the few, the masters, and rested on a
perpetuation or freezing of the historical impasse of a master-slave
society; there could be no collective fulfillment. Brown rejects the
logic of public domination which Nietzsche accepted as the inevitable price for the fulfillment of the few. The highest praise one
can give to Brown's book is that, apart from its all-important attempt to penetrate and further the insights of Freud, it is the first
major attempt to formulate an eschatology of immanence in the
seventy years since Nietzsche.

[1961]

Happenings:
an art of radical
juxtaposition

THERE has appeared in New York recently a new, and still esoteric, genre of spectacle. At first sight apparently a cross between art exhibit and theatrical performance, these events have been given the modest and somewhat teasing name of "Happenings." They have taken place in lofts, small art galleries, backyards, and small theaters before audiences averaging between thirty and one hundred persons. To describe a Happening for those who have not seen one means dwelling on what Happenings are not. They don't take place on a stage conventionally understood, but *in* a dense object-clogged setting which may be made, assembled, or found, or all three. In this setting a number of participants, not actors, perform movements and handle objects antiphonally and in concert to the accompaniment (sometimes) of words, wordless sounds, music, flashing lights, and odors. The Happening has no plot, though it is an action, or rather a series of actions and events. It also shuns continuous rational discourse, though it may contain words like "Help!", "*Voglio un bic-chiere di acqua*," "Love me," "Car," "One, two, three . . ." Speech is purified and condensed by disparateness (there is only the speech of need) and then expanded by ineffectuality, by the lack of relation between the persons enacting the Happening.

Those who do Happenings in New York—but they are not just a New York phenomenon; similar activities have been reported in Osaka, Stockholm, Cologne, Milan, and Paris by groups unrelated to each other—are young, in their late twenties or early thirties. They are mostly painters (Allan Kaprow, Jim Dine, Red Grooms, Robert Whitman, Claes Oldenburg, Al Hansen, George Brecht, Yoko Ono, Carolee Schneemann) and a few musicians (Dick Higgins, Philip Corner, LaMonte Young). Allan Kaprow, the man who more than anyone else is responsible for stating and working out the genre, is the only academic among them; he formerly taught art and art history at Rutgers and now teaches at the State University of New York on Long Island. For Kaprow, a painter and (for a year) a student of John Cage, doing Happenings since 1957 has replaced painting; Happenings are, as he puts it, what his painting has become. But for most of the others, this is not the case; they have continued to paint or compose music in addition to occasionally producing a Happening or performing in the Happening devised by a friend.

The first Happening in public was Allan Kaprow's *Eighteen Happenings in Six Parts*, presented in October, 1959, at the opening of the Reuben Gallery, which Kaprow, among others, helped to form. For a couple of years, the Reuben Gallery, the Judson Gallery, and later the Green Gallery, were the principal showcases of Happenings in New York by Kaprow, Red Grooms, Jim Dine, Robert Whitman, and others; in the recent years, the only series of Happenings were those of Claes Oldenburg, presented every weekend in the three tiny back rooms of his "store" on East Second Street. In the five years since the Happenings have been presented in public, the group has enlarged from an original circle of close friends, and the members have diverged in their conceptions; no statement about what Happenings are as a genre will be acceptable to all the people now doing them. Some Happenings are more sparse, others more crowded with incident; some are violent, others are witty; some are like haiku, others are epic; some are vignettes, others more theatrical. Nevertheless, it is possible to discern an essential unity in the form, and to draw certain conclusions about the relevance of Happenings to the arts of painting and theater. Kaprow, by the way, has written the best article yet to appear on Happenings, their meaning in general in the context of the contemporary art scene, and their evolution for him in particular, in the May, 1961, *Art News*, to which the reader is referred for a fuller description of what literally "happens" than I shall attempt in this article.

Perhaps the most striking feature of the Happening is its treatment (this is the only word for it) of the audience. The event seems designed to tease and abuse the audience. The performers may sprinkle water on the audience, or fling pennies or sneeze-producing detergent powder at it. Someone may be making near-deafening noises on an oil drum, or waving an acetylene torch in the direction of the spectators. Several radios may be playing simultaneously. The audience may be made to stand uncomfortably in a crowded room, or fight for space to stand on boards laid in a few inches of water. There is no attempt to cater to the audience's desire to see everything. In fact this is often deliberately frustrated, by performing some of the events in semi-darkness or by having events go on in different rooms simultaneously. In Allan Kaprow's *A Spring Happening*, presented in March, 1961, at the Reuben Gallery, the spectators were confined inside a long box-like structure resembling a cattle car; peep-holes had been bored in the wooden walls of this enclosure through which the spectators could strain to see the events taking place outside; when the Happening was over, the walls collapsed, and the spectators were driven out by someone operating a power lawnmower.

(This abusive involvement of the audience seems to provide, in default of anything else, the dramatic spine of the Happening. When the Happening is more purely spectacle, and the audience simply spectators, as in Allan Kaprow's *The Courtyard*, presented in November, 1962, at the Renaissance House, the event is considerably less dense and compelling.)

Another striking feature of Happenings is their treatment of time. The duration of a Happening is unpredictable; it may be anywhere from ten to forty-five minutes; the average one is about a half-hour in length. I have noticed, in attending a fair number of them over the last two years, that the audience of Happenings, a loyal, appreciative, and for the most part experienced audience, frequently does not know when they are over, and has to be signalled to leave. The fact that in the audiences one sees mostly the same faces again and again indicates this is not due to a lack of familiarity with the form. The unpredictable duration, and content, of each individual Happening is essential to its effect. This is because the Happening has no plot, no story, and therefore no element of suspense (which would then entail the satisfaction of suspense).

The Happening operates by creating an asymmetrical network of surprises, without climax or consummation; this is the alogic of dreams rather than the logic of most art. Dreams have no sense of time. Neither do the Happenings. Lacking a plot and continuous rational discourse, they have no past. As the name itself suggests, Happenings are always in the present tense. The same words, if there are any, are said over and over; speech is reduced to a stutter. The same actions, too, are frequently repeated throughout a single Happening—a kind of gestural stutter, or done in slow motion, to convey a sense of the arrest of time. Occasionally the entire Happening takes a circular form, opening and concluding with the same act or gesture.

One way in which the Happenings state their freedom from time is in their deliberate impermanence. A painter or sculptor who makes Happenings does not make anything that can be purchased. One cannot buy a Happening; one can only support it. It is consumed on the premises. This would seem to make Happenings a form of theater, for one can only attend a theatrical performance, but can't take it home. But in the theater, there is a text, a complete "score" for the performance which is printed, can be bought, read, and has an existence independent of any performance of it. Happenings are not theater either, if by theater we mean plays. However, it is not true (as some Happening-goers suppose) that

Happenings are improvised on the spot. They are carefully rehearsed for any time from a week to several months—though the script or score is minimal, usually no more than a page of general directions for movements and descriptions of materials. Much of what goes on in the performance has been worked out or choreographed in rehearsal by the performers themselves; and if the Happening is done for several evenings consecutively it is likely to vary a good deal from performance to performance, far more than in the theater. But while the same Happening might be given several nights in a row, it is not meant to enter into a repertory which can be repeated. Once dismantled after a given performance or series of performances, it is never revived, never performed again. In part, this has to do with the deliberately occasional materials which go into Happenings—paper, wooden crates, tin cans, burlap sacks, foods, walls painted for the occasion—materials which are often literally consumed, or destroyed, in the course of the performance.

What is primary in a Happening is materials—and their modulations as hard and soft, dirty and clean. This preoccupation with materials, which might seem to make the Happenings more like painting than theater, is also expressed in the use or treatment of persons as material objects rather than "characters." The people in the Happenings are often made to look like objects, by enclosing them in burlap sacks, elaborate paper wrappings, shrouds, and masks. (Or, the person may be used as a still-life, as in Allan Kaprow's *Untitled Happening*, given in the basement boiler room of the Maidman Theater in March, 1962, in which a naked woman lay on a ladder strung above the space in which the Happenings took place.) Much of the action, violent and otherwise, of Happenings involves this use of the person as a material object. There is a great deal of violent using of the physical persons of the performers by the person himself (jumping, falling) and by each other (lifting, chasing, throwing, pushing, hitting, wrestling); and sometimes a slower, more sensuous use of the person (caressing, menacing, gazing) by others or by the person himself. Another way in which people are employed is in the discovery or the impassioned, repetitive use of materials for their sensuous properties rather than their conventional uses: dropping pieces of bread into a bucket of water, setting a table for a meal, rolling a huge paper-screen hoop along the floor, hanging up laundry. Jim Dine's *Car Crash*, done at the Reuben Gallery in November, 1960, ended with a man smashing and grinding pieces of colored chalk into a blackboard. Simple acts like coughing and carrying, a man shaving himself, or a group of people eating, will be prolonged, repetitively, to a point of demoniacal frenzy.

Of the materials used, it might be noted that one cannot distinguish among set, props, and costumes in a Happening, as one can in the theater. The underwear or thrift-shop oddments which a performer may wear are as much a part of the whole composition as the paint-spattered papier-mâché shapes which protrude from the wall or the trash which is strewn on the floor. Unlike the theater and like some modern painting, in the Happening objects are not *placed*, but rather scattered about and heaped together. The Happening takes place in what can best be called an "environment," and this environment typically is messy and disorderly and crowded in the extreme, constructed of some materials which are rather fragile, such as paper and cloth, and others which are chosen for their abused, dirty, and dangerous condition. The Happenings thereby register (in a real, not simply an ideological way) a protest against the museum conception of art—the idea that the job of the artist is to make things to be preserved and cherished. One cannot hold on to a Happening, and one can only cherish it as one cherishes a firecracker going off dangerously close to one's face.

Happenings have been called by some "painters' theater," which means—aside from the fact that most of the people who do them are painters—that they can be described as animated paintings, more accurately as "animated collages" or "trompe l'oeil brought to life." Further, the appearance of Happenings can be described as one logical development of the New York school of painting of the fifties. The gigantic size of many of the canvases painted in New York in the last decade, designed to overwhelm and envelop the spectator, plus the increasing use of materials other than paint to adhere to, and later extend from, the canvas, indicate the latent intention of this type of painting to project itself into a three-dimensional form. This is exactly what some people started to do. The crucial next step was taken with the work done in the middle and late fifties by Robert Rauschenberg, Allan Kaprow, and others in a new form called "assemblages," a hybrid of painting, collage, and sculpture, using a sardonic variety of materials, mainly in the state of debris, including license plates, newspaper clippings, pieces of glass, machine parts, and the artist's socks. From the assemblage to the whole room or "environment" is only one further step. The final step, the Happening, simply puts people into the environment and sets it in motion. There is no doubt that much of the style of the Happening—its general look of messiness, its fondness for incorporating ready-made materials of no artistic prestige, particularly the junk of urban civilization—owes to the experience and pressures of New York painting. (It should be mentioned, however, that Kaprow for one thinks the use of urban junk is not a necessary element of the Happening form, and contends that Happenings can as well be composed and put on in pastoral surroundings, using the "clean" materials of nature.)

Thus recent painting supplies one way of explaining the look and something of the style of Happenings. Yet it does not explain their form. For this we must look beyond painting and particularly to Surrealism. By Surrealism, I do not mean a specific movement in painting inaugurated by André Breton's manifesto in 1924 and to which we associate the names of Max Ernst, Dali, Chirico, Magritte, and others. I mean a mode of sensibility which cuts across all the arts in the 20th century. There is a Surrealist tradition in the theater, in painting, in poetry, in the cinema, in music, and in the novel; even in architecture there is, if not a tradition, at least one candidate, the Spanish architect Gaudí. The Surrealist tradition in all these arts is united by the idea of destroying conventional meanings, and creating new meanings or counter-meanings through radical juxtaposition (the "collage principle"). Beauty, in the words of Lautréamont, is "the fortuitous encounter of a sewing machine and an umbrella on a dissecting table." Art so understood is obviously animated by aggression, aggression toward the presumed conventionality of its audience and, above all, aggression toward the medium itself. The Surrealist sensibility aims to shock, through its techniques of radical juxtaposition. Even one of the classical methods of psychoanalysis, free association, can be interpreted as another working-out of the Surrealist principle of radical juxtaposition. By its accepting as relevant every unpremeditated statement made by the patient, the Freudian technique of interpretation shows itself to be based on the same logic of coherence behind contradiction to which we are accustomed in modern art. Using the same logic, the Dadaist Kurt Schwitters made his brilliant Merz constructions of the early twenties out of deliberately unartistic materials; one of his collages, for example, is assembled from the gutter-pickings of a single city block. This recalls Freud's description of his method as divining meaning from "the rubbish-heap . . . of our observations," from the collation of the most insignificant details; as a time limit the analyst's daily hour with the patient is no less arbitrary than the space limit of one block from whose gutter the rubbish was selected; everything depends on the creative accidents of arrangement and insight. One may also see a kind of involuntary collage-principle in many of the artifacts of the modern city: the brutal disharmony of buildings in size and style, the wild juxtaposition of store signs, the clamorous layout of the modern newspaper, etc.

The art of radical juxtaposition can serve different uses, however. A great deal of the content of Surrealism has served the purposes of wit—either the delicious joke in itself of what is inane, childish, extravagant, obsessional; or social satire. This is particularly the purpose of Dada; and of the Surrealism that is represented in the International Surrealist Exhibition in Paris in January, 1938, and the exhibits in New York in 1942 and 1960. Simone de Beauvoir in the second volume of her memoirs describes the 1938 spook-house as follows:

In the entrance hall stood one of Dali's special creations: a taxi cab, rain streaming out of it, with a blonde, swooning female dummy posed inside, surrounded by a sort of lettuce-and-chicory salad all smothered with snails. The "Rue Surréaliste" contained other similar figures, clothed or nude, by Man Ray, Max Ernst, Dominguez, and Maurice Henry. Masson's [was] a face imprisoned in a cage and gagged with a pansy. The main salon had been arranged by Marcel Duchamp to look like a grotto; it contained, among other things, a pond and four beds grouped around a brazier, while the ceiling was covered with coal bags. The whole place smelled of Brazilian coffee, and various objects loomed up out of the carefully contrived semi-darkness: a fur-lined dish, an occasional table with the legs of a woman. On all sides ordinary things like walls and doors and flower vases were breaking free from human restraint. I don't think surrealism had any direct influence on us, but it had impregnated the very air we breathed. It was the surrealists, for instance, who made it fashionable to frequent the Flea Market where Sartre and Olga and I often spent our Sunday afternoons.

The last line of this quote is particularly interesting, for it recalls how the Surrealist principle has given rise to a certain kind of witty appreciation of the derelict, inane, démodé objects of modern civilization—the taste for a certain kind of passionate non-art that is known as "camp." The fur-lined teacup, the portrait executed out of Pepsi-Cola bottle caps, the perambulating toilet bowl, are attempts to create objects which have built into them a kind of wit which the sophisticated beholder with his eyes opened by camp can bring to the enjoyment of Cecil B. DeMille movies, comic books, and art nouveau lampshades. The main requirement for such wit is that the objects not be high art or good taste in any normally valued sense; the more despised the material or the more banal the sentiments expressed, the better.

But the Surrealist principle can be made to serve other purposes than wit, whether the disinterested wit of sophistication or the polemical wit of satire. It can be conceived more seriously, thera-peutically—for the purpose of reeducating the senses (in art) or the character (in psychoanalysis). And finally, it can be made to serve the purposes of terror. If the meaning of modern art is its discovery beneath the logic of everyday life of the alogic of dreams, then we may expect the art which has the freedom of dreaming also to have its emotional range. There are witty dreams, solemn dreams, and there are nightmares.

The examples of terror in the use of the Surrealist principle are more easily illustrated in arts with a dominant figurative tradition, like literature and the film, than in music (Varèse, Scheffer, Stockhausen, Cage) or painting (de Kooning, Bacon). In literature, one thinks of Lautréamont's *Maldoror* and Kafka's tales and novels and the morgue poems of Gottfried Benn. From the film, examples are two by Buñuel and Dali, *Le Chien Andalou* and *L'Âge d'Or*, Franju's *Le Sang des Bêtes*, and, more recently, two short films, the Polish *Life Is Beautiful* and the American Bruce Connor's *A Movie*, and certain moments in the films of Alfred Hitchcock, H. G. Clouzot, and Kon Ichikawa. But the best understanding of the Surrealist principle employed for purposes of terrorization is to be found in the writings of Antonin Artaud, a Frenchman who had four important and model careers: as a poet, a lunatic, a film actor, and a theoretician of the theater. In his collection of essays, *The Theater and Its Double*, Artaud envisages nothing less than a complete repudiation of the modern Western theater, with its cult of masterpieces, its primary emphasis on the written text (the word), its tame emotional range. Artaud writes: "The theater must make itself the equal of life—not an individual life, that individual aspect of life in which characters triumph, but the sort of liberated life which sweeps away human individuality." This transcendence of the burden and limitations of personal individuality—also a hopeful theme in D. H. Lawrence and Jung—is executed through recourse to the preeminently collective contents of dreaming. Only in our dreams do we nightly strike below the shallow level of what Artaud calls, contemptuously, "psychological and social man." But dreaming does not mean for Artaud simply poetry, fantasy; it means violence, insanity, nightmare. The connection with the dream will necessarily give rise to what Artaud calls a "theater of cruelty," the title of two of his manifestoes. The theater must furnish "the spectator with the truthful precipitates of dreams, in which his taste for crime, his erotic obsessions, his savagery, his chimeras, his Utopian sense of life and matter, even his cannibalism, pour out, on a level not counterfeit and illusory, but interior. . . . The theater, like dreams, must be bloody and inhuman."

The prescriptions which Artaud offers in *The Theater and Its Double* describe better than anything else what Happenings are.

Artaud shows the connection between three typical features of the Happening: first, its supra-personal or impersonal treatment of persons; second, its emphasis on spectacle and sound, and disregard for the word; and third, its professed aim to assault the audience.

The appetite for violence in art is hardly a new phenomenon. As Ruskin noted in 1880 in the course of an attack on "the modern novel" (his examples are *Guy Mannering* and *Bleak House!*), the taste for the fantastic, the outré, the rejected, and the willingness to be shocked are perhaps the most remarkable characteristics of modern audiences. Inevitably, this drives the artist to ever greater and more intense attempts to arouse a reaction from his audience. The question is only whether a reaction need always be provoked by terrorization. It seems to be the implicit consensus of those who do Happenings that other kinds of arousal (for example, sexual arousal) are in fact less effective, and that the last bastion of the emotional life is fear.

Yet it is also interesting to note that this art form which is designed to stir the modern audience from its cozy emotional anesthesia operates with images of anesthetized persons, acting in a kind of slow-motion disjunction with each other, and gives us an image of action characterized above all by ceremoniousness and ineffectuality. At this point the Surrealist arts of terror link up with the deepest meaning of comedy: the assertion of invulnerability. In the heart of comedy, there is emotional anesthesia. What permits us to laugh at painful and grotesque events is that we observe that the people to whom these events happen are really underreacting. No matter how much they scream or prance about or inveigh to heaven or lament their misfortune, the audience knows they are really not feeling very much. The protagonists of great comedy all have something of the automaton or robot in them. This is the secret of such different examples of comedy as Aristophanes' *The Clouds*, *Gulliver's Travels*, Tex Avery cartoons, *Candide*, *Kind Hearts and Coronets*, the films of Buster Keaton, *Ubu Roi*, the Goon Show. The secret of comedy is the dead-pan—or the exaggerated reaction or the misplaced reaction that is a parody of a true response. Comedy, as much as tragedy, works by a certain stylization of emotional response. In the case of tragedy, it is by a heightening of the norm of feeling; in the case of comedy, it is by underreacting and misreacting according to the norms of feeling.

Surrealism is perhaps the farthest extension of the idea of comedy, running the full range from wit to terror. It is "comic" rather than "tragic" because Surrealism (in all its examples, which include Happenings) stresses the extremes of disrelation—which is preeminently the subject of comedy, as "relatedness" is the subject and source of tragedy. I, and other people in the audience, often laugh during Happenings. I don't think this is simply because we are embarrassed or made nervous by violent and absurd actions. I think we laugh because what goes on in the Happenings is, in the deepest sense, funny. This does not make it any less terrifying. There is something that moves one to laughter, if only our social pieties and highly conventional sense of the serious would allow it, in the most terrible of modern catastrophes and atrocities. There is something comic in modern experience as such, a demonic, not a divine comedy, precisely to the extent that modern experience is characterized by meaningless mechanized situations of disrelation.

Comedy is not any less comic because it is punitive. As in tragedy, every comedy needs a scapegoat, someone who will be punished and expelled from the social order represented mimetically in the spectacle. What goes on in the Happenings merely follows Artaud's prescription for a spectacle which will eliminate the stage, that is, the distance between spectators and performers, and "will physically envelop the spectator." In the Happening this scapegoat is the audience.

[1962]

Notes on
"Camp"

MANY things in the world
have not been named; and many things, even if they have been
named, have never been described. One of these is the sensibility
—unmistakably modern, a variant of sophistication but hardly
identical with it—that goes by the cult name of "Camp."

A sensibility (as distinct from an idea) is one of the hardest
things to talk about; but there are special reasons why Camp, in
particular, has never been discussed. It is not a natural mode of sensibility, if there be any such. Indeed the essence of Camp is its love
of the unnatural: of artifice and exaggeration. And Camp is
esoteric—something of a private code, a badge of identity even,
among small urban cliques. Apart from a lazy two-page sketch in
Christopher Isherwood's novel *The World in the Evening* (1954),
it has hardly broken into print. To talk about Camp is therefore to
betray it. If the betrayal can be defended, it will be for the edifica-

tion it provides, or the dignity of the conflict it resolves. For myself, I plead the goal of self-edification, and the goad of a sharp conflict in my own sensibility. I am strongly drawn to Camp, and almost as strongly offended by it. That is why I want to talk about it, and why I can. For no one who wholeheartedly shares in a given sensibility can analyze it; he can only, whatever his intention, exhibit it. To name a sensibility, to draw its contours and to recount its history, requires a deep sympathy modified by revulsion.

Though I am speaking about sensibility only—and about a sensibility that, among other things, converts the serious into the frivolous—these are grave matters. Most people think of sensibility or taste as the realm of purely subjective preferences, those mysterious attractions, mainly sensual, that have not been brought under the sovereignty of reason. They allow that considerations of taste play a part in their reactions to people and to works of art. But this attitude is naïve. And even worse. To patronize the faculty of taste is to patronize oneself. For taste governs every free—as opposed to rote—human response. Nothing is more decisive. There is taste in people, visual taste, taste in emotion—and there is taste in acts, taste in morality. Intelligence, as well, is really a kind of taste: taste in ideas. (One of the facts to be reckoned with is that taste tends to develop very unevenly. It's rare that the same person has good visual taste and good taste in people and taste in ideas.)

Taste has no system and no proofs. But there is something like a logic of taste: the consistent sensibility which underlies and gives rise to a certain taste. A sensibility is almost, but not quite, ineffable. Any sensibility which can be crammed into the mold of a system, or handled with the rough tools of proof, is no longer a sensibility at all. It has hardened into an idea. . . .

To snare a sensibility in words, especially one that is alive and powerful,* one must be tentative and nimble. The form of jottings, rather than an essay (with its claim to a linear, consecutive argument), seemed more appropriate for getting down something

---

* The sensibility of an era is not only its most decisive, but also its most perishable, aspect. One may capture the ideas (intellectual history) and the behavior (social history) of an epoch without ever touching upon the sensibility or taste which informed those ideas, that behavior. Rare are those historical studies—like Huizinga on the late Middle Ages, Febvre on 16th century France—which do tell us something about the sensibility of the period.

of this particular fugitive sensibility. It's embarrassing to be solemn and treatise-like about Camp. One runs the risk of having, oneself, produced a very inferior piece of Camp.

These notes are for Oscar Wilde.

"One should either be a work of art, or wear a work of art."
—*Phrases & Philosophies for the Use of the Young*

1. To start very generally: Camp is a certain mode of aestheticism. It is one way of seeing the world as an aesthetic phenomenon. That way, the way of Camp, is not in terms of beauty, but in terms of the degree of artifice, of stylization.

2. To emphasize style is to slight content, or to introduce an attitude which is neutral with respect to content. It goes without saying that the Camp sensibility is disengaged, depoliticized—or at least apolitical.

3. Not only is there a Camp vision, a Camp way of looking at things. Camp is as well a quality discoverable in objects and the behavior of persons. There are "campy" movies, clothes, furniture, popular songs, novels, people, buildings. . . . This distinction is important. True, the Camp eye has the power to transform experience. But not everything can be seen as Camp. It's not *all* in the eye of the beholder.

4. Random examples of items which are part of the canon of Camp:

> Zuleika Dobson
> Tiffany lamps
> Scopitone films
> The Brown Derby restaurant on Sunset Boulevard in LA
> The Enquirer, headlines and stories
> Aubrey Beardsley drawings
> Swan Lake
> Bellini's operas
> Visconti's direction of *Salome* and *'Tis Pity She's a Whore*
> certain turn-of-the-century picture postcards
> Schoedsack's *King Kong*

> the Cuban pop singer La Lupe
> Lynn Ward's novel in woodcuts, *God's Man*
> the old Flash Gordon comics
> women's clothes of the twenties (feather boas, fringed and beaded dresses, etc.)
> the novels of Ronald Firbank and Ivy Compton-Burnett
> stag movies seen without lust

5. Camp taste has an affinity for certain arts rather than others. Clothes, furniture, all the elements of visual décor, for instance, make up a large part of Camp. For Camp art is often decorative art, emphasizing texture, sensuous surface, and style at the expense of content. Concert music, though, because it is contentless, is rarely Camp. It offers no opportunity, say, for a contrast between silly or extravagant content and rich form. . . . Sometimes whole art forms become saturated with Camp. Classical ballet, opera, movies have seemed so for a long time. In the last two years, popular music (post rock-'n'-roll, what the French call yé yé) has been annexed. And movie criticism (like lists of "The 10 Best Bad Movies I Have Seen") is probably the greatest popularizer of Camp taste today, because most people still go to the movies in a high-spirited and unpretentious way.

6. There is a sense in which it is correct to say: "It's too good to be Camp." Or "too important," not marginal enough. (More on this later.) Thus, the personality and many of the works of Jean Cocteau are Camp, but not those of André Gide; the operas of Richard Strauss, but not those of Wagner; concoctions of Tin Pan Alley and Liverpool, but not jazz. Many examples of Camp are things which, from a "serious" point of view, are either bad art or kitsch. Not all, though. Not only is Camp not necessarily bad art, but some art which can be approached as Camp (example: the major films of Louis Feuillade) merits the most serious admiration and study.

"The more we study Art, the less we care for Nature."
—*The Decay of Lying*

7. All Camp objects, and persons, contain a large element of artifice. Nothing in nature can be campy. . . . Rural Camp is still man-made, and most campy objects are urban. (Yet, they often have a serenity—or a naïveté—which is the equivalent of pastoral. A great deal of Camp suggests Empson's phrase, "urban pastoral.")

8. Camp is a vision of the world in terms of style—but a particular kind of style. It is the love of the exaggerated, the "off," of things-being-what-they-are-not. The best example is in Art Nouveau, the most typical and fully developed Camp style. Art Nouveau objects, typically, convert one thing into something else: the lighting fixtures in the form of flowering plants, the living room which is really a grotto. A remarkable example: the Paris Métro entrances designed by Hector Guimard in the late 1890s in the shape of cast-iron orchid stalks.

9. As a taste in persons, Camp responds particularly to the markedly attenuated and to the strongly exaggerated. The androgyne is certainly one of the great images of Camp sensibility. Examples: the swooning, slim, sinuous figures of pre-Raphaelite painting and poetry; the thin, flowing, sexless bodies in Art Nouveau prints and posters, presented in relief on lamps and ashtrays; the haunting androgynous vacancy behind the perfect beauty of Greta Garbo. Here, Camp taste draws on a mostly unacknowledged truth of taste: the most refined form of sexual attractiveness (as well as the most refined form of sexual pleasure) consists in going against the grain of one's sex. What is most beautiful in virile men is something feminine; what is most beautiful in feminine women is something masculine. . . . Allied to the Camp taste for the androgynous is something that seems quite different but isn't: a relish for the exaggeration of sexual characteristics and personality mannerisms. For obvious reasons, the best examples that can be cited are movie stars. The corny flamboyant femaleness of Jayne Mansfield, Gina Lollobrigida, Jane Russell, Virginia Mayo; the exaggerated he-man-ness of Steve Reeves, Victor Mature. The great stylists of temperament and mannerism, like Bette

Davis, Barbara Stanwyck, Tallulah Bankhead, Edwige Feuillière.

10. Camp sees everything in quotation marks. It's not a lamp, but a "lamp"; not a woman, but a "woman." To perceive Camp in objects and persons is to understand Being-as-Playing-a-Role. It is the farthest extension, in sensibility, of the metaphor of life as theater.

11. Camp is the triumph of the epicene style. (The convertibility of "man" and "woman," "person" and "thing.") But all style, that is, artifice, is, ultimately, epicene. Life is not stylish. Neither is nature.

12. The question isn't, "Why travesty, impersonation, theatricality?" The question is, rather, "When does travesty, impersonation, theatricality acquire the special flavor of Camp?" Why is the atmosphere of Shakespeare's comedies (*As You Like It*, etc.) not epicene, while that of *Der Rosenkavalier* is?

13. The dividing line seems to fall in the 18th century; there the origins of Camp taste are to be found (Gothic novels, Chinoiserie, caricature, artificial ruins, and so forth.) But the relation to nature was quite different then. In the 18th century, people of taste either patronized nature (Strawberry Hill) or attempted to remake it into something artificial (Versailles). They also indefatigably patronized the past. Today's Camp taste effaces nature, or else contradicts it outright. And the relation of Camp taste to the past is extremely sentimental.

14. A pocket history of Camp might, of course, begin farther back—with the mannerist artists like Pontormo, Rosso, and Caravaggio, or the extraordinarily theatrical painting of Georges de La Tour, or Euphuism (Lyly, etc.) in literature. Still, the soundest starting point seems to be the late 17th and early 18th century, because of that period's extraordinary feeling for artifice, for surface, for symmetry; its taste for the picturesque and the thrilling, its elegant conventions for representing instant feeling and the total presence of character—the epigram and the rhymed couplet (in words), the flourish (in gesture and in music). The late 17th and early 18th century is the great period of Camp: Pope, Congreve, Walpole, etc., but not Swift; *les précieux* in France; the rococo churches of Munich; Pergolesi. Somewhat later: much of Mozart. But in the 19th cen-

tury, what had been distributed throughout all of high culture now becomes a special taste; it takes on overtones of the acute, the esoteric, the perverse. Confining the story to England alone, we see Camp continuing wanly through 19th century aestheticism (Burne-Jones, Pater, Ruskin, Tennyson), emerging full-blown with the Art Nouveau movement in the visual and decorative arts, and finding its conscious ideologists in such "wits" as Wilde and Firbank.

15. Of course, to say all these things are Camp is not to argue they are simply that. A full analysis of Art Nouveau, for instance, would scarcely equate it with Camp. But such an analysis cannot ignore what in Art Nouveau allows it to be experienced as Camp. Art Nouveau is full of "content," even of a political-moral sort; it was a revolutionary movement in the arts, spurred on by a utopian vision (somewhere between William Morris and the Bauhaus group) of an organic politics and taste. Yet there is also a feature of the Art Nouveau objects which suggests a disengaged, unserious, "aesthete's" vision. This tells us something important about Art Nouveau—and about what the lens of Camp, which blocks out content, is.

16. Thus, the Camp sensibility is one that is alive to a double sense in which some things can be taken. But this is not the familiar split-level construction of a literal meaning, on the one hand, and a symbolic meaning, on the other. It is the difference, rather, between the thing as meaning something, anything, and the thing as pure artifice.

17. This comes out clearly in the vulgar use of the word Camp as a verb, "to camp," something that people do. To camp is a mode of seduction—one which employs flamboyant mannerisms susceptible of a double interpretation; gestures full of duplicity, with a witty meaning for cognoscenti and another, more impersonal, for outsiders. Equally and by extension, when the word becomes a noun, when a person or a thing is "a camp," a duplicity is involved. Behind the "straight" public sense in which something can be taken, one has found a private zany experience of the thing.

"To be natural is such a very difficult pose to keep up."
—*An Ideal Husband*

18. One must distinguish between naïve and deliberate Camp. Pure Camp is always naïve. Camp which knows itself to be Camp ("camping") is usually less satisfying.

19. The pure examples of Camp are unintentional; they are dead serious. The Art Nouveau craftsman who makes a lamp with a snake coiled around it is not kidding, nor is he trying to be charming. He is saying, in all earnestness: Voilà! the Orient! Genuine Camp—for instance, the numbers devised for the Warner Brothers musicals of the early thirties (*42nd Street*; *The Golddiggers of 1933*; . . . *of 1935*; . . . *of 1937*; etc.) by Busby Berkeley—does not mean to be funny. Camping—say, the plays of Noel Coward—does. It seems unlikely that much of the traditional opera repertoire could be such satisfying Camp if the melodramatic absurdities of most opera plots had not been taken seriously by their composers. One doesn't need to know the artist's private intentions. The work tells all. (Compare a typical 19th century opera with Samuel Barber's *Vanessa*, a piece of manufactured, calculated Camp, and the difference is clear.)

20. Probably, intending to be campy is always harmful. The perfection of *Trouble in Paradise* and *The Maltese Falcon*, among the greatest Camp movies ever made, comes from the effortless smooth way in which tone is maintained. This is not so with such famous would-be Camp films of the fifties as *All About Eve* and *Beat the Devil*. These more recent movies have their fine moments, but the first is so slick and the second so hysterical; they want so badly to be campy that they're continually losing the beat. . . . Perhaps, though, it is not so much a question of the unintended effect versus the conscious intention, as of the delicate relation between parody and self-parody in Camp. The films of Hitchcock are a showcase for this problem. When self-parody lacks ebullience but instead reveals (even sporadically) a contempt for one's themes and one's materials—as in *To Catch a Thief*, *Rear Window*, *North by Northwest*—the results are forced and heavy-handed, rarely Camp. Successful Camp—a movie like Carné's *Drôle de Drame*; the film

performances of Mae West and Edward Everett Horton; portions of the Goon Show—even when it reveals self-parody, reeks of self-love.

21. So, again, Camp rests on innocence. That means Camp discloses innocence, but also, when it can, corrupts it. Objects, being objects, don't change when they are singled out by the Camp vision. Persons, however, respond to their audiences. Persons begin "camping": Mae West, Bea Lillie, La Lupe, Tallulah Bankhead in *Lifeboat*, Bette Davis in *All About Eve*. (Persons can even be induced to camp without their knowing it. Consider the way Fellini got Anita Ekberg to parody herself in *La Dolce Vita*.)

22. Considered a little less strictly, Camp is either completely naïve or else wholly conscious (when one plays at being campy). An example of the latter: Wilde's epigrams themselves.

"It's absurd to divide people into good and bad. People are either charming or tedious."

—*Lady Windemere's Fan*

23. In naïve, or pure, Camp, the essential element is seriousness, a seriousness that fails. Of course, not all seriousness that fails can be redeemed as Camp. Only that which has the proper mixture of the exaggerated, the fantastic, the passionate, and the naïve.

24. When something is just bad (rather than Camp), it's often because it is too mediocre in its ambition. The artist hasn't attempted to do anything really outlandish. ("It's too much," "It's too fantastic," "It's not to be believed," are standard phrases of Camp enthusiasm.)

25. The hallmark of Camp is the spirit of extravagance. Camp is a woman walking around in a dress made of three million feathers. Camp is the paintings of Carlo Crivelli, with their real jewels and *trompe-l'oeil* insects and cracks in the masonry. Camp is the outrageous aestheticism of Sternberg's six American movies with Dietrich, all six, but especially the last, *The Devil Is a Woman*. . . . In Camp there is often something *démesuré* in the quality of the ambition, not only in the style of the work itself. Gaudí's lurid and beautiful buildings in Barcelona are Camp not only because of their

style but because they reveal—most notably in the Cathedral of the Sagrada Familia—the ambition on the part of one man to do what it takes a generation, a whole culture to accomplish.

26. Camp is art that proposes itself seriously, but cannot be taken altogether seriously because it is "too much." *Titus Andronicus* and *Strange Interlude* are almost Camp, or could be played as Camp. The public manner and rhetoric of de Gaulle, often, are pure Camp.

27. A work can come close to Camp, but not make it, because it succeeds. Eisenstein's films are seldom Camp because, despite all exaggeration, they do succeed (dramatically) without surplus. If they were a little more "off," they could be great Camp—particularly *Ivan the Terrible I & II*. The same for Blake's drawings and paintings, weird and mannered as they are. They aren't Camp; though Art Nouveau, influenced by Blake, is.

What is extravagant in an inconsistent or an unpassionate way is not Camp. Neither can anything be Camp that does not seem to spring from an irrepressible, a virtually uncontrolled sensibility. Without passion, one gets pseudo-Camp—what is merely decorative, safe, in a word, chic. On the barren edge of Camp lie a number of attractive things: the sleek fantasies of Dali, the haute couture preciosity of Albicocco's *The Girl with the Golden Eyes*. But the two things—Camp and preciosity—must not be confused.

28. Again, Camp is the attempt to do something extraordinary. But extraordinary in the sense, often, of being special, glamorous. (The curved line, the extravagant gesture.) Not extraordinary merely in the sense of effort. Ripley's Believe-It-Or-Not items are rarely campy. These items, either natural oddities (the two-headed rooster, the eggplant in the shape of a cross) or else the products of immense labor (the man who walked from here to China on his hands, the woman who engraved the New Testament on the head of a pin), lack the visual reward—the glamour, the theatricality—that marks off certain extravagances as Camp.

29. The reason a movie like *On the Beach*, books like *Winesburg, Ohio* and *For Whom the Bell Tolls* are bad to the point of being laughable, but not bad to the point of being enjoyable, is that they are too dogged and pretentious. They lack fantasy. There is

Camp in such bad movies as *The Prodigal* and *Samson and Delilah*, the series of Italian color spectacles featuring the super-hero Maciste, numerous Japanese science fiction films (*Rodan, The Mysterians, The H-Man*) because, in their relative unpretentiousness and vulgarity, they are more extreme and irresponsible in their fantasy—and therefore touching and quite enjoyable.

30. Of course, the canon of Camp can change. Time has a great deal to do with it. Time may enhance what seems simply dogged or lacking in fantasy now because we are too close to it, because it resembles too closely our own everyday fantasies, the fantastic nature of which we don't perceive. We are better able to enjoy a fantasy as fantasy when it is not our own.

31. This is why so many of the objects prized by Camp taste are old-fashioned, out-of-date, démodé. It's not a love of the old as such. It's simply that the process of aging or deterioration provides the necessary detachment—or arouses a necessary sympathy. When the theme is important, and contemporary, the failure of a work of art may make us indignant. Time can change that. Time liberates the work of art from moral relevance, delivering it over to the Camp sensibility. . . . Another effect: time contracts the sphere of banality. (Banality is, strictly speaking, always a category of the contemporary.) What was banal can, with the passage of time, become fantastic. Many people who listen with delight to the style of Rudy Vallee revived by the English pop group, The Temperance Seven, would have been driven up the wall by Rudy Vallee in his heyday.

Thus, things are campy, not when they become old—but when we become less involved in them, and can enjoy, instead of be frustrated by, the failure of the attempt. But the effect of time is unpredictable. Maybe Method acting (James Dean, Rod Steiger, Warren Beatty) will seem as Camp some day as Ruby Keeler's does now—or as Sarah Bernhardt's does, in the films she made at the end of her career. And maybe not.

32. Camp is the glorification of "character." The statement is of no importance—except, of course, to the person (Loie Fuller, Gaudí, Cecil B. De Mille, Crivelli, de Gaulle, etc.) who makes it. What the Camp eye appreciates is the unity, the force of the per-

son. In every move the aging Martha Graham makes she's being Martha Graham, etc., etc. . . . This is clear in the case of the great serious idol of Camp taste, Greta Garbo. Garbo's incompetence (at the least, lack of depth) as an actress enhances her beauty. She's always herself.

33. What Camp taste responds to is "instant character" (this is, of course, very 18th century); and, conversely, what it is not stirred by is the sense of the development of character. Character is understood as a state of continual incandescence—a person being one, very intense thing. This attitude toward character is a key element of the theatricalization of experience embodied in the Camp sensibility. And it helps account for the fact that opera and ballet are experienced as such rich treasures of Camp, for neither of these forms can easily do justice to the complexity of human nature. Wherever there is development of character, Camp is reduced. Among operas, for example, La Traviata (which has some small development of character) is less campy than Il Trovatore (which has none).

"Life is too important a thing ever to talk seriously about it."
—Vera, or The Nihilists

34. Camp taste turns its back on the good-bad axis of ordinary aesthetic judgment. Camp doesn't reverse things. It doesn't argue that the good is bad, or the bad is good. What it does is to offer for art (and life) a different—a supplementary—set of standards.

35. Ordinarily we value a work of art because of the seriousness and dignity of what it achieves. We value it because it succeeds—in being what it is and, presumably, in fulfilling the intention that lies behind it. We assume a proper, that is to say, straightforward relation between intention and performance. By such standards, we appraise The Iliad, Aristophanes' plays, The Art of the Fugue, Middlemarch, the paintings of Rembrandt, Chartres, the poetry of Donne, The Divine Comedy, Beethoven's quartets, and—among people—Socrates, Jesus, St. Francis, Napoleon, Savonarola. In short, the pantheon of high culture: truth, beauty, and seriousness.

36. But there are other creative sensibilities besides the seriousness (both tragic and comic) of high culture and of the high style

of evaluating people. And one cheats oneself, as a human being, if one has respect only for the style of high culture, whatever else one may do or feel on the sly.

For instance, there is the kind of seriousness whose trademark is anguish, cruelty, derangement. Here we do accept a disparity between intention and result. I am speaking, obviously, of a style of personal existence as well as of a style in art; but the examples had best come from art. Think of Bosch, Sade, Rimbaud, Jarry, Kafka, Artaud, think of most of the important works of art of the 20th century, that is, art whose goal is not that of creating harmonies but of overstraining the medium and introducing more and more violent, and unresolvable, subject-matter. This sensibility also insists on the principle that an oeuvre in the old sense (again, in art, but also in life) is not possible. Only "fragments" are possible. . . . Clearly, different standards apply here than to traditional high culture. Something is good not because it is achieved, but because another kind of truth about the human situation, another experience of what it is to be human—in short, another valid sensibility—is being revealed.

And third among the great creative sensibilities is Camp: the sensibility of failed seriousness, of the theatricalization of experience. Camp refuses both the harmonies of traditional seriousness, and the risks of fully identifying with extreme states of feeling.

37. The first sensibility, that of high culture, is basically moralistic. The second sensibility, that of extreme states of feeling, represented in much contemporary "avant-garde" art, gains power by a tension between moral and aesthetic passion. The third, Camp, is wholly aesthetic.

38. Camp is the consistently aesthetic experience of the world. It incarnates a victory of "style" over "content," "aesthetics" over "morality," of irony over tragedy.

39. Camp and tragedy are antitheses. There is seriousness in Camp (seriousness in the degree of the artist's involvement) and, often, pathos. The excruciating is also one of the tonalities of Camp; it is the quality of excruciation in much of Henry James (for instance, The Europeans, The Awkward Age, The Wings of the Dove) that is responsible for the large element of Camp in his writings. But there is never, never tragedy.

40. Style is everything. Genet's ideas, for instance, are very Camp. Genet's statement that "the only criterion of an act is its elegance"* is virtually interchangeable, as a statement, with Wilde's "in matters of great importance, the vital element is not sincerity, but style." But what counts, finally, is the style in which ideas are held. The ideas about morality and politics in, say, Lady Windemere's Fan and in Major Barbara are Camp, but not just because of the nature of the ideas themselves. It is those ideas, held in a special playful way. The Camp ideas in Our Lady of the Flowers are maintained too grimly, and the writing itself is too successfully elevated and serious, for Genet's books to be Camp.

41. The whole point of Camp is to dethrone the serious. Camp is playful, anti-serious. More precisely, Camp involves a new, more complex relation to "the serious." One can be serious about the frivolous, frivolous about the serious.

42. One is drawn to Camp when one realizes that "sincerity" is not enough. Sincerity can be simple philistinism, intellectual narrowness.

43. The traditional means for going beyond straight seriousness —irony, satire—seem feeble today, inadequate to the culturally oversaturated medium in which contemporary sensibility is schooled. Camp introduces a new standard: artifice as an ideal, theatricality.

44. Camp proposes a comic vision of the world. But not a bitter or polemical comedy. If tragedy is an experience of hyperinvolvement, comedy is an experience of underinvolvement, of detachment.

"I adore simple pleasures, they are the last refuge of the complex."
—A Woman of No Importance

45. Detachment is the prerogative of an elite; and as the dandy is the 19th century's surrogate for the aristocrat in matters of culture, so Camp is the modern dandyism. Camp is the answer to the problem: how to be a dandy in the age of mass culture.

* Sartre's gloss on this in Saint Genet is: "Elegance is the quality of conduct which transforms the greatest amount of being into appearing."

46. The dandy was overbred. His posture was disdain, or else *ennui*. He sought rare sensations, undefiled by mass appreciation. (Models: Des Esseintes in Huysmans' *A Rebours*, Marius the Epicurean, Valéry's *Monsieur Teste*.) He was dedicated to "good taste."

The connoisseur of Camp has found more ingenious pleasures. Not in Latin poetry and rare wines and velvet jackets, but in the coarsest, commonest pleasures, in the arts of the masses. Mere use does not defile the objects of his pleasure, since he learns to possess them in a rare way. Camp—Dandyism in the age of mass culture—makes no distinction between the unique object and the mass-produced object. Camp taste transcends the nausea of the replica.

47. Wilde himself is a transitional figure. The man who, when he first came to London, sported a velvet beret, lace shirts, velveteen knee-breeches and black silk stockings, could never depart too far in his life from the pleasures of the old-style dandy; this conservatism is reflected in *The Picture of Dorian Gray*. But many of his attitudes suggest something more modern. It was Wilde who formulated an important element of the Camp sensibility—the equivalence of all objects—when he announced his intention of "living up" to his blue-and-white china, or declared that a doorknob could be as admirable as a painting. When he proclaimed the importance of the necktie, the boutonniere, the chair, Wilde was anticipating the democratic *esprit* of Camp.

48. The old-style dandy hated vulgarity. The new-style dandy, the lover of Camp, appreciates vulgarity. Where the dandy would be continually offended or bored, the connoisseur of Camp is continually amused, delighted. The dandy held a perfumed handkerchief to his nostrils and was liable to swoon; the connoisseur of Camp sniffs the stink and prides himself on his strong nerves.

49. It is a feat, of course. A feat goaded on, in the last analysis, by the threat of boredom. The relation between boredom and Camp taste cannot be overestimated. Camp taste is by its nature possible only in affluent societies, in societies or circles capable of experiencing the psychopathology of affluence.

"What is abnormal in Life stands in normal relations to Art. It is the only thing in Life that stands in normal relations to Art."
—*A Few Maxims for the Instruction of the Over-Educated*

50. Aristocracy is a position vis-à-vis culture (as well as vis-à-vis power), and the history of Camp taste is part of the history of snob taste. But since no authentic aristocrats in the old sense exist today to sponsor special tastes, who is the bearer of this taste? Answer: an improvised self-elected class, mainly homosexuals, who constitute themselves as aristocrats of taste.

51. The peculiar relation beween Camp taste and homosexuality has to be explained. While it's not true that Camp taste *is* homosexual taste, there is no doubt a peculiar affinity and overlap. Not all liberals are Jews, but Jews have shown a peculiar affinity for liberal and reformist causes. So, not all homosexuals have Camp taste. But homosexuals, by and large, constitute the vanguard—and the most articulate audience—of Camp. (The analogy is not frivolously chosen. Jews and homosexuals are the outstanding creative minorities in contemporary urban culture. Creative, that is, in the truest sense: they are creators of sensibilities. The two pioneering forces of modern sensibility are Jewish moral seriousness and homosexual aestheticism and irony.)

52. The reason for the flourishing of the aristocratic posture among homosexuals also seems to parallel the Jewish case. For every sensibility is self-serving to the group that promotes it. Jewish liberalism is a gesture of self-legitimization. So is Camp taste, which definitely has something propagandistic about it. Needless to say, the propaganda operates in exactly the opposite direction. The Jews pinned their hopes for integrating into modern society on promoting the moral sense. Homosexuals have pinned their integration into society on promoting the aesthetic sense. Camp is a solvent of morality. It neutralizes moral indignation, sponsors playfulness.

53. Nevertheless, even though homosexuals have been its vanguard, Camp taste is much more than homosexual taste. Obviously, its metaphor of life as theater is peculiarly suited as a justification and projection of a certain aspect of the situation of homosexuals. (The Camp insistence on not being "serious,"on playing,

also connects with the homosexual's desire to remain youthful.) Yet one feels that if homosexuals hadn't more or less invented Camp, someone else would. For the aristocratic posture with relation to culture cannot die, though it may persist only in increasingly arbitrary and ingenious ways. Camp is (to repeat) the relation to style in a time in which the adoption of style—as such—has become altogether questionable. (In the modern era, each new style, unless frankly anachronistic, has come on the scene as an anti-style.)

"One must have a heart of stone to read the death of Little Nell without laughing."

—*In conversation*

54. The experiences of Camp are based on the great discovery that the sensibility of high culture has no monopoly upon refinement. Camp asserts that good taste is not simply good taste; that there exists, indeed, a good taste of bad taste. (Genet talks about this in *Our Lady of the Flowers*.) The discovery of the good taste of bad taste can be very liberating. The man who insists on high and serious pleasures is depriving himself of pleasure; he continually restricts what he can enjoy; in the constant exercise of his good taste he will eventually price himself out of the market, so to speak. Here Camp taste supervenes upon good taste as a daring and witty hedonism. It makes the man of good taste cheerful, where before he ran the risk of being chronically frustrated. It is good for the digestion.

55. Camp taste is, above all, a mode of enjoyment, of appreciation—not judgment. Camp is generous. It wants to enjoy. It only seems like malice, cynicism. (Or, if it is cynicism, it's not a ruthless but a sweet cynicism.) Camp taste doesn't propose that it is in bad taste to be serious; it doesn't sneer at someone who succeeds in being seriously dramatic. What it does is to find the success in certain passionate failures.

56. Camp taste is a kind of love, love for human nature. It relishes, rather than judges, the little triumphs and awkward intensities of "character." . . . Camp taste identifies with what it is en-

joying. People who share this sensibility are not laughing at the thing they label as "a camp," they're enjoying it. Camp is a *tender* feeling.

(Here, one may compare Camp with much of Pop Art, which—when it is not just Camp—embodies an attitude that is related, but still very different. Pop Art is more flat and more dry, more serious, more detached, ultimately nihilistic.)

57. Camp taste nourishes itself on the love that has gone into certain objects and personal styles. The absence of this love is the reason why such kitsch items as *Peyton Place* (the book) and the Tishman Building aren't Camp.

58. The ultimate Camp statement: it's good *because* it's awful. . . . Of course, one can't always say that. Only under certain conditions, those which I've tried to sketch in these notes.

[1964]

One culture and
the new sensibility

IN THE last few years there has been a good deal of discussion of a purported chasm which opened up some two centuries ago, with the advent of the Industrial Revolution, between "two cultures," the literary-artistic and the scientific. According to this diagnosis, any intelligent and articulate modern person is likely to inhabit one culture to the exclusion of the other. He will be concerned with different documents, different techniques, different problems; he will speak a different language. Most important, the type of effort required for the mastery of these two cultures will differ vastly. For the literary-artistic culture is understood as a general culture. It is addressed to man insofar as he is man; it is culture or, rather, it promotes culture, in the sense of culture defined by Ortega y Gasset: that which a man has in his possession when he has forgotten everything that he has read. The scientific culture, in contrast, is a culture for specialists; it is founded on remembering and is set down in ways that require complete dedication of the effort to comprehend. While the literary-artistic culture aims at internalization, ingestion —in other words, cultivation—the scientific culture aims at accumulation and externalization in complex instruments for problem-solving and specific techniques for mastery.

Though T. S. Eliot derived the chasm between the two cultures from a period more remote in modern history, speaking in a famous essay of a "dissociation of sensibility" which opened up in the 17th century, the connection of the problem with the Industrial Revolution seems well taken. There is a historic antipathy on the part of many literary intellectuals and artists to those changes which characterize modern society—above all, industrialization and those of its effects which everyone has experienced, such as the proliferation of huge impersonal cities and the predominance of the anonymous style of urban life. It has mattered little whether industrialization, the creature of modern "science," is seen on the 19th and early 20th century model, as noisy smoky artificial processes which defile nature and standardize culture or on the newer model, the clean automated technology that is coming into being in the second half of the 20th century. The judgment has been mostly the same. Literary men, feeling that the status of humanity itself was being challenged by the new science and the new technology, abhorred and deplored the change. But the literary men, whether one thinks of Emerson and Thoreau and Ruskin in the 19th century, or of 20th century intellectuals who talk of modern society as being in some new way incomprehensible, "alienated," are inevitably on the defensive. They know that the scientific culture, the coming of the machine, cannot be stopped.

The standard response to the problem of "the two cultures"— and the issue long antedates by many decades the crude and philistine statement of the problem by C. P. Snow in a famous lecture some years ago—has been a facile defense of the function of the arts (in terms of an ever vaguer ideology of "humanism") or a premature surrender of the function of the arts to science. By the second response, I am not referring to the philistinism of scientists (and those of their party among artists and philosophers) who dismiss the arts as imprecise, untrue, at best mere toys. I am speaking of serious doubts which have arisen among those who are passionately engaged in the arts. The role of the individual artist, in the business of making unique objects for the purpose of giving pleasure and educating conscience and sensibility, has repeatedly been called into question. Some literary intellectuals and artists have gone so far as to prophesy the ultimate demise of the art-making activity of man. Art, in an automated scientific society, would be unfunctional, useless.

But this conclusion, I should argue, is plainly unwarranted. Indeed, the whole issue seems to me crudely put. For the question of "the two cultures" assumes that science and technology are changing, in motion, while the arts are static, fulfilling some perennial generic human function (consolation? edification? diversion?). Only on the basis of this false assumption would anyone reason that the arts might be in danger of becoming obsolete.

Art does not progress, in the sense that science and technology do. But the arts do develop and change. For instance, in our own time, art is becoming increasingly the terrain of specialists. The most interesting and creative art of our time is not open to the generally educated; it demands special effort; it speaks a specialized language. The music of Milton Babbitt and Morton Feldman, the painting of Mark Rothko and Frank Stella, the dance of Merce Cunningham and James Waring demand an education of sensibility whose difficulties and length of apprenticeship are at least comparable to the difficulties of mastering physics or engineering. (Only the novel, among the arts, at least in America, fails to provide similar examples.) The parallel between the abstruseness of contemporary art and that of modern science is too obvious to be missed. Another likeness to the scientific culture is the history-mindedness of contemporary art. The most interesting works of contemporary art are full of references to the history of the medium; so far as they comment on past art, they demand a knowledge of at least the recent past. As Harold Rosenberg has pointed out, contemporary paintings are themselves acts of criticism as much as of creation. The point could be made as well of much recent work in the films, music, the dance, poetry, and (in Europe) literature. Again, a similarity with the style of science—this time, with the accumulative aspect of science—can be discerned.

The conflict between "the two cultures" is in fact an illusion, a temporary phenomenon born of a period of profound and bewildering historical change. What we are witnessing is not so much a conflict of cultures as the creation of a new (potentially unitary) kind of sensibility. This new sensibility is rooted, as it must be, in our experience, experiences which are new in the history of humanity—in extreme social and physical mobility; in the crowdedness of the human scene (both people and material commodities multiplying at a dizzying rate); in the availability of new sensations such as speed (physical speed, as in airplane travel; speed of images, as in the cinema); and in the pan-cultural perspective on the arts that is possible through the mass reproduction of art objects.

What we are getting is not the demise of art, but a transformation of the function of art. Art, which arose in human society as a magical-religious operation, and passed over into a technique for depicting and commenting on secular reality, has in our own time arrogated to itself a new function—neither religious, nor serving a secularized religious function, nor merely secular or profane (a notion which breaks down when its opposite, the "religious" or "sacred," becomes obsolescent). Art today is a new kind of instrument, an instrument for modifying consciousness and organizing new modes of sensibility. And the means for practicing art have been radically extended. Indeed, in response to this new function (more felt than clearly articulated), artists have had to become self-conscious aestheticians: continually challenging their means, their materials and methods. Often, the conquest and exploitation of new materials and methods drawn from the world of "non-art"— for example, from industrial technology, from commercial processes and imagery, from purely private and subjective fantasies and dreams—seems to be the principal effort of many artists. Painters no longer feel themselves confined to canvas and paint, but employ hair, photographs, wax, sand, bicycle tires, their own toothbrushes and socks. Musicians have reached beyond the sounds of the traditional instruments to use tampered instruments and (usually on tape) synthetic sounds and industrial noises.

All kinds of conventionally accepted boundaries have thereby been challenged: not just the one between the "scientific" and the "literary-artistic" cultures, or the one between "art" and "non-art"; but also many established distinctions within the world of culture itself—that between form and content, the frivolous and the serious, and (a favorite of literary intellectuals) "high" and "low" culture.

The distinction between "high" and "low" (or "mass" or "popular") culture is based partly on an evaluation of the difference between unique and mass-produced objects. In an era of mass technological reproduction, the work of the serious artist had a special value simply because it was unique, because it bore his personal, individual signature. The works of popular culture (and even films were for a long time included in this category) were seen as having little value because they were manufactured objects, bearing no individual stamp—group concoctions made for an undifferentiated audience. But in the light of contemporary practice in the arts, this distinction appears extremely shallow. Many of the serious works of art of recent decades have a decidedly impersonal character. The work of art is reasserting its existence as "object" (even as manufactured or mass-produced object, drawing on the popular arts) rather than as "individual personal expression."

The exploration of the impersonal (and trans-personal) in contemporary art is the new classicism; at least, a reaction against what is understood as the romantic spirit dominates most of the interesting art of today. Today's art, with its insistence on coolness, its refusal of what it considers to be sentimentality, its spirit of exactness, its sense of "research" and "problems," is closer to the spirit of science than of art in the old-fashioned sense. Often, the artist's work is only his idea, his concept. This is a familiar practice in architecture, of course. And one remembers that painters in the Renaissance often left parts of their canvases to be worked out by students, and that in the flourishing period of the concerto the cadenza at the end of the first movement was left to the inventiveness and discretion of the performing soloist. But similar practices have a different, more polemical meaning today, in the present post-romantic era of the arts. When painters such as Joseph Albers,

Ellsworth Kelly, and Andy Warhol assign portions of the work, say, the painting in of the colors themselves, to a friend or the local gardener; when musicians such as Stockhausen, John Cage, and Luigi Nono invite collaboration from performers by leaving opportunities for random effects, switching around the order of the score, and improvisations—they are changing the ground rules which most of us employ to recognize a work of art. They are saying what art need not be. At least, not necessarily.

The primary feature of the new sensibility is that its model product is not the literary work, above all, the novel. A new non-literary culture exists today, of whose very existence, not to mention significance, most literary intellectuals are entirely unaware. This new establishment includes certain painters, sculptors, architects, social planners, film-makers, TV technicians, neurologists, musicians, electronics engineers, dancers, philosophers, and sociologists. (A few poets and prose writers can be included.) Some of the basic texts for this new cultural alignment are to be found in the writings of Nietzsche, Wittgenstein, Antonin Artaud, C. S. Sherrington, Buckminster Fuller, Marshall McLuhan, John Cage, André Breton, Roland Barthes, Claude Lévi-Strauss, Siegfried Gidieon, Norman O. Brown, and Gyorgy Kepes.

Those who worry about the gap between "the two cultures," and this means virtually all literary intellectuals in England and America, take for granted a notion of culture which decidedly needs reexamining. It is the notion perhaps best expressed by Matthew Arnold (in which the central cultural act is the making of literature, which is itself understood as the criticism of culture). Simply ignorant of the vital and enthralling (so called "avant-garde") developments in the other arts, and blinded by their personal investment in the perpetuation of the older notion of culture, they continue to cling to literature as the model for creative statement.

What gives literature its preeminence is its heavy burden of "content," both reportage and moral judgment. (This makes it possible for most English and American literary critics to use literary works mainly as texts, or even pretexts, for social and cultural diagnosis—rather than concentrating on the properties of, say, a given novel or a play, as an art work.) But the model arts of our time are actually those with much less content, and a much cooler mode of moral judgment—like music, films, dance, architecture, painting, sculpture. The practice of these arts—all of which draw profusely, naturally, and without embarrassment, upon science and technology—are the locus of the new sensibility.

The problem of "the two cultures," in short, rests upon an uneducated, uncontemporary grasp of our present cultural situation. It arises from the ignorance of literary intellectuals (and of scientists with a shallow knowledge of the arts, like the scientist-novelist C. P. Snow himself) of a new culture, and its emerging sensibility. In fact, there can be no divorce between science and technology, on the one hand, and art, on the other, any more than there can be a divorce between art and the forms of social life. Works of art, psychological forms, and social forms all reflect each other, and change with each other. But, of course, most people are slow to come to terms with such changes—especially today, when the changes are occurring with an unprecedented rapidity. Marshall McLuhan has described human history as a succession of acts of technological extension of human capacity, each of which works a radical change upon our environment and our ways of thinking, feeling, and valuing. The tendency, he remarks, is to upgrade the old environment into art form (thus Nature became a vessel of aesthetic and spiritual values in the new industrial environment) "while the new conditions are regarded as corrupt and degrading." Typically, it is only certain artists in any given era who "have the resources and temerity to live in immediate contact with the environment of their age . . . That is why they may seem to be 'ahead of their time' . . . More timid people prefer to accept the . . . previous environment's values as the continuing reality of their time. Our natural bias is to accept the new gimmick (automation, say) as a thing that can be accommodated in the old ethical order." Only in the terms of what McLuhan calls the old ethical order does the problem of "the two cultures" appear to be a genuine problem. It is not a problem for most of the creative artists of our time (among whom one could include very few novelists) because most of these artists have broken, whether they know it or not, with the Matthew Arnold notion of culture, finding it historically and humanly obsolescent.

The Matthew Arnold notion of culture defines art as the criticism of life—this being understood as the propounding of moral, social, and political ideas. The new sensibility understands art as the extension of life—this being understood as the representation of (new) modes of vivacity. There is no necessary denial of the role of moral evaluation here. Only the scale has changed; it has become less gross, and what it sacrifices in discursive explicitness it gains in accuracy and subliminal power. For we are what we are able to see (hear, taste, smell, feel) even more powerfully and profoundly than we are what furniture of ideas we have stocked in our heads. Of course, the proponents of "the two cultures" crisis continue to observe a desperate contrast between unintelligible, morally neutral science and technology, on the one hand, and morally committed, human-scale art on the other. But matters are not that simple, and never were. A great work of art is never simply (or even mainly) a vehicle of ideas or of moral sentiments. It is, first of all, an object modifying our consciousness and sensibility, changing the composition, however slightly, of the humus that nourishes all specific ideas and sentiments. Outraged humanists, please note. There is no need for alarm. A work of art does not cease being a moment in the conscience of mankind, when moral conscience is understood as only one of the functions of consciousness.

Sensations, feelings, the abstract forms and styles of sensibility count. It is to these that contemporary art addresses itself. The basic unit for contemporary art is not the idea, but the analysis of and extension of sensations. (Or if it is an "idea," it is about the form of sensibility.) Rilke described the artist as someone who works "toward an extension of the regions of the individual senses"; McLuhan calls artists "experts in sensory awareness." And the most interesting works of contemporary art (one can begin at least as far back as French symbolist poetry) are adventures in sensation, new "sensory mixes." Such art is, in principle, experimental—not out of an elitist disdain for what is accessible to the majority, but precisely in the sense that science is experimental. Such an art is also notably apolitical and undidactic, or, rather, infra-didactic.

When Ortega y Gasset wrote his famous essay The Dehumanization of Art in the early 1920s, he ascribed the qualities of modern art (such as impersonality, the ban on pathos, hostility to the past, playfulness, willful stylization, absence of ethical and political commitment) to the spirit of youth which he thought dominated our age.* In retrospect, it seems this "dehumanization" did not signify the recovery of childlike innocence, but was rather a very adult, knowing response. What other response than anguish, followed by anesthesia and then by wit and the elevating of intelligence over sentiment, is possible as a response to the social disorder and mass atrocities of our time, and—equally important for our sensibilities, but less often remarked on—to the unprecedented change in what rules our environment from the intelligible and visible to that which is only with difficulty intelligible, and is invisible? Art, which I have characterized as an instrument for modifying and educating sensibility and consciousness, now operates in an environment which cannot be grasped by the senses.

Buckminister Fuller has written:

In World War I industry suddenly went from the visible to the invisible base, from the track to the trackless, from the wire to the wireless, from visible structuring to invisible structuring in alloys. The big thing about World War I is that man went off the sensorial spectrum forever as the prime criterion of accrediting innovations . . . All major advances since World War I have been in the infra and the ultrasensorial frequencies of the electromagnetic spectrum. All the important technical affairs of men today are invisible . . . The old masters, who were sensorialists, have unleased a Pandora's box of non-sensorially controllable phenomena, which they had avoided accrediting up to that time . . . Suddenly they lost their true mastery, because from then on they didn't personally understand what was going on. If you don't understand you cannot master . . . Since World War I, the old masters have been extinct . . .

But, of course, art remains permanently tied to the senses. Just as one cannot float colors in space (a painter needs some sort of

* Ortega remarks, in this essay: "Were art to redeem man, it could do so only by saving him from the seriousness of life and restoring him to an unexpected boyishness."

surface, like a canvas, however neutral and textureless), one cannot have a work of art that does not impinge upon the human sensorium. But it is important to realize that human sensory awareness has not merely a biology but a specific history, each culture
placing a premium on certain senses and inhibiting others. (The
same is true for the range of primary human emotions.) Here is
where art (among other things) enters, and why the interesting
art of our time has such a feeling of anguish and crisis about it,
however playful and abstract and ostensibly neutral morally it may
appear. Western man may be said to have been undergoing a massive sensory anesthesia (a concomitant of the process that Max
Weber calls "bureaucratic rationalization") at least since the Industrial Revolution, with modern art functioning as a kind of shock
therapy for both confounding and unclosing our senses.

One important consequence of the new sensibility (with its
abandonment of the Matthew Arnold idea of culture) has already
been alluded to—namely, that the distinction between "high" and
"low" culture seems less and less meaningful. For such a distinction—inseparable from the Matthew Arnold apparatus—simply
does not make sense for a creative community of artists and scientists engaged in programming sensations, uninterested in art as a
species of moral journalism. Art has always been more than that,
anyway.

Another way of characterizing the present cultural situation, in
its most creative aspects, would be to speak of a new attitude toward pleasure. In one sense, the new art and the new sensibility
take a rather dim view of pleasure. (The great contemporary
French composer, Pierre Boulez, entitled an important essay of his
twelve years ago, "Against Hedonism in Music.") The seriousness
of modern art precludes pleasure in the familiar sense—the pleasure of a melody that one can hum after leaving the concert hall, of
characters in a novel or play whom one can recognize, identify
with, and dissect in terms of realistic psychological motives, of a
beautiful landscape or a dramatic moment represented on a canvas.
If hedonism means sustaining the old ways in which we have
found pleasure in art (the old sensory and psychic modalities), then

the new art is anti-hedonistic. Having one's sensorium challenged or stretched hurts. The new serious music hurts one's ears, the new painting does not graciously reward one's sight, the new films and the few interesting new prose works do not go down easily. The commonest complaint about the films of Antonioni or the narratives of Beckett or Burroughs is that they are hard to look at or to read, that they are "boring." But the charge of boredom is really hypocritical. There is, in a sense, no such thing as boredom. Boredom is only another name for a certain species of frustration. And the new languages which the interesting art of our time speaks are frustrating to the sensibilities of most educated people.

But the purpose of art is always, ultimately, to give pleasure—though our sensibilities may take time to catch up with the forms of pleasure that art in a given time may offer. And, one can also say that, balancing the ostensible anti-hedonism of serious contemporary art, the modern sensibility is more involved with pleasure in the familiar sense than ever. Because the new sensibility demands less "content" in art, and is more open to the pleasures of "form" and style, it is also less snobbish, less moralistic—in that it does not demand that pleasure in art necessarily be associated with edification. If art is understood as a form of discipline of the feelings and a programming of sensations, then the feeling (or sensation) given off by a Rauschenberg painting might be like that of a song by the Supremes. The brio and elegance of Budd Boetticher's *The Rise and Fall of Legs Diamond* or the singing style of Dionne Warwick can be appreciated as a complex and pleasurable event. They are experienced without condescension.

This last point seems to me worth underscoring. For it is important to understand that the affection which many younger artists and intellectuals feel for the popular arts is not a new philistinism (as has so often been charged) or a species of anti-intellectualism or some kind of abdication from culture. The fact that many of the most serious American painters, for example, are also fans of "the new sound" in popular music is not the result of the search for mere diversion or relaxation; it is not, say, like Schoenberg also playing tennis. It reflects a new, more open way of looking at the world and at things in the world, our world. It does not mean the renunciation of all standards: there is plenty of stupid popular music, as well as inferior and pretentious "avant-garde" paintings, films, and music. The point is that there are new standards, new standards of beauty and style and taste. The new sensibility is defiantly pluralistic; it is dedicated both to an excruciating seriousness and to fun and wit and nostalgia. It is also extremely history-conscious; and the voracity of its enthusiasms (and of the supercession of these enthusiasms) is very high-speed and hectic. From the vantage point of this new sensibility, the beauty of a machine or of the solution to a mathematical problem, of a painting by Jasper Johns, of a film by Jean-Luc Godard, and of the personalities and music of the Beatles is equally accessible.

[1965]

Susan Sontag

IN AMERICA

'The ultimate force of this fine book lies in its rich descriptions and lively incidents, in the concrete wealth of detail in which the novel abounds'
Sunday Times

In 1876 a group of Poles led by Maryna Załężowska, Poland's greatest actress, emigrate to the United States and travel to California to found a 'utopian' commune outside the village of Anaheim. Maryna, who has renounced her career for this venture, is accompanied by her small son and her husband, an aristocrat in revolt against his family; in her entourage is a rising young writer who is in love with her. Sontag's gripping narrative shows us an exotic, still largely empty, up-for-grabs southern California, with European newcomers lording it over native Californians and Native Americas.

When the commune fails and most of the émigrés return to Poland, Maryna stays, learns English, and – as Marina Zalenska – forges a new, even more triumphant career on the American stage. A diva on a par with Sarah Bernhardt, Maryna soon forms her own company and crisscrosses the country in her private railroad car, year after year, eventually playing opposite Edwin Booth, the great American actor of the age.

VINTAGE